SHAPERS
OF
BAPTIST
THOUGHT

SHAPERS
OF
BAPTIST
THOUGHT

James E. Tull

JUDSON PRESS • VALLEY FORGE

SHAPERS OF BAPTIST THOUGHT

Copyright © 1972

Judson Press
Valley Forge, Pa. 19481

Library of Congress Cataloging in Publication Data

Tull, James E.
  Shapers of Baptist thought.

  Includes bibliographical references.
  1. Baptists—Doctrinal and controversial works.
  2. Baptists—Biography. I. Title.
BX6331.2.T84   286'.092'2 [B]   72-75359
ISBN 0-8170-0503-X

Printed in the U.S.A.   286.09

P918a

175101

CONTENTS

FOREWORD

The purpose of this volume is to present the thought of representative Baptist thinkers. The subjects of the various chapters are not depicted as Baptist "heroes." If this task were attempted, it is quite likely that, in most cases, other subjects would have been chosen. Neither is it to be inferred that the figures here discussed are necessarily the very greatest "thinkers" that are to be found in Baptist history.

The Baptist leaders who are considered in this work were men who stood within the ranks of significant movements which have influenced Baptist history. John Smyth stood at the headwaters of Baptist origins. Roger Williams was a prophetic figure whose name is synonymous with religious liberty, a cause to which Baptists have been proud to attach their names as a people. Isaac Backus was an important and representative leader of a denomination of Baptists which, though now long extinct, has had a profound influence upon American Baptists for two hundred years, and particularly upon Baptists of the South. This denomination was called the Separate Baptists. Andrew Fuller was the theologian of the Baptist missionary movement at the time when Baptists in England were breaking away from a hyper-Calvinism which nullified all missionary effort. Fuller is chosen for discussion here rather than William Carey because Fuller, not Carey, was the "thinker" of the movement. Alexander Campbell was the controversial figure who caused a crucial break in the Baptist ranks of America during the first half of the nineteenth century. Although Campbell's stay with the Baptists was brief (twelve years) and troubled, he and the movement which he sponsored had a profound impact upon the Baptist denomination. J. R. Graves, another highly controversial figure, defined the norm for a Baptist ecclesiastical orthodoxy among Baptists of the South for many years. His influence over a wide area is still tenacious and pervasive. William Newton Clarke is included in this volume because he was a representative of a phase of theological liberalism in this country. Since many Baptists were involved in the liberal movement, the influential thought of this prominent theologian may profitably be studied by Baptists of our own time. Walter Rauschenbusch, the great exponent of the social gospel, was a Baptist whose contribution should not be forgotten. Similarly, the name of the last figure here discussed, Martin Luther King, Jr., is indelibly associated with the civil rights movement in which many Baptists have had a prominent part.

It is hoped that this study will contribute to an understanding of the Baptist heritage by calling attention to these representative figures who stood at important turning points of Baptist history.

Why were not other prominent figures included? Why not, for example, John Bunyan, William Kiffin, John Gill, William Carey, Robert Hall, Jr., Richard Furman, Luther Rice, William Bullein Johnson, Jesse Mercer, John A. Broadus, A. T. Robertson, H. Wheeler Robinson, H. H. Rowley, T. R. Glover, John Clifford, Charles Haddon Spurgeon, E. Y. Mullins, Shailer Mathews, G. B. Foster, D. C. Macintosh, George W. Truett, Harry Emerson Fosdick, Harvey Cox, and others? The answer to this question has been given above, at least in part. However, such a roster of distinguished Baptist names calls attention to the fact that Baptist life and thought have been larger in scope, and more diverse in character, than this book indicates. Nevertheless, it is to be hoped that what is done here may point out the varied lines in which the Baptist witness has run, and at the same time call attention to the fact that there is something valuable to the whole church in that part of it which is called "Baptist."

I-JOHN SMYTH-
Baptist Pathfinder

John Smyth's life was profoundly influenced by the tortuous course of the English Reformation. Smyth, in turn, was a leader in one stream of that Reformation which flowed through Puritanism and Separatism to the beginnings of Baptist life.

THE REFORMATION IN ENGLAND

The Protestant Reformation in England, begun during the reign of Henry VIII (1509–1547), was mixed with a great deal of political calculation. Henry, it has been said, wanted popery but not a pope. He made himself the supreme head of the Church of England. He plundered the monasteries for revenue, but by the Act of Six Articles (1539) he made it a crime punishable by death to deny transubstantiation. To repudiate clerical celibacy, auricular confession, and private masses became a felony.

During the short reign of Edward VI, who succeeded his father to the throne in 1547, many English people who had been driven into exile by Henry's repressive policies came back from Lutheran Germany and from Calvinistic Zurich, Geneva, and Strassburg. They brought with them the doctrines of the continental reformation. Some abuses in the English church were purged. The clergy were allowed to marry; images and shrines were abolished; the Sacrament was administered in two kinds; and the Prayer Book underwent a number of revisions.

The accession of Mary to the throne in 1553 brought a Roman reaction of such cruelty that another stream of Protestant exiles fled to the continent. Most of these, numbering about eight hundred persons, settled at such reformed centers as Zurich, Geneva, Basel, Strassburg, Frankfort, and Emden, imbibing, meanwhile, the spirit and the ideals of the reformation on the continent.

When Elizabeth became queen in 1558, many of these "Marian

9

exiles" came back to England and formed the nucleus of a Puritan party in the home country.

Elizabeth's official policy toward the dynamic religious situation in her realm was shrewdly and energetically administered. Ruling over the church through Parliament, she made herself the "Supreme Governor" of the church. She reimposed the Book of Common Prayer. She made attendance upon the parish churches mandatory by law. She reduced the Articles of Religion to thirty-nine and required subscription to these articles by all the clergy. The hierarchy was retained, without allegiance to Rome.

THE PURITANS

The Puritan party first came into prominence during the reign of Elizabeth. The Puritans did not want to secede from the Church of England. They wanted instead to reform it, to "purify" it. Reform involved getting rid of Roman Catholic accretions and impurities in the worship and polity of the church. Puritan efforts for reform were prosecuted with such energy and power that they incurred heavy opposition from Elizabeth and from her ecclesiastical lieutenants, as well as from large numbers of the ministers of the establishment who agreed with state policy.

Three factors in the complex Puritan movement should be emphasized here. The first is the conviction held by many Puritans that the church should be composed, insofar as possible, of saints.[1] In 1572 John Field, a Puritan of note, defined a church as

a company or congregatione of the faythfull called and gathered out of the worlde by the preachinge of the Gospell, who followinge and embraceinge true religione, do in one unitie of Spirite strengthen and comforte one another, dayelie growinge and increasinge in true faythe, framinge their lyves, governmente, orders and ceremonies according to the worde of God.[2]

The second factor to note here derives from a Puritan conviction exemplified in the above statement by Field. The Puritans believed that Christian life and worship, orders and ceremonies, should be "according to the worde of God." All church polity, the Puritans held, must have biblical warrant. This, according to Perry Miller, was the Puritan's "basic assumption." [3] The Puritans contended that every detail of church organization and practice had been prescribed by Christ and consequently could not be changed without contravening the will of Christ.[4]

This rigid biblical norm was acquired by the Puritans in Geneva, and they gave this norm radical application. Worship and polity must conform to biblical requirement, and abuses in the church were defined by practices which did not adhere to this norm.

However, by the close of Elizabeth's reign, the church, by Puritan standards, was still far from being adequately reformed.

In the year 1600 a Puritan listed ninety-one things still wrong with the Church of England. Among other offenses, he objected to the use of the Apocrypha, to liturgies and set forms of prayers, to prohibitions of marriage and of eating meat at certain times, to the rituals used in baptism, in the Lord's Supper, in marriages and burials; he objected to confirmation, to popish vestments, to the neglect of preaching, to tithes, canon law, bishop's courts, and to the very existence of archbishops, lord bishops, and some thirty-odd other offices recognized by the church.[5]

The third factor which helps to characterize the Puritan protest is to be seen in the kind of biblical interpretation to which the Puritans pledged themselves. There were, of course, many differences of viewpoint within Puritanism, as in any great movement. The majority of Puritans, however, read the mandates of biblical ecclesiastical polity through Genevan, that is, through Calvinistic, eyes. The Puritan majority were Presbyterians, and they may be described as the right wing of the Puritan movement. Their ancestry went back to the efforts of Elizabethan Puritans, such as Thomas Cartright and Walter Travers, to bring the Church of England into conformity with the faith and order of the Reformed churches. Faith and practice were dictated by the Word of God, and the Word prescribed Presbyterianism. Presbyterianism "intended only the substitution of the Genevan régime for that which prevailed, but it expected no other alterations." [6]

The Word was to be interpreted by godly ministers, but this did not mean the entire separation of the church from the civil power. Indeed, the king, who was supreme in civil matters, was obligated to enforce the true church order and worship. The government was therefore to be a partner of the church in the protection and enforcement of true religion.

The Presbyterians intended for the church to be a national church, embracing the whole population in its membership. Dissent was not to be allowed; membership was compulsory. Everyone was to have his children baptized and to pay tithes. On this point there was to be little difference from the church as already established.

The Presbyterian concept of a church membership coextensive with the whole society was incompatible with the ideal expressed by John Field, quoted above, in an earlier period — the ideal of a church membership made up of "the faithful." The tension in Puritanism between these concepts of the church later led to the demand for the pure church ideal in Separatism.

THE SEPARATISTS

Near the end of the reign of Queen Elizabeth, there appeared in England small groups of Puritans who felt that it was impossible to reform the established church, and that it was sinful to stay within that church if it remained unreformed. One of these groups originated at Norwich about 1580, under the leadership of Robert Browne. Browne was the first church leader of this period to defend publicly the act of separating from the Church of England. Though he later recanted and went back into the established church, Browne's voice and pen as an early Separatist became a rallying cry for persons of like mind. No one knows how many Separatist churches were organized during Elizabeth's reign, but the number was small. It is probable that the combined membership of all the Separatist churches did not exceed a thousand.[7]

The compelling reason for withdrawal from the established church was the Separatist conviction that the established church had become a false church because, contrary to biblical commandment, it included the wicked with the saints. The Separatists believed that a church must retain the power to purge itself by expelling the wicked and the unconverted, and that it must vigilantly exercise this power. If the church has not power to redress gross sins, "or rebelliously refuseth to redresse them, then it ceaseth to be the Church of God."[8] "Whosoever are not gathered from all false Churches, & from their false gouvernment," said Browne, "can neither be the Church of God, nor preachers in the same."[9]

The Separatists believed that the church is made up of "visible saints." A true church was formed when these saints came together by voluntary association, professed their faith, and entered into a covenant of allegiance to Christ as their prophet and king. Each local congregation was to be self-governing, independent of other congregations, and independent of any higher ecclesiastical organization. The ministry was to be supported by the voluntary contributions of the congregation rather than by tithes or contributions from the civil government. The preaching of the gospel, the celebration of the sacraments, the election of officers, and the exercise of discipline were rights and obligations belonging to the local congregation alone. In other words, the Separatists were strict congregationalists in church polity.

The Separatists were just as insistent as other Puritans that the faith and order of their churches were in conformity with scriptural precedent and prescription. True faith, they thought, was to be found only in "assemblies of believers." True order could exist only where true saints observed and administered this faith.

Despite their strong preference for congregationalism over the presbyterianism of the orthodox Puritans, Separatists shared with the latter the belief that the true faith and order should be enforced by the state. They held that it was the duty of princes

> to suppress and root out by their authoritie all false ministeries, voluntarie Relligions and counterfeyt worship of God . . . [and], to establish & mayntein by their lawes every part of God's word his pure Relligion and true ministerie . . . yea, to enforce al their Subjects whether Ecclesiasticall or civile, to do their dutyes to God and men. . . .[10]

As might have been expected, the Separatists incurred the bitter hostility of the government, the hierarchy, and of non-separating Puritans. Separation was adjudged to be schism, and schism was reckoned to be sedition. Numbers of Separatists fled to Holland to escape government persecution at home. Three of their London leaders, Henry Barrow, John Greenwood, and John Penry, were hanged in 1593. One of their prominent leaders who escaped to Holland with his congregation was John Smyth.

JOHN SMYTH

Many of the details of Smyth's life will appear in connection with the material which follows. Here only a brief biographical sketch will be given.

BIOGRAPHICAL SKETCH

The exact date and place of Smyth's birth are unknown. In 1586 he matriculated as a sizar at Christ's College, Cambridge. At this time, Cambridge was a Puritan center. Smyth's tutor was Francis Johnson, who already was showing Puritan sympathies, and who later became the pastor of a church of English Separatists which fled to Holland.

In 1594 Smyth received ordination from the Bishop of Lincoln and was designated a fellow of his college. In 1600 he was appointed lecturer to the city of Lincoln. Two years later, he was dismissed from this office, after incurring the opposition of certain local political dignitaries.

After losing his position as lecturer, Smyth for a time supported himself as a physician. About the year 1606, he appears to have decided to separate from the Church of England. Finding a congregation of Separatists at Gainsborough, he associated himself with them and was ordained their pastor. In 1608 this church, accompanied by Smyth, emigrated to Amsterdam. Thomas Helwys of Broxtowe Hall, Nottinghamshire, a well-to-do layman in the church, probably provided the funds for the move.

In Amsterdam, Smyth came into close contact with other English Separatists. One congregation was under the leadership of Francis Johnson, Smyth's old tutor. Another was led by John Robinson. The latter church, which later moved to Leyden, furnished the core of the "Pilgrim Fathers," who were destined to play a distinguished part in the opening up of the New World. While living at Amsterdam, Smyth carried on a running discussion and debate with Johnson, Robinson, and other Separatist leaders concerning points of church polity.

In 1608 Smyth came to the conclusion that baptism upon a profession of faith was the New Testament method of admitting believers to church fellowship and that there was no sanction in the New Testament, therefore, for infant baptism. Believing that the baptism which he and his fellow church members had already received was false, and therefore a nullity, he led his church to disband and to declare itself no church. Smyth then baptized himself and the rest of his congregation, constituting the new church fellowship on the basis of believer's baptism.

Perhaps a self-baptism was not without known precedent in Smyth's time, but it was highly untraditional, and it brought Smyth much sharp criticism. He was asked why he had not applied for baptism to some of the Dutch Anabaptists, who also practiced believer's baptism. In due course, Smyth requested admission for himself and his congregation to a local church of Waterlander Mennonites located in Amsterdam.

However, Thomas Helwys and ten other members balked at Smyth's overtures to the Mennonites and formed a separate church on the basis of the baptism which they had already received at Smyth's hands.

The negotiations with the Mennonites dragged on until after Smyth's death. His church was finally absorbed by the Waterlanders and was lost as an independent congregation. In 1612 Helwys and the little congregation of which he was pastor returned to England and became the first Baptist church on English soil.

Smyth, active in his ministry almost to the end of his life, was cut down in his prime. He died of consumption toward the end of August, 1612, forty-five (or less) years of age.

THE PURITAN PHASE

Richard Bernard, one of Smyth's friends who later became an enemy, noted that Smyth was not entirely a conformist even at the time of his ordination. Smyth is known to have sided with the Puritan majority in a college election. Like Bernard, he was in this period of his life a Puritan to whom many of the ceremonies of the established church and to whom several parts of the Book of Common Prayer were regarded with distaste. At the outset of his public career, therefore, he belonged to a class of clergy who were most closely watched by the bishops. Town lecturers and preachers were usually drawn from this class. Puritans who accepted such positions were less accessible to the direct authority of the bishops, because the lectureships were supported by the subscriptions of the townsmen or by grants from corporation funds.[11]

Two books issued from Smyth's pen during his Puritan phase. *The Bright Morning Starre,* published in 1603, was based upon a series of sermons which Smyth preached in Lincoln in 1601. *A Paterne of True Prayer,* published in 1605, also appears to have been a series of sermons at Lincoln. Since he left Lincoln in 1602, both works came out in book form after his departure from that city. These two works were not intended by Smyth to be expositions of Puritanism. In fact, the Puritan elements in them appear to be almost incidental and therefore do not furnish a checklist by which to number Smyth's Puritan tendencies.

The Bright Morning Starre is an exposition of the Twenty-second Psalm. There is little in it which would seem remarkable today. Some of the book, from a modern viewpoint, is marred by a kind of syllogistic logic-chopping in the manner of the time in which it was written.

Psalm 22, Smyth thought, was used by the Jews at the time of the morning sacrifice.

> . . . this psalme was an exposition and comentarie of the sacrifice: the sacrifice was a type of Christ; this Psalme teacheth the signification of the sacrifice: & so this Psalme annexed to the sacrifice did every day traine up the Church of the Iewes with a continuall meditation and expectation of the promised Messias, whose sufferings and glorie are in this psalme expressed.[12]

At a number of points, Smyth appears thoroughly orthodox in this work. A consideration of the question why Christ the God-man needed to pray led to a rather conventional treatment of the person of Christ, and of the Trinity.[13] His doctrine of the work of Christ was Anselmic. "Christ," he said, ". . . sustayned the wrath of God, striued with it, and subdued it; that is, he deliuered both himselfe and us from it, and so perfectly finished the worke of our redemption." [14] "Christ if hee had beene a meere man, could not haue excaped part of the damnation of hel, when gods wrath was so fully powred out upon him . . . but because Christ was God also, his godhead did infinitely strengthen and grace his manhood. . . ." [15]

Insofar as there is a polemical strain in this writing, it is most overtly expressed against the Papists. Smyth insisted that the minister is a preacher and not a priest, and that the Eucharist "is a sacrament and not a sacrifice . . . unbloody . . . and not propitiatory." [16] The papists are always mentioned in terms of sharp hostility. In this attitude, Smyth was not greatly different from many English protestants.

Smyth found the Scriptures to be an absolute rule of faith.

We are not to adde to, or detract any thing from the writte[n] word of God, or to alter any whitte thereof, which whosoeuer presumeth to doe, derogateth from the propheticall office of Christ: the scriptures indeede may be expounded, but they must not be altered, augmented or diminished.[17]

In contrast with orthodox churchmen, Smyth appears not to have recognized the authority of a hierarchical church government. In public worship, he thought, preaching is to be exalted. Ministers are referred to as pastors and teachers, not as priests and bishops. The end of the ministry is the glory of God and the salvation of souls.[18]

Smyth was dismissed from his office as preacher to the city of Lincoln in 1602. Of the dispute which preceded this action little need be said here. The mayor with the consent of his council made representations to the lord bishop regarding some of Smyth's "erroneous doctrine" and "personal preaching at men in the city." [19] In his preface to *A Paterne of True Prayer*, Smyth says, "I have become strangely traduced for the doctrine I taught out of the Lord's Prayer." [20] He believed, however, that *"there is no one doctrine or opinion contrarie to the doctrine of this* [the Anglican] *Church in all this tractate."* [21]

The very title of his book, *A Paterne of True Prayer*, indicated that Smyth believed that the Lord's Prayer was designed to be primarily a model prayer rather than a prayer to be formally repeated verbatim. The value of the prayer is as follows:

This prayer containeth the whole Scripture: for it is an Epitome or abridgement of the whole Scripture: a Catechisme in forme of a prayer, containing all the vertues of the Law and Gospell, and all the good we can pray for, all the graces and blessings wee can giue thankes for, all the euill we can pray against: and to these heads may the whole Scripture be referred. . . . All the prayers which haue been, are, or shall be made, must be measured by this prayer.[22]

Since the *Pater Noster* had been much abused in the Roman church by a popular belief that some magical efficacy resulted from its mere recital, and since, in the minds of convinced Protestants, it had become a perfunctory part of an empty and stylized Anglican ritual, its use as a part of public worship had been discontinued by many Separatists and was looked upon with suspicion by some non-separating Puritans. Smyth spoke relevantly to this problem by taking a mediating position. In his preface "to the Christian reader," he stated his disagreement with the members of the Separation who thought that the use of "a set forme of prayer" was unlawful.[23] "Christ," he said, "leaueth it arbitrarie unto us, as a thing indifferent when we pray to say this prayer, or not to say it, so be that we say it in faith and feeling." [24]

The phrase "in faith and feeling" gives the key to Smyth's interpretation. The Lord's Prayer, he thought, gives us the content, scope, and attitude of all true prayer, but it must be prayer in which heart, tongue, and mind accord. The "true and holy use" of the Lord's Prayer, Smyth said, involved four particulars:

1. Knowledge: for a man must understand what he prayeth.
2. Faith: which is an assurance of obtaining that we aske.
3. Repentance: which is bewailing our sins and wants, and a practizing of our prayers.
4. Deuotion: which is a due disposition in time of prayer.[25]

The prayer may be "said" if the saying is one of the heart as well as of the lips. Its "saying" may be omitted if its substance informs the adoration and petition of the believing mind and heart.

The particular use of the Lord's Prayer in worship raised the larger question of the lawfulness and appropriateness of set forms of worship. On this point, Smyth was moderately conservative. In private prayer, he thought, "it seemeth most expedient and profitable that he [the worshipper] powre out his soule unto God with such a forme of words as hee can. . . ." [26] Nevertheless, in public worship, "an uniforme order of publike prayer in the seruice of God is necessarie." [27] Smyth cited precedent for this position from the Old and New Testaments, and from the reformed churches.[28]

In the light of Smyth's later subscription to an Arminian theology, it is interesting to observe in this book his firm Calvinism. Christ, he noted, did not pray for the world. It is not God's will that all men should be converted and saved. Yet, because we cannot know which man is reprobate, it is our duty to pray for any particular man.[29] If we do discern a person to be reprobate, that is, one who commits the sin against the Holy Ghost, we are "directly and particularly to pray for his speedy damnation, and all the meanes effecting the same." [30]

A few years after this writing, Smyth became a courageous advocate of religious freedom. Here he affirms, however, "that Magistrates should cause all men to worship the true God, or else punish them with imprisonment, confiscation of goods, or death as the qualitie of the cause requireth." [31] The king, he says, is the supreme governor in all matters, ecclesiastical as well as civil. The appointment of "ecclesiastical magistrates," however, which are designated bishops, is to be done "according to the word." One wonders whether the term "according to the word" may not be a Puritan rider here!

Smyth nowhere condones overt rebellion against "evil magistrates," or "wicked and irreligious lawes and statutes." But it is lawful to *pray* against them. Prayer should be made for the salvation of wicked magistrates. "But it is lawfull also to pray against their proceedings against the truth, that God would discomfit them in battel, bridle their corruption, abate their pride, asswage their malice, and confound their deuices." [32]

W. T. Whitley's judgment about Smyth at this stage of the latter's life would seem to be an accurate one: ". . . he seems a fair specimen of a moderate Puritan, accepting set forms of prayer, vocal and instrumental music in church, as he had heard for the last twelve years at college." [33]

THE SEPARATIST PHASE

Shortly before leaving England, or perhaps shortly after arriving at Amsterdam, Smyth published *Principles and Inferences Concerning the Visible Church*. Not long afterward *Parallels, Censures and Observations* came from the press. A third book, *The Differences of the Churches of the Separation*, appeared in 1608. These three books comprise the principal materials for a study of Smyth's Separatist affiliation.

Principles and Inferences is a systematic, practical, and positive exposition of the nature, authority, and composition of a church, according to New Testament principles, and according to inferences which may legitimately be drawn from these principles. The various propositions are amply buttressed by scriptural references. The work gives a valuable exposition in brief compass of the way in which Smyth conceived the church to be "gathered, ordered, and governed." [34]

Smyth accepted the traditional belief of both Catholicism and Protestantism that the church is both invisible and visible. The invisible church is composed of the elect and is known only to God. Smyth, however, was more concerned with the visible church, and his Separatist convictions appear in relation to the visible church.

> A visibe communion of Saincts is of two, three, or moe Saincts joyned together by covenant with God & themselves, freely to use al the holy things of God, according to the word, for their mutual edification, & God's glory. . . . This visible communion of Saincts is a visible Church.[35]

Smyth urged three things as requisite to a true visible church: "(1) True matter, (2) true form, (3) true properties." Each of these requisites should be given more consideration.

1. True matter. The true matter of a church is that the church is composed of "saints." "Saincts are men separated from all knowne syn, practising the whol will of God knowne unto the[m] . . . growing in grace and knowledg . . . continuing to the end." [36]

2. True form. The *inward* form of the church is determined by the presence of the Holy Spirit; by faith, which unites the members to Christ their Head; and by love, which unites the members of the body with each other. The *outward* form of the church is a "covenant betwixt God and the Saints." [37] In the covenant relationship, God promises to be the God of his people, to give them Christ, and with Christ, "al things els." On their part, the saints promise in the covenant bond to obey all the commandments of God and to love each other.[38]

3. True properties. The properties of a true church are: the presence of Christ, the benefits of Christ, and the power of Christ. The "presence of Christ" means that the living Christ is present in his body, the church. The "benefits of Christ" is a term by which Smyth indicates that the church retains the "meanes of salvation and almes." The means of salvation are: "the word, Sacraments, prayers, Censures, and the ordinances of Christ for the dispensing of them all." [39] The "power of Christ" in the church is

threefold: (1) power to receive; (2) power to "preserve and keep within"; (3) power to "cast out."

The power to receive is first the power which Christ has given to the church to receive members into church fellowship and, second, to receive officers into office. The way by which the church receives members is by the candidate's declaration of faith "testified by obedience." [40] The way by which the church receives officers into office involves a threefold procedure which is designated election, approbation, and ordination. [41]

A person who is proposed for an office in the church must receive the endorsement of a majority of the members of the church by popular vote. This is election. Approbation is the examining of the elected candidate in order to determine, again in church meeting, whether he is fitted for his office, and the approval of his qualifications. If he is not adjudged to be qualified, his election is voided, and the church proceeds to the selection of another in his place. Ordination is the dedication of the officer to his office after he has been fully approved by the congregation. The laying on of hands is the ceremony used in ordination. This ceremony conveys no sacerdotal power, but rather indicates that the church has set the officer aside for the duties of a particular office. The laying on of hands is also observed in order "to signifie and to assure the officer to be ordeyned that the Lord by the church giveth him power to administer." [42]

Smyth stipulated that any person admitted to an office must be a member of the church in which he holds office; that the church, under Christ, has the power to select its own officers and to discharge them; and even that "none of those that are without may cast of their goods into the treasurie lest the treasury be polluted." [43]

The power of the church to "preserve and keep within" is concerned with the edification, purity, and witness of the church. The point here is that preserving and keeping is the duty and prerogative of the whole church, the task of each and all. Each officer and each member has his own particular function for the sake of the whole church. [44]

The power of casting out which belongs to the church includes the casting of officers out of office, and of members out of membership. The church firmly retains this power in its own hands. Of particular interest is Smyth's assertion that the "end of excommunicatio[n] is not the destruction of the offender, but the mortification of his synne, and the salvation of his soule." [45] The excommunicated party is not to be treated as an enemy; he is rather to be admonished as a brother.

The strict congregationalist position of this illuminating book is consistently maintained throughout. Smyth departed from both the Anglican and the Genevan orders in seeing church officers to be of two sorts: bishops and deacons. Bishops, he said, are also called elders or presbyters. Jointly, the bishops or elders are called the "Eldership" or "Presbyterie." Bishops or elders may be further denominated pastors, teachers, or governors. All of these officers are of equal rank. "The Deacons are officers occupied about the works of mercy respecting the body or outward man." [46] The congregationalist order is also disclosed in Smyth's contention that every visible church enjoys equal power with all other visible churches and has from Christ the authority to correct all abuses within its own fellowship.[47]

Parallels, Censures, and Observations belongs to the same immediate period of Smyth's life as does *Principles and Inferences.* The two books are concerned with similar points of ecclesiology, and much of the same material is duplicated. They are, however, very different in method and tone. For whereas the latter is positive and constructive, the former is argumentative and, indeed, sharply and sometimes harshly polemical.

The *Parallels* contains Smyth's side of a debate with Richard Bernard, formerly a Puritan friend who had shown Separatist leanings. Eventually Bernard drew back and became a resolute antagonist of the Separatists. The *Parallels* is an answer point by point to Bernard's indictment of the Separatist movement.[48] The value of Smyth's reply is not only that it furnishes an elaboration of Smyth's main positions as a Separatist, but also that it shows how seriously Smyth held these positions.

Smyth's main point is that a church must be faithful to the constitution of the church as revealed in the New Testament in order to be a true church. An ecclesiastical organization which does not have the same matter, form, and properties prescribed in the New Testament is a false church, an idol.

To Smyth, the supreme disqualifying characteristic of a false church is that it contains a mixed membership. ". . . wicked men joyned with Godly men in a Church, doe not produce a true Church, but a false Church. . . ." [49] This does not mean that there are not true saints in false churches.[50] It is, however, incumbent upon saints who are in false churches to depart from them. "The Children of God, must come out from the unbeleevers . . . yea &

must be seperated from the[m]: & must touch none of there uncleanness." [51]

Despite the fact that saints may live in the mixed membership of false churches, they are not while so living "subjects of Christ's Kingdome." They cannot be, because "the visible Church truly constituted is the only Kingdome of Christ." [52]

Here the driving passion of Smyth's conviction shows through. He earnestly desired that the invisible church and the invisible kingdom of Christ become luminously visible in the visible church. The kingdom is denied, and the true church is subverted, in so-called churches of mixed membership.

The test of fitness for membership in the true church is the manifestation of "an outward visible faith," confirmed by subsequent obedience to Christ. The member, "by reason of his outward true calling, true profession of the true faith, and true baptisme is discerned & judged to be inwardly called, inwardly to have faith, and to be inwardly baptized. . . ." [53] Perseverance is a built-in requirement. "Iff afterward men Apostate finally then wee chandg our mynd & say they were never of us for had they been of us they would have continued with us." [54]

While Smyth strongly argued the indispensability of a regenerate church membership for the constitution of a true church, he also held that the whole church order of a New Testament church must be observed if a religious organization is to be recognized as a true church. The apostles, he said, baptized into the "whole New Testament of Christ, & al the ordinances thereof." [55] The Church of England was a false church, not only because it contained unconverted people, but because it contained many other impurities and unscriptural institutions.

1. Christ is not their King, seing he onely ruleth by his own Lawes and Officers, and not by Antichristian Lords, and Lawes, such as are their Prelates, and their Officers, Courts, and Canons. 2. Christ is not their priest to ratifie unto them by his blood that ordinance of Church, Ministery, Worship, and Government which they retaine among them. . . . 3. Christ is not their Prophett to teach them by their false Prophetts the instruments of Antichrist. . . . [56]

If the Church of England was a false church, as Smyth charged, it followed that its ministry was false,[57] its worship was false,[58] and its baptism was false. When one is converted to the Church of England, he is converted to "your false repentance, false Faith, false Church, false Ministery, false Worship, false Government. . . ." [59]

Smyth's stringent congregationalism appeared in his belief that the church receives from Christ complete authority for the conduct of its own life. He was particularly interested in showing that there is no authority which resides in the ministry parallel to or separate from the authority of the church itself. ". . . the Church," he said, "hath from Christ the head al powre, & al the members & officers of the Church have al their powre from the body, which they hold & use in the body & not Seperated from the body. . . ." [60] Again, "whatsoever the Elders have, they have it from the Church by delegation. . . ." [61]

Finally, it may be noted that Smyth made a polemical thrust at the doctrine of ministerial succession. A true church has the covenant, the promises, and ministerial power given to it, not through a carnal line of succession, but directly and immediately, by Christ. The church receives these "from Christ's hand out of heaven." This immediate authority is given, not to the pope, to the bishops, or to the presbytery, but to the body of the church.[62]

Smyth's book *The Differences of the Churches of the Separation* has been called one of the curiosities of religious literature. It discloses points which were at issue between Smyth and the "Ancient Church of Amsterdam," to which Smyth and his congregation attached themselves for a time after their arrival in Holland. In this writing, Smyth debated with the pastor of the church, Francis Johnson, such matters as the authority of the presbytery, the use of the Bible in public worship, the use of Bible translations in the church service, and the observance of set forms of worship.

Little exposition of this curious book needs to be given here. The central thrust of it shows Smyth's quest for a deeply spiritual worship. The Spirit, he said, must be "at liberty." [63] Saying set forms of worship by rote is "quenching the Spirit." The same may be said of reading forms of worship out of a book.[64]

The same principle is to be observed even in the reading of the Scriptures. Christ at the synagogue read from the book and then shut the book "to signifie that that ceremony of bookworship, or the ministerie of the lettre was now exspired, & finished." [65]

Smyth's argument was in no sense intended to be a denigration of the Scriptures, which Smyth called the "Fountayne of all truth," and "the ground the foundacion of our fayth." The Scriptures are to be read and studied in the church and by the church, and interpreted with reverent diligence. Nevertheless, they are not to be "reteyned as helps before the eye in tyme of Spirituall worship." [66] The reading of the Scriptures was to be done prior to worship and was not to constitute an integral part of worship. The meaning of this procedure was that the Scripture must become internalized before it becomes a part of worship. ". . . whither we pray, prophesy, or sing," Smyth said, "it must be the word of scripture, not out of the book, but out of the hart." [67]

Smyth revealed in this work that he had a low opinion of Bible translations. No translation, he believed, "can possibly expresse all the matter of the holy originalls. . . ." [68] In the service of worship, the minister should translate the Scripture freely for the congregation from the original languages. The originals should be used, so that the minister may have contact with the original matter and content of the word. The translations should be free, so that the living Spirit may be in free communication with the hearers.[69]

Burgess notes that Smyth was disposed to a sharp distinction between what he called the "Kingdom of the Saynts" and the "priesthood of the Saynts." As members of the "kingdom," the saints transact the business of the church, study, organize, debate, receive members, excommunicate, etc. As "priests," the church engages in its highest prerogative, the offering up of spiritual sacrifice to the Lord. Thus Smyth marked off the governmental function of the church from the devotional.[70]

THE BAPTIST PHASE

In 1609 Smyth reached another important and crucial doctrinal conviction which took him out of the Separatist camp into a Baptist position. As a Separatist, he had been confident that he and his fellow Separatists had been adhering to the New Testament pattern by constituting their churches on the basis of a mutual covenant. In his study of the New Testament, however, he at length became aware that while the Old Testament said much about covenant, the New Testament said relatively little. The apostles, it now appeared to him, formed churches and admitted members on the basis of baptism upon repentance and a profession of faith.

Smyth reached another far-reaching conclusion also. If baptism was the badge of faith, there seemed to be no scriptural sanction for the retention of infant baptism.

The first of Smyth's writings to be noticed in connection with his Baptist phase is *The Character of the Beast,* published in 1609. This work reveals that Smyth became a Baptist by following through to what he considered to be the logical conclusions of his Separatist positions. He still was an uncompromising congregationalist in his ideas of church polity and in his view that the true church is made up only of saints. On the other hand, the sharp polemical weapons which Smyth had formerly used against the established church, he now directed against the Separatists themselves. "Be it knowne," said Smyth, ". . . to all the Seperation that we account them in respect of their constitution to bee as very an harlot as either her Mother England, or her grandmother Rome is, out of whose loynes she came." [71]

The false constitution of Separatism, Smyth said, springs from the fact that Separatism shares the "mark of the beast" which is found in the state church — i.e., infant baptism. "The true constitution of the Church is of a new creature baptized into the Father, the Sonne, & the holy Ghost: The false constitution is of infants baptized: . . . al those Churches that baptise infants are of the same false constitution." [72]

In *The Character of the Beast,* Smyth debated with an old Separatist friend, Richard Clifton. The argument of Clifton in support of infant baptism was the typical pedobaptist one, and centered upon the Abrahamic covenant. In this view, the seal of the Abrahamic covenant was circumcision. So in the New Testament, the children of the faithful are to receive baptism as the seal of the new covenant. As children in the Old Testament dispensation were engrafted into the covenant by circumcision, so children of the faithful now are engrafted into the new covenant by baptism. The sealing of the covenant to the believing parents with their infants, Clifton said, showed only a changing of the outward sign, from circumcision to infant baptism. [73]

Smyth replied by distinguishing between the two covenants which, he affirmed, God made with Abraham. One covenant was made with Abraham and his "carnal seed." Of that covenant, circumcision was the seal. Another covenant was made with Abraham and his "spiritual seed," and of that covenant, "the holy Spirit of promise is the seale." [74] The spiritual seed of Abraham are those who have faith. These "must first beleeve actually, & be sealed with the Spirit of promise, & then receave the baptisme of water." [75] Infants are incapable of church membership because they are not qualified for baptism. [76] Baptism is to be administered only to one who presents himself voluntarily, and it is conducted by mutual consent of the church and of the candidate. The person who so presents himself "must bee one that confesseth his

Fayth & his sinnes, one that is regenerate & borne againe." [77]

Smyth expressly avoided saying that baptism is the "seal" of the new covenant. Baptism does not, he says, "seale up any promises to the Faithfull, but onely doth visibly declare what promises they already are partakers of, viz: of the Spirit of promise." [78]

Reacting to the charge that the position which he represented was substantially that of Anabaptism, Smyth replied that the baptism of any person except one who had experienced regeneration was not baptism at all, since the true matter and the true form of baptism were lacking. Believer's baptism is therefore not a rebaptism; it is the only true baptism. [79]

Smyth thought that since true baptism had been destroyed by the corruption and falseness of the established churches, it must be recovered and started anew. ". . . when Antichrist hath utterly destroyed the true Temple, the true Church, then must we build it up againe, & when Antichrist hath destroyed the true baptisme, the[n] must we reare it up againe. . . ." [80]

Nothing seemed more scandalous to Smyth's old friends in Separatism, or to his Anglican enemies, for that matter, than his self-baptism after he reached his Baptist convictions. He therefore took some pains to justify this action. Since true baptism had been lost, he reasoned, in "Antichristian" churches, it was incumbent upon the true church to recover "the old Apostolique baptisme which Antichrist had overthrowne." [81] If believers, separating from false churches, come together to form true churches, then the same authority which enables them to form true churches empowers them to set up a true baptism. They assume all the functions and obligations of the church, one of which is baptism. ". . . two men singly are no Church, joyntly they are a Church, & they both of them put a Church uppon themselves, so may two men put baptisme uppon themselves. . . ." [82]

As a Baptist, Smyth still did not accept the view that a historical baptismal succession was necessary to true church order. The succession of the church is only by the spiritual line of faith. True baptism comes by "Spirituall succession uppon that Spirituall Line of Faythfull men confessing their Fayth & their sinnes. . . ." [83]

In 1610 Smyth published a confession of faith, consisting of one hundred articles, under the title *Propositions and Conclusions Concerning True Christian Religion Conteyning a Confession of Faith of Certaine English People, Liuinge at Amsterdam*. By this time, his health was failing, and, indeed, his life was drawing toward its close.

This notable confession, however, indicates that he had not finished traveling, spiritually and intellectually speaking. After an examination of his previous works, the student finds at least two surprises in this confession. The first is the unmistakable Arminian orientation of many of his doctrinal views. Smyth had been for most of his life, it appears, an orthodox Calvinist. Perhaps his move toward Arminianism is to be explained by his contact with the Dutch Mennonites, who were influenced by the theological views of the moderate Dutch Calvinist Jacob Arminius (1560–1609). Arminius believed in a general atonement (Christ died for all men). At any rate, because Smyth and his followers came to believe in a general atonement, they were subsequently called "General Baptists."

Smyth now affirmed that God created man with freedom of will, which man retained after the fall; that original sin is "an idle terme," because God threatened death only to Adam for his disobedience, not to his posterity; that infants are conceived and born in innocence, and that all infants dying in infancy are saved; that God did not hate Adam after his fall, but loved him still, and does not hate any man who suffers Adam's fall, but loves all mankind; that God does not predestinate any man to destruction; that God foresaw before the foundation of the world who would accept life and salvation, but that he has not decreed the choice which any man will make; that Christ's death on the cross reconciles us to God, but not God to us, because God "did never hate us." [84]

The other surprise which confronts us in this confession is the irenic spirit in which it was written. Smyth still held that the visible church consists of believers only. On the other hand, in this confession the emphasis falls upon the spiritual church invisible. ". . . the visible church is a mistycall figure outwardlie, of the true, spirituall invisible church: which consisteth of the spirits of iust and perfect men onlie, that is of the regenerate." [85] Article 69 comprises perhaps the most famous and the most moving words Smyth ever wrote. "I believe," he said,

that all penitent and faithfull Christians are brethre[n] in the communion of the outward church, wherso euer they liue, by what name soeuer they are knowen, which in truth and zeale, follow repentance and faith, though compassed with neuer so manie ignorances and infirmities: and we salute them all with a holie kisse, being hartilie grieved that wee which follow after one faith, and one spirit, one lord, and one God, one bodie, and one baptisme, should be rent into so manie sects, and schismes: and that only for matters of lesse moment.[86]

The confession reaffirmed Smyth's conviction that baptism is to be administered only to believers. Baptism and the Lord's Supper, he said, do not convey grace and regeneration. They have rather "the same use that the word hath: that they are a visible word, and that they teach to the eye of them that understand as the word teacheth the eares of them that have eares to heare." [87] Smyth reaffirmed also that there are two sorts of ministers in the church. One class is called pastors, teachers, or elders, and the other is called deacons — men and women, whose ministry is "to serve tables," and (surprisingly) to "wash the saints feet." [88]

Since Smyth in previously written books had defended the duty of magistrates to superintend true religion, it is a matter of note that in his Baptist phase he defended freedom of conscience. The magistrate, he said, is to "leaue Christian religion free, to euery mans conscience, and to handle onely ciuil transgressions." [89] Members of the outward church are to adjudicate their differences among themselves, and "not to goe to law, before the magistrates." [90]

In the last few months of his life, Smyth took up his pen once more to write a small work, posthumously entitled *The Last Booke of Iohn Smith, Called the Retraction of His Errours, and the Confirmation of the Truth.* He retracted none of the substantive convictions to which he had advanced in his last years. What he retracted was the spirit of censure in which many of his judgments had been made against others. "I protest," he said, "against that my former course of censuringe other persons, and especially for all those hard phrases, wherwith I have in any of my writings, inveighed against either England or the seperation." [91] This spirit, he admitted, "hath broken the rules of loue and charitie, which is the superiour law." [92]

In this last book, however, he found it necessary to defend himself against charges which had emanated from his own congregation, and particularly against charges which had been made by his old friend Thomas Helwys. Two of these charges were important. The first was Helwys' accusation that, by seeking to join the Mennonites, Smyth had reverted to erroneous ideas of succession. To this Smyth replied that he did not believe in any succession "except in the truth." [93] He had come to have misgivings about his self-baptism, however, on the following grounds:

> . . . it is not the truth that two or three priuate persons may baptize, whe[n] ther is a true church and ministers established whence baptisme may orderlie be had: for if Christ himself did fetch his baptisme from John, and the

gentills from the Jewes baptised, and if God be the God of order and not of confusion, then surely wee must obserue this order now, or els disorder is order, and God alloweth disorder. . . .[94]

The second charge was that Smyth subscribed to the Hoffmanite Christology. This was a very docetic view of Christ's person which was held among some of the Mennonites. Advocates of this view in its extreme form contended that Jesus did not have a human body, but that, as a divine being, he passed through the body of his mother as water passes through a pipe. To this charge Smyth replied that he believed that Jesus was of natural flesh, which he received from his mother. Smyth, in other words, subscribed to the Chalcedonian formula which contended that Christ was true God, true man. He did acknowledge, however, that he thought it far more important to know Christ's "spiritual flesh" than to know his "natural flesh,"

for who knoweth not that to knowe and be made conformable to the similitude of Christs death, buriall and resurrection in the mortification of synne and the new creature, to be made flesh of his flesh, and bone of his bone, spiritually in the fellowship of one holy āoynting, which is Christ's spiritual flesh . . . is better then the knowledge of Christs naturall flesh.[95]

The last book of John Smyth was a swan song and remains apparently a small fragment. His last days were fittingly described by W. T. Whitley. "Seven weeks he lingered, declining all debate, teaching his children, comforting his wife, cheering the brethren, 'examining his life, confessing his sins, praying for patience, having always confidence in the mercy and favour of the Lord towards him in the end.' " He died triumphantly with the testimony, "I praise the Lord, He hath now holpen me, and hath taken away my sins." [96]

CONCLUSION

One of the finest tributes ever paid to John Smyth came from the great historian Mandell Creighton:

None of the English Separatists had a finer mind or a more beautiful soul than John Smyth. None of them succeeded in expressing with so much reasonableness and consistency their aspirations after a spiritual system of religious beliefs and practice. None of them founded their opinions on so large and liberal a basis.[97]

Smyth was not destined as a Baptist leader to plant a Baptist church on English soil. That honor was reserved for his friend and former disciple, Thomas Helwys. His own congregation, in the course of a few years, disappeared in Holland by absorption into the fellowship of the Mennonites. Yet the acknowledgment of A. C. Underwood about Smyth is true.

> . . . he stands at the fountain-head of consecutive Baptist history. He may be regarded as the father and founder of the organized Baptists of England and of the General Baptists in particular. After the lapse of three hundred years he must be placed in the vanguard of what is now an ecumenical communion.[98]

Underwood's statement must stand, even though the General Baptist communion which Smyth founded was almost extinct by the end of the seventeenth century, and even though the Particular Baptists, who originated in England later in the century, had little clear connection with Smyth.

Smyth's courageous and pioneering spirit enabled him to break with old traditions and to blaze trails which were followed in later centuries by multitudes. The Baptists, allowing for wide differences and points of view within their fellowship, still stand for convictions which Smyth stood for in his own time, and which originally emanated from the spiritual pilgrimage of his own life. For identifiable historical reasons, of course, his Arminianism was soon abandoned among the great majority of Baptists. Yet his emphasis upon a regenerate church membership, upon the self-government of the church under Christ, his belief in the ministry of one rank, his belief that baptism is the badge of faith and is the constituting principle of church membership, his denial of infant baptism as a valid ordinance because infants are incapable of faith, his belief in religious freedom — all these convictions of Smyth have been written indelibly into the Baptist heritage. It is true also that Smyth contributed to the sectarian spirit which has so often marked Baptist life. Perhaps more than any other man in what Underwood calls "consecutive Baptist history," Smyth deserves the title "Baptist Pathfinder."

2-ROGER WILLIAMS-
Apostle of Religious Liberty

The exact date of birth of Roger Williams is not known. He probably was born in London in 1603, the year in which Queen Elizabeth died and in which James I became king. Forces long held in check by the strong policies of the queen were soon unleashed. There were mutterings of unrest. Divisions which had lain dormant came to the surface. A time of change, of political and religious unrest, in a few years eventuated in open revolution.

Roger Williams grew up in this time of ferment. Questions which in later years interested him profoundly were already in the air. What is the difference between the civil and the religious spheres? Can religion and politics, church and state, be separated? What is freedom for the individual conscience, and what are the limits of this freedom? Can the individual conscience stand against established authority?

Also, during this time adventurers were pushing toward the western horizons. London merchants were making London a world emporium. It was an outward-looking age, marked by a widening vision of the world.

WILLIAMS'S LIFE

A brief survey of his life will help to set the consideration of his contributions in perspective. Williams grew up in a middle-class home. The English middle class of the period became the focus of social discontent and of disrespect for the kind of kingly authority which was vested in a monarch such as James I.

Roger Williams's father was a merchant tailor in London. What influence his father's mercantile interests had upon him is a matter of conjecture. However, Williams was a trader all of his active adult life. This competence served him well in the Rhode Island wilderness.

Williams spent his youth in West Smithfield, near the commercial heart of old London. Nearby were the docks from which merchant ships carried on traffic with peoples who lived oceans away. The community was doubtless alive with news and talk about the New World. Captain John Smyth had been a worshiper at St. Sepulchre's church. Smyth's later exploits in Virginia were bound to have been known to young and old in the neighborhood. As early as 1609, the Merchant Taylors' Company was asked by the Lord Mayor to contribute to a project of colonization.

The area of London in which he grew up also furnished the impressionable young man the opportunity to observe some of the effects of religious persecution. In March, 1611/1612, a young lay preacher named Bartholomew Legate was burned as a heretic close to the Williams's home. Legate was not orthodox in his Christological views. In the same year Edward Wightman was burned in Litchfield. Other Smithfield martyrdoms had occurred many years before. In 1409/1410, for example, John Badby, a tailor, had been burned because he had said that the sacrament was "hallowed bread," not Christ's body. In 1546 Anne Askew, adjudged heretical, had suffered the rack until she died. Nine years later John Rogers, vicar of St. Sepulchre's church, had been burned.

Not far from the Williams's home were Dutch and French refugees who had been granted royal permission to maintain their own preaching, administer their own sacraments and discipline, and elect their own officers in a church which they called "Mother of all Reformed Dutch Churches." Royal permission did not keep them from being ridiculed and ostracized in the community.

The Smithfield neighborhood also contained nonconforming groups which represented various gradations of Dissent and even Separatism. These groups did not enjoy legal immunity. Hence they met secretly in private houses, going and coming with discreet furtiveness. While there is no evidence that young Williams was associated with any of these unorthodox groups, the probability is that he knew about them and about some of their opinions.[1]

Due to the patronage of Sir Edward Coke, Chief Justice of the King's Bench, Williams was admitted to Pembroke College, Cambridge, and graduated in 1626. For a year after his graduation, he was chaplain to the household of Sir William Masham. During his stay in this position, he married a maid of one of the young ladies in the household.

By the time of his marriage, Williams had become a Puritan. Indeed, it appears that he had already moved beyond Puritanism to hold the view that complete separation from the established church was necessary for saints who desired to set up a pure church. Probably due to pressure from Bishop Laud, he set sail for New England in December, 1630, arriving in Boston February 5, 1631.

Shortly after his arrival, Williams was invited to occupy the pulpit of the Boston church, since the church's minister, John Wilson, was about to return to England for a time. Williams refused the invitation, on the ground that the church was not "separated" from the Church of England.

In April, 1631, he became assistant teacher of the church at Salem. By the time he had lived only a few months in Salem, the Boston authorities had become so hostile toward him, mainly because of his Separatist views, that it became necessary for him to move to Plymouth, where he became assistant to the Plymouth pastor, Ralph Smith. In August, 1633, he returned to Salem, and twelve months later he became chief teacher in the Salem church, following the death of the pastor, Samuel Skelton.

His return to Salem brought Williams back under the jurisdiction of the Massachusetts Bay Colony (Plymouth, of course, was a separate colony). By 1635 his standing with the Massachusetts Bay establishment had so deteriorated that the General Court, on October 9, sentenced him to banishment for teaching certain dangerous opinions. John Winthrop, the governor of the colony, summarized the points at issue:

Mr. Williams holds these four particulars.

First, that we have not our land by patent from the King, but that the natives are the true owners of it, and that we ought to repent of such a receiving it by patent.

Secondly, that it is not lawful to call a wicked person to swear, to pray, as being actions of God's worship.

Thirdly, that it is not lawful to hear any of the ministers of the [Anglican] parish assemblies in England.

Fourthly, that the civil magistrate's power extends only to the bodies and goods and outward state of men, etc.[2]

Williams was permitted to remain in his house at Salem until spring, with the understanding that he should not "go about to draw others to his opinions." However, Williams was accused of violating this understanding. In January, 1636, therefore, Captain John Underhill was sent to Salem to apprehend Williams and to transport him to England. The latter, warned by Winthrop, fled, in bitter winter weather, into the "howling wilderness."

By the end of May, Williams had settled at a spot outside the jurisdiction of the Massachusetts Bay Colony. He named the new settlement Providence. Later in the year, he was joined by his wife and his two children. He supported himself and his family by farming and by trading with the Indians, whose language he had learned, and whose friendship he cultivated. In the course of time, he became a mediator between the Indians and the rest of the New England colonies, and in this role he rendered service of incalculable value both to the English and to the Indians.

As the region around the Narragansett filled with settlers, most of them refugees from the Massachusetts colony, the communities which developed in the area suffered from internal rivalries and disunities, as well as from the expansionist ambitions of Massachusetts and Connecticut. Williams went to England in 1643 to procure a charter for the infant colony. There, in 1644, he obtained from Parliament a charter which united the various towns into the colony of Rhode Island. He also published three books during his sojourn in the motherland.

In 1651 he returned to England in a successful effort to save the colony's charter at a time when dissension within the colony seemed to threaten its veritable disintegration. While in England, he published three more books and found himself to be a man of some renown among his countrymen.

Williams was "president" of the Rhode Island colony for three years, 1654–1657. The position was equivalent to his being governor, although the disunity of the colony was so great that he had little real power. He remained active in Indian affairs and continued to make his living by trading and farming. In 1672 he engaged in a public debate with three Quakers. His report on this altercation was published in Boston in 1676. When he was past seventy years of age, he acted both as a soldier and as an intermediary in King Philip's War. In his last years he became an impoverished old man, supported by his son. When he died in the spring of 1683, about eighty years of age, he was buried with military honors.[3]

WILLIAMS'S THOUGHT

Although Roger Williams was branded as something of a heretic by contemporaries who stood in high positions, he has suffered also in more recent times from the interpretations of scholars who have cast him in the role of an enlightened secular democrat. Vernon Louis Parrington, for example, said of Williams:

He was primarily a political philosopher rather than a theologian — one of the acutest and most searching of his generation of Englishmen, the teacher of Vane and Cromwell and Milton, a forerunner of Locke and the natural-rights school, one of the notable democratic thinkers that the English race has produced.[4]

The judgment of H. Richard Niebuhr that Williams was most notably a profoundly religious man is a much more realistic assessment.

> Despite the modern tendency to interpret Roger Williams as primarily a political thinker, it seems impossible that one should read his writings without understanding that he also, like Thomas More and many another Christian statesman, was first of all a churchman. He was a seeker, discontent with every institutional religious organization. . . . In spirit he was the most otherworldly man of all the New Englanders, a Protestant monk.[5]

Williams was an orthodox Calvinist. He agreed with nine-tenths of the doctrines held by men who later became his relentless antagonists, men such as John Winthrop, John Endicott, John Cotton, and Thomas Hooker. He believed firmly in the doctrines of predestination, reprobation, irresistible grace, and the perseverance of the saints, as did the most orthodox of his fellow New Englanders.

The place at which to start in assessing Williams's thought is not with his political theory, nor even with his belief in "soul freedom," but with his belief in the sovereignty of God. "At most," says LeRoy Moore, "Williams' idea of soul freedom was only derivative from his steady insistence upon an unadulterated allegiance to divine sovereignty, which was itself actually his 'great principle.' " [6]

From the idea of the sovereignty of the divine will, Williams derived the conviction of an unconditioned claim of God upon his life and upon the lives of all men. Williams's joy in the will of God received luminous expression in his *Experiments of Spiritual Life and Health,* a devotional classic which he wrote in an effort to encourage and instruct his wife.

THE NEW ENGLAND WAY

The main issue between Williams and his orthodox brethren in New England turned out to be his intransigent and radical separatism. This issue precipitated his confrontation with the Massachusetts establishment. It became the area in which he expended most of his creative energy and achieved his stature as a Christian thinker. A brief description of the New England way will serve to show the background of this confrontation.

The Puritans who went to Massachusetts intended to set up the precise form of church organization and government which they believed to have been prescribed in the New Testament. What they saw in the New Testament was a congregational polity. All churches, they thought, were local congregations. These churches were equal in status and supported no hierarchies, bishops, or presbyteries. Each church was founded on a verbal covenant and was limited to "visible saints," who related their Christian experience before the congregation and demonstrated their intention to keep the covenant in the worship of the church.

In these beliefs, the New Englanders differed from the orthodox Anglicans, and also from the majority of the Puritans, the latter of whom held to a Presbyterian church polity which did not restrict church membership to believers and which did not involve subscription to a church covenant.

While differing from the Puritan majority on matters of church polity, the leaders of Massachusetts Bay were nevertheless Non-separatists. They shared the original Puritan conviction that the Church of England should be purified, not abandoned. With the vast majority of their English contemporaries, they believed that the church should be protected and supported by the civil government.

> . . . they were entirely at one with both their Presbyterian brethren and their Anglican enemies in believing that in any society only one orthodox regime should be allowed and that the civil magistrate should suppress and, if necessary, extirpate every form of ecclesiastical or doctrinal dissent. They were legitimists, wanting to be law-abiding, conservative; they held it axiomatic that the state should protect the orthodox doctrine and way of life (once the clergy had defined it), punish heresy, and compel all inhabitants, whether church members or not, to attend services and pay taxes for the support of the ministry.[7]

The colony's charter, issued by Charles I in 1629, gave the colony the right to suppress heresy and, if necessary, to put subversives to death. This basic position, of course, was a familiar one in the mother country. The difference was that, in New England, Congregationalism became the norm of orthodoxy rather than Anglicanism or Presbyterianism.

John Cotton, the distinguished minister of the church at Boston, became the most articulate and the most learned exponent of the New England way. For this reason, and perhaps also because he had figured prominently in the proceedings which eventuated in Williams's banishment, he became a principal target of Williams's most trenchant writings.

Cotton was eloquent, sophisticated, and urbane. He was a scholar, a gentleman, and, by the standards of his time, a fine thinker. He advocated that a system of checks and balances should be observed in the relations between the church and the state. The church should maintain its own life and government without interference from the state. The state, on the other hand, should be free from church domination. Church and state were to have a cooperative relationship, in which each would observe a careful respect of the duties and prerogatives of the other.

Among the Puritans as a whole, Cotton was left of center in his ideas of church government. However, he was thoroughly orthodox in believing that the Congregational system required a vigorous magistracy for its support.[8] The state had the duty to support and require uniformity in religion. The state could not legitimately interfere in the internal life of the church, but it was obligated to see to it that only the true church was tolerated. The magistrates were to be "nursing fathers" to the church.

A man should be tolerated with respect to his doctrinal errors, Cotton taught, "unless his errors be fundamental, or seditiously and turbulently promoted. . . ." In the case of his holding false doctrines, he should be instructed and exhorted concerning the error of his way. If, after due instruction, he persisted in error, he was to be punished, in which case his punishment would be applied, not "for his conscience, but for sinning against his conscience."[9]

There is as much difference between truth and "anti-Christian doctrines," Cotton said, as between day and night. Therefore, "there is no safe toleration of them, but one of them will be rooting out the other, either lies or the truth will be banished. . . ."[10] It is therefore better to cut off the persistent heretic by banishment or death than that the flock should be "seduced and destroyed."[11] If the civil state, said Cotton, should allow the churches "to corrupt and annoy themselves by pollutions in religion, the staff of the peace of the commonwealth will soon be broken as the purity of religion is broken in the churches. . . ."[12]

THE TWO SPHERES

Williams's dissent from the New England way took the form of a separatism which issued from a profound personal conviction that only God has a right to be Lord of the conscience. Hence, his severance of the civil from the spiritual sphere was dictated by his belief that a confusion or interchange of jurisdiction was first of all fatal to the highest interests of the spiritual life and, secondarily, damaging to the life of secular society.

Williams believed that the mistake which John Cotton made, and which the New England establishment of which Cotton was representative made, was to mix and confuse two spheres which ought always to be kept separate. These spheres were the spiritual and the civil. Williams was scornful of that "commonly received and not questioned opinion, viz., that the civil state and the spiritual, the church and the commonweal, they are like Hippocrates' twins, they are born together, grow up together, laugh together, weep together, sicken and die together." [13]

The divine order for the civil and the spiritual spheres was, in Williams's opinion, one of radical separation. God, to be sure, is the God of the spiritual, the civil, and the natural orders. Natural order, Williams said, "is the same ever and perpetual." Civil order "alters according to the constitutions of peoples and nations." The spiritual order God has changed from the national in the land of Canaan (that is, in the Old Testament era), "to *particular and congregational churches* all the world over." To confound or abrogate these divinely established orders "is to exalt man's folly against the most holy and incomprehensible wisdom of God." [14]

While Williams distinguished three spheres, the natural, the civil, and the spiritual, he actually made little of the natural sphere as a separate category. The focus of his attention was rather on the other two spheres. The reason for this, perhaps, was that he really considered the state to be profoundly a part of the natural world. A "state or land is none else but a part of the world, and if so . . .it is but natural, and so lieth as the whole *world* doth in *wickedness.*" [15]

Williams had a veneration for the Scriptures, and was quite aware of Paul's assertion in Romans 13:6 that "the powers that be are ordained of God." He therefore acknowledged a double ministry, the first in the church, appointed by Christ, and the second in the state, deriving ultimately from God, but deriving immediately from the people who comprise the civil sphere.

. . . as it is most true that magistracy in general is of God for the preservation of mankind in civil order and peace (the world, otherwise, would be like the sea, wherein men, like fishes, would hunt and devour each other and the greater devour the lesser), so also it is true, that magistracy . . . is of man. Now what kind of magistrate soever the people shall agree to set up, whether he receive Christianity before he be set in office, or whether he receive Christianity after, he receives no more power of magistracy than a magistrate that has received no Christianity. For neither of them both can receive more than the commonweal, the body of people and civil state, as men, communicate unto them and betrust them with.

All lawful magistrates in the world . . . have, and can have no more power, than fundamentally lies in the bodies of fountains themselves, which power, might, or authority, is not religious, Christian, etc., but natural, human, and civil.[16]

The State

To those who think of Williams as being primarily a political thinker, it is an embarrassing fact that Williams's thought contains little of an elaborated political theory. In contrast with the view of Cotton and the rulers of New England, the nature of the state, in Williams's view, was completely secular, because it was ordained of God to regulate the material affairs of men. Its function was to maintain order, to effect a tolerable balance of interests in society, and to protect the social order from the molestation of other states from the outside.

Williams's interest in government was primarily in the definition of governmental power and the limitations of its competence. The state passes the limit of its authority, he thought, when it begins to encroach upon the domain of the kingdom of God, whose agent in the world is the church. While competent and obligated in its own sphere, the state is incompetent in the realm of the spirit.

Williams was not concerned to describe in great detail the nature of civil government. Although he has been hailed as the "Irrepressible Democrat," it would be difficult to prove that he subscribed to democracy or to any other specific form of government.

He was irrepressible enough, and noble enough, but it is the irrepressibility and the nobility of a passionate pilgrim who spends his life trying to save souls and to win for them the soul liberty they desire. He would have taken soul liberty gratefully from any government. He is content to enjoy it in Rhode Island either under the authority of Parliament, a Cromwellian dictatorship, or a restored Stuart. When he visits England in the course of the Revolution, it is the struggle for soul liberty that interests him, not the struggle for civil liberty. He has no contacts with the Levellers, the only genuinely democratic party thrown up by Puritanism. When he has to concern himself in Rhode Island with the details of political organization— a task for which he had no particular talent—he shows himself to be a constitutionalist, trying to adapt English representative institutions to a frontier situation, but with no commitment to social democracy.[17]

Since the civil order, in his opinion, was essentially secular, Williams was convinced that government might be as efficient and as wholesome under non-Christian as under Christian auspices.

"Both these *Antichristian states,* and since also the *Turkish Monarchy,* have flourished many *generations* in external and outward prosperity and glory, notwithstanding their *religion* is false." [18] Eventually, God will cause all nations to drink the cup of his wrath for their national sins, but this usually follows "a long course of many *ages* and *generations,*" as in the case of Nineveh, Athens, Constantinople, and Rome.[19]

Williams did not agree that it was the task of the magistrate to "see godliness preserved" in the realm of his jurisdiction. The *bonus magistratus* is not so denominated by his concern for promoting the interests of a particular religion, but by giving his attention to the peculiar concerns of civil government. Williams observed that there are "divers sorts of goodness." One may say "good air, a good ground, a good tree, a good sheep," city, corporation, husband, father, master, physician, lawyer, or seaman, without meaning that the term "good" in reference to these entities involves a Christian quality. So a "good" magistrate may be good without reference to a Christian quality in the exercise of his office. A good magistrate is to be reckoned so with regard to his "civil respects and employments." [20]

In answer to the charge that permission for false religion to flourish in civil society would promote society's destruction, Williams replied that this was not true so long as the adherents of the false religion break no civil law. If civil laws are not broken, "civil peace is not broken." Moreover, if false religion is confined to society, without penetrating the church, it is not capable of damaging the life of the church. "A false religion out of the church will not hurt the church, no more than weeds in the wilderness hurt the enclosed garden, or poison hurt the body when it is not touched or taken, yea, and antidotes are received against it." [21]

The Church

If Williams's theory of the state was neither elaborately nor extensively developed, it may appear even more surprising that a man of such profound religious conviction did not spell out in great detail a definite ecclesiology. His elaboration of a doctrine of the church was in most points fragmentary and inadequate. So much is this true that many of his interpreters find him to have been indifferent to what the Puritans called "the visible church." For example, William Warren Sweet says, ". . . Williams stressed the inner experience, and to him the true Church was an invisible entity made up of the regenerate — an inward experience without physical form. The visible Church, therefore, to Williams was of slight importance. . . ." [22]

Provisional support of this opinion may be found in that although Williams became a Baptist in Rhode Island for a few months in 1636, he soon withdrew from the church which he had joined. He declared himself a Seeker, thenceforth dissatisfied with every insitutional expression of the church, although he did not withdraw from public worship.

The position to which Williams ultimately came, it would appear, was that the church, as an empirical, social, sociological entity, as an institution in the world, was, as Sweet observed, "of slight importance."

In a famous passage, Williams said:

> . . . the church, or company of worshippers, whether true or false, is like unto a body or college of physicians in a city—like unto a corporation, society, or company of East India or Turkey merchants, or any other society or company in London; which companies may hold their courts, keep their records, hold disputations, and in matters concerning their society may dissent, divide, break into schisms and factions, sue and implead each other at the law, yea, wholly break up and dissolve into pieces and nothing, and yet the peace of the city not be in the least measure impaired or disturbed; because the essence or being of the city, and so the well being and peace thereof, is essentially distinct from those particular societies; the city courts, city laws, city punishments distinct from theirs. The city was before them, and stands absolute and entire when such a corporation or society is taken down. [23]

It should be emphasized that the above statement, however remarkable, was intended to indicate only the relative unimportance of the church *as an institution in the civil sphere*. It was not intended to indicate that the church is unimportant as a spiritual fellowship. In a statement just preceding the passage above quoted, Williams asserted that no man can prove the existence of a *true church* in the "many and flourishing cities of the world." Yet, he says, "the peace spiritual" is of "a higher and far different nature" from the peace of the city, since the latter is only civil and human.

In Williams's many references to the church, it is often difficult to tell whether he is speaking about the church as an uninstitutionalized, unorganized spiritual community (the universal spiritual church), or of the church as a concrete, visible entity in the world. In reply to a charge by John Cotton that Williams did not acknowledge the validity of any churches extant, Williams replied that it was true that he was unable to recognize any ecclesiastical institution as a true church of Christ. He sought to make a distinction between the spiritual reality and the empirical institution. The true church, he appears to be saying, expresses itself through various Christian personalities and ecclesiastical arrangements, with varying degrees of clarity, approximation, and distortion.

> Although the Discusser cannot to his *Souls satisfaction* conclude any of the various and several sorts of *Churches* extant to be those pure *golden Candlesticks* framed after the first patterne, *Rev.* 1:12-20. Yet doth he acknowledge *golden Candlesticks* of *Christ Jesus* extant; those golden *Olive trees* and *candlesticks*, his *Martyrs* or *Witnesses*, standing before the *Lord*, and testifying his holy *Truth* during all the *Reign* of the *Beast, Rev.* 11:4. Hence, although we have not *satisfaction* that *Luther* or *Calvin*, or other precious *Witnesses* of *Christ Jesus*, erected *Churches* or *Ministeries*, after the first pattern . . . yet doth he affirm them to have been *Prophets* and *witnesses* against the *Beast*, and furnished sufficiently with *Spirituall Fire* in their *mouthes*, mightily able to consume or humble their *Enemies*, as *Elijah* did with the captains sent out against him. [2 Kings 1:10].[24]

On the other hand, much of Williams's discussion of the church would seem to refer to what might be termed the empirical church. It is possible to infer from various parts of his writings that Williams believed in a congregationalist ecclesiology, both because he believed that the New Testament church, in its visible form, was congregational, and because he thought that any recovery of church purity would involve a gathering of regenerate persons into fellowships separate from polluted organizations which included both Christians and "Anti-Christians." This mixing of church and world was, in his view, the fatal disqualification of the Church of England. And, he charged, it was not less the fatal flaw of the New England churches, which brought the world into the church by the retention of infant baptism, and which polluted themselves by a persecuting alliance with the civil government. ". . . godly and regenerate persons," Williams said, ". . . are not fitted to constitute the true Christian church, until it hath pleased God to convince their souls of the evil of the false church, ministry, worship, &c." [25]

Williams held against Cotton the latter's refusing to go the whole way to separation when, he said, Cotton himself realized the importance of separating the true church from the false. "This Mr. Cotton himself will not deny, if he remembers how little a while it is since the falsehood of a national, provincial, diocesan, and parishional church . . . and the truth of a particular congregation, consisting of holy persons, appeared to him." [26] Instead of following his convictions, Williams charged, Cotton had become the champion of another national church, the Massachusetts establishment! [27]

The Separatists, although they themselves were divided into "many several professions," were yet known by "their exposing themselves for Christ to greater sufferings, and their desiring no civil sword nor arm of flesh, but the two-edged sword of God's Spirit to try out the matter by. . . . Let the inhabitants of the world judge," Williams said, "which come nearest to the doctrine, holiness, poverty, patience, and practice of the Lord Jesus Christ." [28] Cotton, said Williams, would not sanction or practice separation, although he knew that the "generality of every parish in England consisteth of unregenerate persons. . . ." Non-separation resulted in maintaining an alliance with this godless system in the home country. "What are two or three or more of regenerate and godly persons in such communions," Williams asked, "but as two or three roses or lilies in a wilderness? a few grains of good corn in a heap of chaff. . . ?" [29] And Williams believed the same corrupt system was being perpetuated in New England.

Very evidently, there is an ambivalence in Williams's thought about the church. Although he became a Seeker, refusing to recognize the validity of any institutional church, he continued to make references to the church in ways which would apply only to the church in its institutional expressions. His references to the church as a suffering church, for example, had direct exemplification in actual dissenting congregations. "The Christian church," said Williams, "doth not persecute; no more than a lily doth scratch the thorns, or a lamb pursue and tear the wolves, or a turtle-dove hunt the hawks and eagles, or a chaste and modest virgin fight and scratch like whores and harlots." [30]

There is even more applicability to the empirical church in his comparisons of the disciplinary powers of the state with those of the church. "Civil officers bear not the sword in vain," Williams said, "when the *civil state* is assaulted, as the *spiritual officers* and *governors* of the church bear not in vain the *spiritual* and *two-edged sword* coming out of the *mouth* of Christ." [31] Even more pointedly:

. . . when Paul saith, *The weapons of our warfare are not carnal but spiritual,* he denieth no civil weapons of justice to the civil magistrate, Rom. xiii., but only to church officers. And yet the weapons of such officers he acknowledgeth to be such, as though they be spiritual yet are ready to take vengeance of all disobedience, 2 Cor. x. 6; which hath reference, amongst other ordinances, to the censure of the church against scandalous offenders.[32]

How the spiritual church is related to the empirical church in Williams's thought is a question which cannot be further pursued here. It is enough to say that he believed that "the *Church* of *Christ* is a *congregation* of *Saints*";[33] that the saints must separate from false churches; that he repudiated the ordinances of apostate churches; that he insisted upon a regenerate church membership; that he rejected infant baptism; and that he affirmed that the church must be free to pursue its spiritual life without molestation from the state.

Separation of Church and State

Whatever Williams believed about the institutional church, it is evident that he was vitally interested in the spiritual life to which the church ministered. He believed in the separation of church and state to the end that all men might have the "soul liberty" to traffic with God without hindrance. Since the church belonged to the spiritual sphere, and the state to the sphere of nature, the competence, the principles, and the authority of each did not apply in the sphere of the other. Therefore, the church should not attempt to interfere in the life of the state, nor the state in the life of the church. Each had its own autonomy of life apart from the other.

Williams made these spheres so distinct that serious questions can be raised about the value of his thought with regard to this particular point. Can church and state be made as separate as Williams wanted to make them? His own experience and observation told him that when the religious life and the civil life were bound together, the result was a mixing of spheres, the use of the powers and weapons of the one in the domain of the other, and the consequent spoiling and even destruction of both.

If Roger Williams separated the two spheres somewhat unrealistically, his appreciation of the problem was realistic indeed. He had observed in both old and New England, and had felt in his own life, the baleful consequences of the mixing of the two spheres. His conviction was that this mixing resulted in either a tyranny of the church over the state or of the state over the church. If they were in partnership, the result was a collective tyranny over the individual conscience.

To say that church and state in the thought of Williams were separated is not to say that they were unrelated. Rather, their relation was one of separation. It was also one of toleration, in which each, recognizing the rights and prerogatives of the other, agreed to respect those rights and prerogatives without interference.

Perhaps the most eloquent and the most famous passage in all of Williams's writings is a parable of a ship at sea, in which passage he stated his conviction concerning the separation of the civil from the spiritual sphere, while affirming their separate validity and necessity.

> There goes many a ship at sea, with many hundred souls in one ship, whose weal and woe is common, and is a true picture of a commonwealth or a human combination or society. It hath fallen out sometimes that both Papists and Protestants, Jews and Turks, may be embarked in one ship; upon which supposal I affirm that all the liberty of conscience that ever I pleaded for turns upon these two hinges: that none of the Papists, Protestants, Jews, or Turks be forced to come to the ship's prayers or worship, nor compelled from their own particular prayers or worship, if they practice any. I further add that I never denied that, notwithstanding this liberty, the commander of this ship ought to command the ship's course, yea, and also command that justice, peace, and sobriety be kept and practiced, both among the seamen and all the passengers. If any of the seamen refuse to perform their services, or passengers to pay their freight; if any refuse to help, in person or purse, towards the common charges or defense; if any refuse to obey the common laws and orders of the ship concerning their common peace or preservation; if any shall mutiny and rise up against their commanders and officers; if any should preach that there ought to be no commanders or officers because all are equal in Christ, therefore no masters nor officers, no laws nor orders, nor corrections nor punishments—I say, I never denied but in such cases, whatever is pretended, the commander or commanders may judge, resist, compel, and punish such transgressors according to their deserts and merits.[34]

The Scriptural Sanction

A close alignment of responsibility between church and state was justified by the New England fathers on the basis of that court of ultimate appeal, the Scriptures, which were held in veneration by Williams as well as by themselves. The interpretation of the Scriptures became, therefore, crucial in establishing the wide divergencies between Williams's interpretation and theirs.

Perry Miller, a perceptive interpreter of Williams, called Williams's fundamental principle his typological interpretation of the Bible.[35] Certainly the typological interpretation employed by Williams was decisively different from the interpretation of New England orthodoxy.

While typology was a device frequently used by Protestants to relate the Old Testament to the New, it was seldom used as boldly, or with such sweeping conclusions, as Williams used it. The orthodox interpreted the relationship of the Old Testament to the New as an unfolding through history of a perennial covenant between God and man. It was a covenant within which men were still living. By this method of interpretation, the government of Israel was in certain respects a model for the guidance of modern governments. The first four of the Ten Commandments were laws still in force and were to be employed by government in the ordering of society. New England orthodoxy attempted to mold itself by these commandments. The Christian magistrate had as one of his principal duties the support of true worship and the suppression of false worship, after the example of the kings of Israel in the Old Testament. Thus persecution of religious error was given the sanction of biblical mandate.

Williams explicitly repudiated both this method of interpretation and the conclusions which the orthodox had derived therefrom. There was, in his opinion, no less than a radical break between the Old Testament and the New. There was not to be a literal carry-over of the laws and examples of the Old Testament into the Christian era. The Old Testament was full of "types" for the instruction of Christians, but these types were to be given figurative, not literal, interpretation. The nation Israel, the kings and rulers of this nation, the battles which Israel fought, the captivities and deliverances of its people, were to be interpreted for the *spiritual* edification of the people of God, not as legal models.

Williams's pursuit of this methodology was extensive and elaborate. His method of reasoning may be indicated by brief citations.

In *The Bloudy Tenent of Persecution,* Peace asks Truth to "glance at the difference of the wars of this people (Israel) from the wars of other nations, and of their having no antitype but the churches of Christ Jesus." Truth replies that all the nations round about Israel "had indignation" against her. This was a typical representation of the lot of the Israel of the *New* Testament.

Such enemies the Lord Jesus foretold his Israel, The world shall hate you. . . . All that live godly in Christ Jesus must be persecuted, or hunted. . . . And not only by flesh and blood, but also by principalities, powers, spiritual wickedness in high places . . . by the whole pagan world under the Roman emperors, and the whole anti-christian world under the Roman popes . . . by the kings of the earth. . . .[36]

The Israel of God now, men and women, fight under the great Lord General, the Lord Jesus Christ: their weapons, armour, and artillery, are like themselves, spiritual . . . so mighty and so potent that they break down the strongest holds and castles, yea, in the very souls of men, and carry into captivity the very thoughts of men, subjecting them to Christ Jesus.[37]

Also, the following passage is a characteristic and an especially pithy example of Williams's use of the typological method:

. . . only such as are Abraham's seed, circumcised in heart, new-born, Israel
. . . are the antitype of the former Israel; these are only the holy nation,
1 Pet. ii. 9: wonderfully redeemed from the Egypt of this world, Tit. ii. 14;
brought through the Red Sea of baptism, 1 Cor. x. 2; through the wilderness of afflictions, and of the peoples, Deut. viii., Ezek. xx., into the kingdom
of heaven begun below, even that Christian land of promise where flow
the everlasting streams and rivers of spiritual milk and honey.[38]

But New England orthodoxy was not limited to the Old Testament to find explicit sanction for the belief that the civil powers
were to be "nursing fathers" to the church. There were New Testament sanctions for this course also, the principal one of which
was in Romans 13:1 f. (KJV): "Let every soul be subject unto the
higher powers . . . the powers that be are ordained of God. . . ."
The establishment interpreted this injunction to mean that if the
church offended, it is incumbent upon the magistrate "to seek the
healing thereof as a nursing father"; if his advice does not prevail,
then he is to "exercise the superiority of his power in redressing
what is amiss." [39]

Williams observed, however, that Romans 13 took account of
a twofold state, a civil state and a spiritual state. These involved
distinct and characteristic features: civil officers and spiritual officers, civil punishment and spiritual punishment, civil weapons and
spiritual weapons. The powers and weapons of one are incompetent in the realm of the other.[40]

. . . to batter down idolatry, false worship, heresy, schism, blindness, hard-
ness, out of the soul and spirit, it is vain, improper, and unsuitable to bring
those weapons which are used by persecutors, stocks, whips, prisons, swords,
gibbets, stakes . . . but against these spiritual strongholds in the souls of
men, spiritual artillery and weapons are proper, which are mighty through
God to subdue and bring under the very thought to obedience. . . .
Will the Lord Jesus . . . join to his breastplate of righteousness, the
breastplate of iron and steel? to the helmet of righteousness and salvation in
Christ, a helmet and crest of iron, brass, or steel? [41]

With telling insight, Williams observed that any system of
partnership between state and church really turned the power of
decision over to the civil magistrate.

. . . since the magistrate is bound . . . to see the church, the church officers,
and members do their duty, he must therefore judge what is the church's
duty, and when she performs or not performs it, or when she exceeds; so
likewise when the ministers perform their duty, or when they exceed it:—
And if the magistrate must judge, then certainly by his own eye, and
not by the eyes of others. . . .
Then also, upon his judgment must the people rest, as upon the mind
and judgment of Christ. . . .[42]

The church must judge when the magistrate offends; and yet the magistrate must judge when the church offends. . . . And therefore, though the church make him a delinquent at the bar, yet by their confession God hath made him a judge on the bench. What blood, what tumults, have been and must be spilt upon these grounds.[43]

In such a system, Williams charged, men have more confidence "in the *sword* of *steel* that hangs by the side of the *civil officer,* than in the two-edged sword" which proceeds from the mouth of Christ. Thus, it makes *"Christ's spiritual sword* but *serviceable* and *subordinate* unto the *temporal* or worldly *powers. . . ."* [44]

Soul Liberty

Williams held that Christians are to be subject even to pagan magistrates in civil matters but are not to obey them in matters of faith and worship, or in matters pertaining to the government of the church. Christians are not to yield an inch of their Christian convictions to tyranny. The only thing they are to yield is "so many hundred thousand of their *bodies,* as the bodies of *Lambs* to the devouring jaws of those *bloody lions* and *devilish monsters,* of more than barbarous cruelty." [45] In other words, the church's resistance is to be nonviolent, but unyielding, to the force of civil coercion. Even when the saints are persecuted and slain, they do not fight for themselves "with any other *weapons* than by the *word* of their *prophecy,* the *blood* of the *Lamb,* their patient *sufferings,* the not loving their lives unto the *death."* [46]

Williams was discerning enough to see the profound hypocrisy which lay behind the practice of persecution. He saw that the fundamentals of faith are not as clear as Cotton undertook to make them, and certainly not enough to justify coercion of belief.[47] Besides, he asked, why should "Master Cotton's conscience" and ministry be maintained by the sword, any more than the consciences and ministries of Cotton's fellow-subjects? [48] The hypocrisy of the persecutors is shown by the fact that no one ever admits to persecuting the Son of God. He rather clothes himself in the garments of self-righteousness.

No, saith Pharaoh, the Israelites are idle, and therefore they speak of sacrificing. David is risen up in conspiracy against Saul, therefore persecute him. Naboth hath blasphemed God and the king, therefore stone him. Christ is a seducer of the people, a blasphemer against God, and traitor against Caesar, therefore hang him. Christians are schismatical, factious, heretical, therefore persecute them. The devil hath deluded John Huss, therefore crown him with a paper of devils, and burn him. . . .[49]

It is the self-righteousness of both popish and Protestant sects which makes them persecutors. Each one cries out:

> We are *righteous,* my title is good, and the *best.* We are *holy,* we are *orthodox* and *godly:* You must spare *us,* believe *us,* honour *us,* feed *us,* protect and defend *us* in peace and quietness. Others are *Heretics, Apostates, Seducers, Idolators, Blasphemers;* starve *them,* imprison *them,* banish *them,* yea hang *them,* burne *them* with fire and sword pursue them.[50]

Persecution, Williams asserted, is never justified. Indeed, the persecutor is a soul-murderer. The compelling of conscience is a greater crime than if one "blew up parliaments, and cut the throats of kings or emperors, so precious is that invaluable jewel of a soul. . . ." The persecutor will pay life for life and soul for soul, although the exaction of this payment is in the hands of God alone.[51] In the meantime, we are to obey God's admonition to show gentleness toward all men, even toward our oppressors, for "It may be, God may *give them repentance."* Complete freedom of conscience in religious concerns is to be granted to the Jews, the Turks, the papists, and toward those of all other persuasions, for freedom of conscience is no more than their right.[52]

> Grant a man to be a false teacher, a heretic, a Balaam, a spiritual witch, a wolf, a persecutor, breathing out blasphemies against Christ and slaughters against his followers, as Paul did, Acts ix. 1, I say, these who appear soul-killers today, by the grace of Christ may prove, as Paul, soul-savers to-morrow.[53]

Despite the fact that Williams demanded complete freedom of conscience, he believed that the civil magistrate did have certain obligations to "religion and worship." To that worship which the magistrate believes is true, he owes personal commitment, respect, and protection. To that worship which he does not believe to be true, he owes permission, and protection, "that no injury be offered either to the persons or goods of any." [54]

WILLIAMS'S CONTRIBUTION

A discussion which focuses upon Roger Williams as an advocate of religious liberty, however important his contribution was in this vital area, nevertheless runs the risk of obscuring the impressive breadth of the man. His life with the Indians, his love for them and theirs for him; his efforts to learn their language, and his relative mastery of their tongue; his work among them as a mediator by which he was able repeatedly to render for them and for the New England colonies a heroic service; his adroit and effective diplomacy in England to obtain a charter for Rhode Island, and to protect and sustain the struggling colony; his access in

England to some of the foremost men of the country, such as Vane, Milton, and Cromwell, who respected and admired him; his ability to maintain friendships with men with whom he sometimes radically disagreed, such as Governor John Winthrop of Massachusetts Bay; his hard work in the meantime to sustain himself and his loved ones by trading and farming; his devotion to his family; his solid contributions as a citizen and a public official in the colony, despite misunderstandings and personal differences — all of these varied labors and achievements have to be considered in measuring the man.

Ola Winslow, one of Williams's most discerning biographers, says of him:

> As Roger Williams met the "barbarous distractions" of his near half century on the fringe of the Narragansett country, he also lived another life of study, of thought, of religious satisfactions, of inward growth, to which the outer background of his life gives little clue. His mind roamed far places; his very large correspondence with men in England, as well as in other colonies, brought him in touch with the ongoing life of those who spoke his language; he read; he learned. The wilderness extended his view, not only by making the universe more vast to his eyes, but also by resolving its contrasts and strengthening the sense of unity in its vastness and diversity. In this unity he found a sustaining comfort. His life with the Indians also enlarged his view, and made him hospitable to ideas sharply different from his own. This should not be a hard lesson for an individualist to learn, but it was hard for Roger Williams. In the wilderness he also learned quietness, inner quietness.[55]

Even so, Williams's greatest contribution lay in the area of religious liberty. Roger Williams was not the first man in modern history, of course, to advocate liberty of conscience. It had been championed by the anti-pedobaptists of the sixteenth century, and by some of the leaders of the General Baptists in the early seventeenth century. John Smyth, for example, had said:

> [We believe] that the magistrate is not by vertue of his office to meddle with religion, or matters of conscience, to force and compell men to this or that form of religion or doctrine: but to leaue the Christian religion free, to euery mans conscience, and to handle onely ciuil transgressions, injuries and wronges of men against man, in murther, Adulterie, theft, etc., for Christ onelie is the king and lawgiuer of the church and conscience.[56]

Likewise, Thomas Helwys made a militant defense of religious liberty in his book entitled *A short Declaration of the Mistery of Iniquity*, published in 1612. The substance of this book is expressed in the following famous passage:

> Our lord the king is but an earthly king, and he hath no authority as a king but in earthly causes, and if the king's people be obedient and true

subjects, obeying all human laws made by the king, our lord and king can require no more: for men's religion to God is betwixt God and themselves; the king shall not answer for it, neither may the king be judge between God and man. Let them be heretics, Turks, Jews, or whatsoever, it appertains not to the earthly power to punish them in the least measure.[57]

W. K. Jordan, author of the monumental work entitled *The Development of Religious Toleration in England,* believed that Williams was not a great creative writer, nor an especially important contributor to the task of developing the philosophical foundations of religious liberty. Williams was indebted not only to earlier Baptist theorists, but also to the radical Independents in England with whom he was closely associated, and whom he militantly supported during his visits back in the mother country. Nevertheless, his books championing the rights of conscience were written at the right time to deliver a powerful blow for liberty in the highly charged atmosphere of the religious and political situation to which they were addressed, both in England and in New England. His work was widely recognized as having been tested by years of controversy with ecclesiastics in America and by a remarkable experiment in religious liberty in Rhode Island. His views were backed up by his life and were successfully embodied in the civil constitution of his little colony. In Rhode Island for the first time in modern history, religious liberty had become the law of the land.

It would not be correct to say that Roger Williams was the principal architect of the great achievements of religious liberty, and of the separation of church and state, as these finally developed on the American religious scene. The actual development of these achievements derived from such diverse historical sources, and from the contributions of so many thinkers who were not directly indebted to Williams, that this claim cannot be made. At the same time, the work of Williams may be said to have, as Sidney Mead indicates, a "long-term symbolic value."[58] For the history of what later became the United States, says Perry Miller,

. . . Roger Williams possesses one indubitable importance, that he stands at the beginning of it. Just as some great experience in the youth of a person is ever afterward a determinant of his personality, so the American character has inevitably been molded by the fact that in the first years of colonization there arose this prophet of religious liberty. . . . As a figure and a reputation he was always there to remind Americans that no other conclusion than absolute religious freedom was feasible in this society.[59]

Although John Mecklin perhaps unduly depreciated the value of Williams's thought, he was certainly correct in saying that "the story of his struggle for religious liberty, which he thought so futile, has become part of our most precious spiritual heritage." [60]

While the contribution of Roger Williams to the concept of religious liberty is relatively clear, his relationship to Baptist life and thought is ambiguous. Williams remained in formal connection with a Baptist church for only a few months. In 1649 he wrote to John Winthrop concerning the Baptist practice of baptism:

> I believe their practice comes nearer the first practice of our great Founder Christ than other practices of religion doe, and yet I have not satisfaction neither in the authoritie by which it is done, nor in the manner: nor in the prophecies concerning the rising of Christs Kingdome after the desolations of Rome, &c.[61]

Shortly after he had led in the founding of the Baptist church in Providence, Williams appears to have reached the conclusion that all existing churches, including the one at Providence, lacked a proper foundation. This foundation could be supplied only by a new apostolic dispensation. New apostles, divinely commissioned, would have to appear, to set up again the true church. Until that happened, Williams thought, there would be no true churches in existence. Williams's prompt withdrawal from the Providence church makes the observation of Henry C. Vedder a just one, i.e., that the part played by Williams in the institutional life of the Baptists has been a "ludicrously small" one, "when the facts are compared to the ink that has been shed on the subject." [62] More recently, Robert G. Torbet remains duly cautious in assessing Williams's relationship to the Baptists. The significance of Williams to the Baptists, according to Torbet, was his devotion to religious liberty and the creation of a climate where the Baptists could be heard.[63]

A statement by historian A. H. Newman, nevertheless, brings us nearer to the truth concerning Williams's relationship to the Baptists. "[Williams] remained a Baptist," said Newman, "in everything except in his demand for direct divine sanction for the restoration of the ordinances long since hopelessly lost." [64] Although he gave up his membership in a Baptist church, he retained throughout his life theological convictions which were identifiably Baptist. He believed in a congregational church government, a regenerate church membership, a rejection of infant baptism, and the baptism of believers only. These were Baptist positions.

However, the Baptists insistently claim him still at the point of his distinguished and heroic advocacy of religious liberty. Here he is a foremost representative of one of the Baptists' most cherished convictions. They claim him as their most illustrious champion of a principle with which they have eagerly associated themselves in the brightest hours of their own history. In this sense, the name of Roger Williams will always add luster to the Baptist cause.

3 - ISAAC BACKUS -
Leader of the Separate Baptists

Isaac Backus has been chosen as the subject of this chapter because he was a prominent representative figure in the rise of a significant new movement among the Baptists of America. This movement led to the emergence of a new Baptist denomination, the Separate Baptists, whose influence upon Baptists in the United States has been far-reaching. Backus was both a child of this movement and its most articulate spokesman. His contribution will be described within the context of the rise and progress of the Separate Baptists. A summary account of the historical and cultural factors pertinent to the larger inquiry must first be attempted.

THE SEPARATE BAPTISTS

The setting for the consideration of the emergence of the Separate Baptists is colonial New England. The beginnings of Baptists in this area are quite obscure. Perhaps no one knows exactly how many Baptist churches and church members there were in the region in the early eighteenth century. Isaac Backus knew of thirteen Baptist churches which existed in New England in 1730. Only three of these were Particular (Calvinistic) Baptist churches. The other ten appear to have been of General (Arminian) Baptist background.[1] As early as 1670, four General Baptist churches had organized in Rhode Island the first Baptist association of churches in America. By 1729 this association comprised thirteen churches in Massachusetts, Connecticut, and New York.[2]

On fundamental theological conceptions pertaining to the Bible, the ordinances, sin, salvation, the Trinity, heaven, hell, and the final judgment, the Baptists shared many points of agreement with the New England Congregationalists, the dominant religious group in the region. For this reason, Cotton Mather, who was no friend of the Baptists, could say that the Baptists "have infinitely more of Christianity among them than the Quakers and have indeed been useful defenders of Christianity against the assaults of the Quakers." [3]

Except in Rhode Island, however, the Baptists were not welcome in New England. Their churches were illegal in status; their members were denied voting rights; they were taxed for the support of the state churches. In many cases, they were annoyed and harassed, hailed into court, imprisoned, and sometimes beaten for practicing their faith.

The points at issue between the Baptists and the established church were succinctly summarized by Isaac Backus: First, "the extending of the gospel ordinance of baptism to subjects who are in a state of nature"; second, "limiting the church of Christ to human schools for ministers"; and, third, "compelling all to support such and only such. . . ." [4] The Baptist answers to these issues were characteristic. They were believer's baptism, a spiritual call to the ministry, and religious liberty.

The Baptist witness was, however, too small to be very effective. The status of the Baptists as a disinherited, illegal group had placed them under crippling disadvantages. Their scattered, isolated congregations lacked any overall cohesion. They were unaggressive and only halfheartedly evangelistic. They were caught in the general spiritual lethargy of the times and were slowly verging toward decline.

One of the most remarkable episodes in American colonial history is commonly referred to by historians as the Great Awakening. It was a veritable blaze of religious interest and revival. While the New England phase of the Awakening began at Northampton, Massachusetts, in 1734 under the preaching of Jonathan Edwards, its most dramatic phase began with the visit to New England of the great English evangelist George Whitefield. Whitefield's tour of six weeks in 1740 drew tremendous crowds. His impassioned oratory, striking dramatic power, sonorous voice, the intense earnestness of his preaching, and the authentic evangelical note in his message produced everywhere a profound impression.

Whitefield's efforts were reinforced by the work of a host of lesser luminaries, who preached in the open air, itinerated widely, and brought the effects of the revival not only to the cities, but also to village and hamlet and open countryside.

The Revival was much more than the fiery ministrations of Whitefield, Tennent, and Davenport. The Awakening was "Great" because it was general: none escaped its influence or avoided its controversy. In both coastal and frontier areas, within cities and rural communities, in churches and in open fields, people gathered to hear an earnest evangelistic gospel, be it preached by their own minister, a neighboring pastor, a trespassing itinerant, or an exhorter. Men whose words had never before been heeded now proclaimed, wrote, and published their zealous defense or their acrimonious contempt of the "present extraordinary work of God." New England's printing presses vastly increased their output, giving to religious subjects significant precedence. Executive, legislative, and judicial officials were obliged to note and to deal with this upsurge of religious interest. Over the most keenly intellectual or the most grossly credulous, the revival had its sway.[5]

After Whitefield's return to England, some of New England's strongest Congregationalist ministers, such as Jonathan Edwards, Eleazor Wheelock, and Joseph Bellamy, became, for the time being, itinerant evangelists. To the surprise of these evangelists, some of the meetings were marred by emotional excesses which served to bring the revival (and revivalism) into considerable disfavor. Certain individuals among the evangelists, of whom James Davenport was a notable example, gained unsavory reputations as rabble-rousers.

The Great Awakening continued to have sporadic manifestations for some years, but the crest of its power had definitely passed by 1744. Between 1740 and 1760 many thousands of members were added to the churches of New England. One hundred and fifty new Congregationalist churches were founded. Although it is impossible to say exactly how many Baptist and Separate congregations sprang into existence, the number was surprisingly large.[6]

"OLD LIGHTS" AND "NEW LIGHTS"

The Puritan fathers of New England had insisted upon a conversion experience as a prerequisite to membership in their churches. For many years before the Great Awakening, however, a general cooling of religious enthusiasm had relaxed the churches' insistence upon a conscious experience of conversion. Conversion, it was held, was so inward and so subtle that it could transpire without, perhaps, even being recognized by oneself. Anyone who lived a respectable moral life, "owned" the church covenant, and maintained a conventional observance of his church duties was presumed to be converted.

The strict congregationalist ideal of a pure church composed of "visible saints" only was seriously compromised by the widespread adoption of the "Halfway Covenant" (1657, 1662). By the terms of this covenant, the infants of unconverted church members (which members had been baptized in infancy and had grown up in the churches without ever being converted) were themselves permitted to receive baptism by the churches. The Halfway Covenant

> . . . admitted that persons baptized in infancy, even though not professing Christians, were connected somehow with the visible church and were capable of passing along to their children the same degree of membership that they themselves possessed. They were permitted to present their children for baptism, provided they themselves were of upright life and would "own the covenant" into which they had been born. They were not, however, to partake of the Lord's Supper or vote in church affairs; hence they were "halfway" members.[7]

In 1700, Solomon Stoddard, of Northampton, Massachusetts, made an open appeal to admit unconverted church members to the Lord's Supper on the ground that the Lord's Supper was a converting ordinance, as well as an ordinance for those already converted. "Stoddardeanism," though opposed by many critics, became an accepted practice in many New England churches.

The doctrine of the "new birth," pointing to an ascertainable change as a necessary precedent to salvation, was not generally held in any Christian circles in New England when the revival began. The conversion experience became, however, under the leadership of the revivalists, the central emphasis of the Great Awakening. As a corollary to this emphasis upon an inward experience, the revivalists believed that a convert might certainly be distinguished from those who had not experienced regeneration. They believed that those who manifested no discernible change should be considered unregenerate and should be debarred from Communion.[8]

The revival soon focused attention upon the spiritual leaders of the people — the ministers. Before the Great Awakening, it does not appear that the established churches in New England required a conversion experience for their ministerial candidates, and they did not have the idea of an internal or spiritual call. In 1712, the ministers of Connecticut, at their general association, recommended that a candidate for the ministry should be required to show proficiency in Hebrew, Greek, Latin, logic, and philosophy. He should demonstrate acquaintance with the main principles of the Christian religion. He should acknowledge his assent to the confession of faith which was publicly held by the churches of the colony and should give evidence of "sober and religious conversation."[9] No acquaintance with "experimental religion" was deemed necessary.

Some, at least, of the revivalists believed that many of the parish ministers were strangers to a conversion experience. Gilbert Tennent's sermon "On the Danger of an Unconverted Ministry" caused much bad feeling, and the eccentric James Davenport was disposed to pronounce almost any minister unconverted who did not agree with him. Whitefield himself voiced the opinion that many ministers were unconverted.

> The Lord enabled me to open my mouth against unconverted ministers; to caution tutors to take care of their pupils; and also to advise ministers particularly to examine into the experiences of candidates for ordination. For I am verily persuaded the generality of preachers talk of an unknown and unfelt Christ; and the reasons why congregations have been so dead is, because they have had dead men preaching to them.[10]

The revival message was carried to every geographical area through the wide itineracy of its heralds. Since a settled custom in New England was that no one preached in a given parish without the express invitation and permission of its minister, the practice of indiscriminate itineracy aroused both dismay and antagonism. James Davenport, already mentioned above, caused much hostility by his unsparing condemnation of the parish clergy during his preaching tours. Other persons, unordained and uncommissioned by any of the churches, traveled up and down the land, preaching to the people of the uneducated classes and denouncing the parish clergy in unmeasured terms.

The revival divided the established church of New England into two groups. One party sanctioned the new evangelism and approved the work of reputable itinerant evangelists. The other party stood in opposition to the aims and methods of the new evangelism. The party favoring the revival were nicknamed "New Lights"; those opposing were called "Old Lights."

Actually, these nicknames were suggestive without being completely definitive. Gaustad is more specific.

> The theological divisions which followed in the wake of the revival were more complex than the familiar Old Light—New Light dichotomy. Four parties may be distinguished. The extremists, least important of the four, were hyperzealous New Lights who were characterized either by theological novelty or theological vacuity. The traditional orthodoxy, that which existed before the Awakening and which tried desperately to maintain itself after, came to be known as "Old Calvinism." A third party, the Liberals, comprised a left wing within the older orthodoxy which spoke with new vigor and clarity. Finally, the Strict Calvinists or New Divinity men fully displayed and effectively extended the theological bias of the revival.[11]

THE RISE OF THE SEPARATES

Ezra Stiles, a prominent New England minister, estimated that of the four hundred ministers in New England, "one hundred and thirty were 'New Lights — & of these only 30 violent.' " [12] Perhaps about an equal number actively opposed the revival, while the rest remained uncommitted. Charles Chauncy, the most intelligent leader of the liberal wing of the "Old Lights," attempted to bring about a general repudiation of the revival. Jonathan Edwards led the defense of the revival's basic aims. The defense was not radical enough for some Congregationalists, who conceived that separation from the established churches was the only recourse left to them. Separatist churches organized between 1740 and the latter 1760's and eventually formed an independent denomination called the Separates. While the movement leading to the emergence of the Separates was fairly widespread in New England, its center was located in eastern Connecticut and was composed of radical "New Lights."

In 1744 the "Associated Ministers of the County of Windham" (in Connecticut) formulated a letter in which they enumerated the points of contention between themselves and the Separates. This letter stated some of the basic issues between the Separates and the Standing Order. According to the Windham ministers, "some of the most considerable errors of the Separates" were:

1. That it is the will of God to have a pure church on earth, in this sense, that all the converted should be separated from the unconverted.

2. That the saints certainly know one another, and know who are Christ's true ministers, by their own inward feelings, or a communion between them in the inward actings of their own souls.

3. That no other call is necessary to a person undertaking to preach the gospel, but his being a true Christian, and having an inward motion of the Spirit, or a persuasion in his own mind, that it is the will of God that he should preach and perform ministerial acts: the consequence of which is, that there is no standing instituted ministry in the Christian church, which may be known by the visible laws of Christ's kingdom.

4. That God disowns the ministry and churches in this land, and the ordinances as administered by them.

5. That at such meetings of lay preaching and exhorting, they have more of the presence of God than in his ordinances, and under the ministration of the present ministry, and the administration of the ordinances in these churches.[13]

Without being especially notable for precision of statement, the above has the value of a contemporary document which discloses some of the Separates' principal concerns: first, the concern for a converted church membership, a concern so intensely felt that the Separates were willing to withdraw from the established churches in order to achieve this objective in their own fellowships; second, the concern to affirm that a converted state is consciously known, both by the converted person and by his fellow saints; third, a concern for a divinely called ministry, which contrasts sharply with the merely trained ministers in the churches of the Standing Order; fourth, a concern to repudiate the churches of the establishment, to the extent of calling them false churches; and, last, a concern to affirm the validity of lay preaching and exhortation which is animated by the spirit of God, even though it may not have had the formal sanction of the established churches.

The Separates were especially offended by the Saybrook Platform, which referred matters of ecclesiastical importance, including the ordination of ministers, to the decision of a synod composed of the regular ministers in each county. The Separates, in reply to this restriction, emphatically asserted the right of each church to regulate its own internal affairs.[14]

This right, they believed, applied also to the selection of ministers. They held that each church had the authority to select its own minister without the jurisdiction of a synod. In addition, the Separate conception of an inward "spiritual" call removed the necessity for ecclesiastical confirmation or commission, beyond that performed by a local church. Far from standing in awe of the learned clergymen of the establishment, the Separates esteemed spiritual discernment far more highly than classical learning. They believed:

> That every brother that is qualified by God for the same, has a right to preach according to the measure of faith, and that the essential qualification for preaching is wrought by the Spirit of God; and that the knowledge of the tongues and liberal sciences are not absolutely necessary; yet they are convenient, and will doubtless be profitable if rightly used; but if brought in to supply the want of the Spirit of God, they prove a snare to those that use them and all that follow them.[15]

The Separates flagrantly disregarded the established parish system in their aggressive campaigns of itinerant evangelism. The Separate ministers ranged near and far, preaching to everyone who would hear them, paying slight regard to parish lines, and repeatedly trespassing on fields which were claimed by ministers of the Standing Order. The preaching of these sometimes rude and uncouth, unordained and unwanted preachers and exhorters became an open scandal and brought down upon the Separates not only public odium, but also harsh and repressive legislation.

It remains a moot question whether there would have been a more favorable reaction if the Separates had been less arrogant.

ISAAC BACKUS — SEPARATE

Isaac Backus (1724–1806) was in many respects a representative figure among the Separates. He was born in Norwich, Connecticut, where a tradition of "pure Congregationalism" had manifested itself by a considerable degree of hostility toward the Halfway Covenant and the Saybrook Platform of 1708. During the revival, the region had come under the influence of such revival preachers as Eleazor Wheelock, Benjamin Pomeroy, James Davenport, and others.

Backus experienced a somewhat typical conversion in 1741. Referring to himself, he said:

> But in May, 1741, his eyes were opened to see, that time was not at his command, and that eternity was directly before him, into which he might justly be called the next moment. . . . On August 24, as he was alone in the field, it was demonstrated to his mind and conscience, that he had done his utmost to make himself better, without obtaining any such thing; but that he was a guilty sinner in the hands of a holy God, who had a right to do with him as seemed good in God's sight; which he then yielded to, and all his objections against it were silenced. And soon upon this a way of relief was opened to his soul, which he never had any true idea of before, wherein truth and justice shine with lustre, in the bestowment of free mercy and salvation upon objects who have nothing in themselves but badness. And while this divine glory engaged all his attention, his burthen of guilt and evil dispositions was gone. . . .[16]

Backus and other converts were reluctant to join the church at Norwich, because the pastor, Benjamin Lord, although friendly to the revival, continued to hold to the terms of the Halfway Covenant and to advocate that the Lord's Supper was a converting ordinance, in the tradition of "Stoddardeanism."

Backus finally joined the church in 1742. Two years later, however, he and other dissatisfied New Lights in the church withdrew. They organized a Separate church in October, 1745. The reasons which Backus and his associates assigned for this action reflected characteristic New Light sentiments:

> . . . that persons were received into the church who gave no satisfactory evidence of conversion; that many were suffered to remain as regular members, without being dealt with, whose walk was evidently contrary to the Gospel; that the pastor declared his strong attachment to the Saybrook Platform, which had been renounced by the church before settling him. . . .[17]

They also complained that the nature of true piety and of experimental religion "were not clearly set forth" by the pastor.

Backus could never have qualified for a position among the established ministry, for he had received only a common-school education. Nevertheless, in September, 1746, he received what he considered to be an internal call from God to preach the gospel.[18] Subsequently, with true New Light zeal, he spent fourteen months as an itinerant evangelist, traveling widely and laboring diligently through eastern Connecticut, Rhode Island, and eastern Massachusetts.

At length, Backus was attracted to a group of New Lights at Titicut, Massachusetts, a new parish between Middleboro and Bridgewater. On February 16, 1748, this group became a Separate church. On April 13, Backus became their pastor. For the rest of his life, comprising a ministry of fifty-eight years, he labored as a pastor in this geographical location (though not in the same church).[19]

Although Backus appears to have been heart and soul a Separate, he was all his adult life a keen-minded, intelligent man. The excesses and shortcomings of the Separates were delineated in later years by this man who had been one of their most gifted leaders.

Backus discerned that the Separate movement attracted disaffected elements in the established churches. He saw that many Separates, in their desire to secure a freedom which had been denied them, embraced a fanatical individualism. Some held to a dry and rigid legalism, while others tended toward antinomianism.

The excesses of the movement upon its fringes gave opportunity to its enemies to stigmatize the whole Separate cause. The Separate reaction to this treatment was "to guard their minds against receiving any instruction or correction from the men who had treated them so abusively." [20]

> A first principle of their separation was, that the leadings of the divine Spirit are ever to be followed, and not fleshly wisdom, nor man's inventions; but how little was the meaning and right application of this principle understood? When it was asserted, that none but the regenerate ought to be admitted to full communion, ministers would answer, You cannot know who they are. And when it was mentioned, that our Lord says, Ye shall know them by their fruits; the question was shifted, whether they held to a satisfactory or an infallible knowledge? which dispute was often carried to extremes on both sides. And while many would confine the word *fruits* to dry morality, others ran to the opposite extreme, and formed their judgments of persons by their inwards feelings towards them, rather than upon an intelligent view of what came from them by words and actions.[21]

The repression exerted upon them by the Establishment made the Separates veer toward an extremely democratic church polity. They insisted not only upon the rule of the majority, but also upon unanimous consent in many of their church acts. Sometimes this system, Backus observed, allowed a single member to obstruct the wishes of the whole church if he chose to be obstinate.[22]

While some of the Separates bluntly contended that God disowned the churches, the ministry, and the ordinances of the Establishment, others were more charitable. The churches of the Establishment, they felt, were churches of Christ, though "greatly degenerated and corrupted." The differences of opinion on this subject, however, did not cause serious division within the Separate fellowship.

Yet in the light of the fact that the Separates strongly insisted that their church fellowships be made up only of converted persons, the rise of a most serious internal issue might have been anticipated. This issue was the status of infant baptism. C. C. Goen says:

> One effect of discussions about the Halfway Covenant from its inception in 1657 was to revive concern as to the importance of baptism and its relation to membership in the visible church. That question became much more urgent when converts of the Great Awakening attacked the Halfway Covenant as an evil compromise with the world whose effect was to dilute the purity of the churches. In professing to return to the pure church ideal, the Separates almost inevitably came to the conclusion that if churches were to be composed only of the regenerate, the rite of admission should be restricted to confessed believers. The baptism of infants, whether of believing parents or not, appeared to deny the strict standard of church membership and to undo the work of reformation in one generation. If this practice were not repudiated, the unregenerate were not explicitly excluded from the church and the basic presuppositions of a worldly religious establishment were still retained. The gravitation of many Separates to the practice of believer's baptism, therefore, was a logical termination of their quest for the true church in all its purity. It would have been strange if such a development had not taken place.[23]

The issue brought about a travail of spirit among the Separates. Backus's own experience was again typical of that of many others in the Separate fellowship.

In 1749 Backus found that there were at least two members of his church at Titicut who held Baptist views concerning infant baptism and who propagated these views with open zeal. Backus was led to begin a careful study of the question. In the midst of this period, he said, there was a "disagreeable temper," and "much heat in debates" in the church for three weeks. At last, rather impulsively, Backus was led to a "sudden conclusion" to the effect "that the Baptist way is right, because nature so fights against it." He could hardly wait to preach this newly discovered conviction to his people the next day, which caused, he said, "confusion among the hearers, and returned with a horrible gloom over his own mind; and he was turned back to his former practice." [24]

After an extended period of inward turmoil, Backus made known to his church in July, 1751, that he had come to the settled conviction that there was no scriptural warrant for infant baptism. Most of the members of his church held contrary views, but Backus implemented his change of sentiments by receiving baptism by immersion on profession of faith, July 27, 1751. Six other members of his congregation were baptized at the same time.

There were now seventeen immersed members of the Titicut church. For the time being, Backus continued as pastor.

From the distress and dispute in the church over infant baptism versus believer's baptism, another issue soon emerged. Could a congregation which held differing convictions, and which observed differing practices concerning infant baptism, observe Communion in a way that would allow the different parties to abide in amicable church fellowship? The strife engendered by the baptismal and Communion questions greatly demoralized the church at Titicut. A number of councils, bringing together representatives from other Separate churches, many of whom were having similar problems, found the Separates unable to deal cogently with the problem.

The church undertook to keep peace in a divided house. Backus refused to baptize infants, but it was arranged that a neighboring minister should officiate at services of infant baptism. New members who wished to receive believer's baptism by immersion were baptized by Backus. In the meantime, the differing factions of the church observed the Lord's Supper together.

Sharp differences over the same questions appear to have been general among the Separate churches. In some cases, the minister of a church was obligated to baptize infants or not, according to the disposition or request of the parents. On the other hand, some of the churches made the baptism of infants a test of fellowship. The vacillation and volatility of the Separates on the mooted questions injected an element of instability into the whole denomination.

A general council representing twenty-seven Separate churches met at Exeter in 1753. After long deliberation, the delegates concluded:

(1) That we do not find it to be a censurable evil for one who has professed and practiced the baptism of minors, to turn from that to the baptism of adults by immersion; and (2) That we do not find it to be a censurable evil for one who has professed and practised re-baptizing by immersion to turn from it and give up his children or minors in baptism.[25]

Regarding this action, Backus commented, "A strong persuasion was still held by many, that if a right temper was in exercise, Christians might, and ought to, commune together, although of different judgments about baptism." [26] The Titicut church attempted to abide by the council's decision, but found that the proposed solution was instead a point of division and marred the fellowship of the church, so that the Pedobaptist and the Baptist factions could not commune together.

In 1756 Backus and his church came to a parting of the ways. On January 16, he and his wife and four others of Baptist sentiments established a Baptist church at Middleboro. He was destined to remain the pastor of this church for the remainder of his life.

Concerning the Separates as a whole, their inability to reach a consistent stand concerning infant baptism impelled their two principal factions in opposite directions. Those who subscribed to believer's baptism were forced toward a further separation on grounds which were authentically Baptist. Those who continued to hold to infant baptism were constrained toward reabsorption into the Congregationalist fold. With the relaxation of persecution, the Separates declined in zeal, and, by degrees, many of them returned to the Congregationalist churches. More generally, they united with the Baptists.[27] By 1818 the Separates had ceased to exist as a denomination.

ISAAC BACKUS — SEPARATE BAPTIST

The Separate Baptists sprang from that wing of the Separate denomination which held to believer's baptism and opposed infant baptism. The issues which disturbed the hearts and minds of these children of the Great Awakening are strikingly manifest in the spiritual pilgrimage of their greatest leader, Isaac Backus. Although the course followed by Backus, and by the church of which he was pastor, indicates a pattern among the Separates, this pattern had, of course, variations. C. C. Goen discusses these at more length than space permits in this chapter. A summary comment by Mr. Goen should, however, be taken into consideration.

> There were four main ways in which Separate Baptist churches, such as the one under Isaac Backus at Middleborough, were formed: the en bloc conversion of entire Separate congregations, the division of mixed-communion churches, individual converts to Baptist principles, and schisms in some of the older Baptist churches.[28]

At any rate, Backus later stated clearly and forcefully the

conviction which led him out of pedobaptism into a Baptist position.

> . . . truth is never to be violated for any one, no, not to save natural life, which all lawful means should be used to preserve. And truth so clearly requires baptism before the Supper, that Paedobaptists do never come to the table with any but such as are baptized in their esteem. Neither could we understandingly act in being buried in baptism, until we were convinced that what was done to us in infancy was not gospel baptism; therefore to commune at the Lord's table with any who were only sprinkled in infancy, is parting with truth, by practically saying they are baptized when we do not believe they are.[29]

As a Baptist, Isaac Backus achieved his full stature. During the next decade or more, he worked industriously and fruitfully in his pastoral field, was much in demand as a counselor for sister churches, and itinerated on wide-ranging evangelistic tours. Alvah Hovey, his biographer, says that in the eleven years after the organization of the Baptist church at Middleboro, Backus traveled 14,691 miles, preached 2,412 sermons, and baptized 62 persons.[30]

He also became a prolific writer. Carefully gathering materials relative to Baptist history, about 1770 he began writing his most important work, *A History of New England. With Particular Reference to the Denomination of Christians Called Baptists.* This writing was originally published in three volumes, in 1777, 1784, and 1796. Backus, said George Bancroft, is " 'one of the most exact of our New England historians,' whose work is marked by 'ingenuousness, clear discernment, and determined accuracy.' "[31] T. B. Maston says of his other writings:

> Fully as voluminous as his history and probably more influential in his age were his numerous (thirty-seven) pamphlets. They touched on a wide variety of subjects but practically all of them dealt with some current theological or practical problem and most of them were in propagation or defense of some truth or position held by Baptists. . . . The tracts of Backus, in spite of the financial and transportation difficulties of his age, were circulated rather widely. They, with his books, won him many friends and opened avenues of service.[32]

A characteristic of sectarianism is to emphasize a few doctrinal points of principal concern, rather than to give a large consideration to the body of divinity. The doctrinal points emphasized by the Separates were a converted church membership, the immediate leadership of the Holy Spirit, the necessity of a divine call to preach the gospel, the validity of lay preaching, and the self-government of the local church. The Separate Baptists took over all of these emphases, adding a strong emphasis upon believer's baptism and strict close Communion. Like the Separates, the Separate Baptists also tended to disparage the value of an educated ministry, to accentuate itineracy, and to place strong value upon an emotional response in the religious experience.

In nearly all of these points, Backus was a fairly typical Separate Baptist. He was quite cautious, however, in guarding the prerogatives of the ministry of the church in the administration of the ordinances. He was therefore insistent upon the duty of a church to ordain its minister in a formal manner.

Neither did Backus share the prejudice of many Separates and Separate Baptists against an educated ministry. His own schooling was meager, but he was a strong supporter of ministerial education, and he served with loyalty and distinction for many years upon the board of trustees of Rhode Island College (later Brown University).

The Separate Baptists were such moderate Calvinists that they were suspected by many of the Particular (Calvinistic) Baptists of having Arminian tendencies. Their enthusiastic proclamation of the gospel to all who would hear and their open invitations to embrace salvation indicate, at the most, a rather qualified subscription to the doctrines of particular election and limited atonement. Backus himself retained through life a firm allegiance to an evangelical Calvinism.

A man of Backus's signal ability, however truly representative of his people he might have been, was able to view their common body of convictions in a much wider scope, and at a much deeper level, than most of his fellows were able to do. In the second volume of his history, Backus undertook to "give a distinct account of what the faith and order of these Baptist churches are, against which such opposition has been made." He affirmed that "their faith and practice come the nearest to that of the first planters of New England, of any churches now in the land, excepting in the single article of sprinkling infants." Then follow fourteen points, in which it is asserted that all men fell in Adam, "the public head of all mankind"; that God "gave a certain number of the children of men to his beloved Son, before the world was," and that he, by his "obedience and sufferings, has procured eternal redemption for them"; that these persons individually are "effectually" called and saved in time; that their justification is by the righteousness of Christ "received by faith"; that every such soul will be preserved unto eternal salvation; that only regenerate persons are valid materials for Christian churches;

"that the right way of building such churches is by giving a personal, verbal account to the church of what God has done for their souls, to the satisfaction of the church"; that the power of calling, ordaining, and deposing its officers is in the hands of the local church; although a church may want the advice and assistance of sister churches, that the power of church discipline is also in the hands of the local church; that the government of the church should be according to the laws of Christ, "and not at all by the secular arm"; that ministers ought to be supported by voluntary contributions, not by civil taxation and compulsion; that ordinarily "ministers ought to preach, and not read their sermons"; "that free liberty ought to be allowed for every saint to improve his gifts according to the gospel . . ."; "that officers, when chosen and ordained, have no arbitrary, lordly, or imposing power, but are to rule and minister with the consent of the brethren, who ought not to be called *The Laity,* but to be treated as men and brethren in Christ." [33]

In common with most of the early Separate Baptists of New England, Backus had a strongly sectarian concept of the authority of the local church. He began his two-volume history of the Baptists of New England with a lengthy first chapter on the ecclesiological views of John Robinson, the seventeenth-century Separatist. Particular attention was given to Robinson's book, written in 1610, on *A Justification of Separation from the Church of England.* With obvious approval, Backus quoted Robinson concerning the nature of the church:

> There is no true visible church of Christ, but a particular congregation only. . . . Every true visible church of Christ, or ordinary assembly of the faithful, hath, by Christ's ordinance, power in itself immediately under Christ to elect, to ordain, deprive and depose their ministers, and to execute all other ecclesiastical censures.[34]

The Saybrook Platform, adopted by Connecticut Congregationalists in 1708, was criticized by Backus because he held that the ecclesiastical arrangements provided by this platform directly subverted the principles of the original New England churches, taking away the autonomy of the local church as the supreme earthly authority in church government. The platform also, said Backus, became an engine for the persecution of dissenting churches.

When the Warren Baptist Association was organized in 1767, the moving spirits in its organization were James Manning, president of Rhode Island College, and John Gano, an able Baptist leader from Massachusetts. Both of these men had worked previously in the Philadelphia Baptist Association, which was made up of Baptist churches with a Particular Baptist background. Backus was present at the organizational meeting and was elected clerk. Only four churches consented to join the Association at the first meeting, and Backus noted in his diary: "I did not see my way clear to join now, if ever I do." [35]

Backus and other Separate Baptists were afraid that the Association would assume a tyrannical power over the churches. At the suggestion of Backus, Manning revised the plan of the Association to include the stipulation that the Association might not violate "the independency and power of particular churches, because it pretends to be no other than an *Advisory council,* utterly disclaiming superiority, jurisdiction, coercive right, and infallibility." [36] This provision allayed the fears of many Separate Baptists, so that eleven additional churches joined the Association by 1772.

The Association proved to be an effective instrument for the Baptist cause in New England, for it was through this body, principally, that the Baptists focused their energies for their great battle to win religious liberty. Isaac Backus became the agent for the Association in 1772, and soon he became a principal leader in the struggle. His leadership was one of the most distinguished contributions of his life. Among Baptists, the Separate Baptists furnished the strongest agitation for religious freedom, and for thirty years Backus stood in the front ranks of their battle for this cause. Only a brief account of this struggle can be given here.

In 1691 the new charter of the Massachusetts Bay colony had granted toleration to Baptists and other dissenters, but it had not exempted them from taxation for the support of the state church. Baptists refused to pay this tax on the ground that an imposed tax for the support of a religious establishment was an infringement upon religious freedom. In consequence, Baptists frequently had their property seized and sold for the defrayment of tax costs. The laws governing the toleration of dissenters were changed in subsequent years, for example, in 1728, 1747, 1753, and 1772. In each case, however, the established church remained in being; dissenting churches remained in an inferior status and under legal obligations to support the state church by the payment of taxes, except by resort to the use of legal provisions which were humiliating.

In addition, Baptists were subjected to frequent mistreatment in local communities, sometimes with the connivance of local authorities. Mobs broke up Baptist meetings, and sometimes their preachers were beaten. In 1769 the minutes of the Warren Association stated that "many letters from the churches mentioned grievous oppressions and persecutions from the Standing order."

In 1774 the Warren Association sent its agent, Isaac Backus, and several other Baptist leaders, including President Manning of Rhode Island College, to the meeting of the First Continental Congress in Philadelphia. The purpose of this mission was to meet with the delegates of Massachusetts to the Congress and thus to secure from them an opportunity to present their grievances before the Continental Congress. The representation which the Baptists made particularly irked Samuel and John Adams, both of whom denied that there were any real restrictions upon religious minorities in Massachusetts.

Throughout the period of the American Revolution, New England Baptists continued aggressively to agitate for the cause of religious liberty under the leadership of Isaac Backus. They supported the revolutionary cause almost to a man, in the hope of obtaining not only political but also religious freedom.

Out of Backus's many writings in support of religious liberty, perhaps the most notable is a pamphlet of some fifty-nine pages entitled *An Appeal to the Public for Religious Liberty, Against the Oppressions of the Present Day*. It was published in Boston in 1773. In this writing, which William G. McLoughlin has called "pietistic America's declaration of spiritual independence," [37] Backus gave an affirmative estimate of the need for civil government. It is a dangerous error, he said, to imagine "that there is any thing in the nature of true government that interferes with true and full liberty." [38]

The heart of Backus's argument is stated as follows:

. . . it appears to us that the true difference and exact limits between ecclesiastical and civil government is this, That the church is armed with *light and truth*, to pull down the strong holds of iniquity, and to gain souls to Christ, and into his church, to be governed by his rules therein; and again to exclude such from their communion, who will not be so governed; while the state is armed with the sword to guard the peace, and the civil rights of all persons and societies, and to punish those who violate the same. And where these two kinds of government, and the weapons which belong to them, are well distinguished, and improved according to the true nature and end of their institution, the effects are happy, and they do not at all interfere with each other; but where they have been confounded together, no tongue nor pen can fully describe the mischiefs that have ensued.[39]

Backus proceeded to make an extensive indictment of the New England establishment. They strove very hard, he said, "to have the church govern the world, till they lost their charter; since which they have yielded to have the world govern the church." [40] Backus was able to capitalize heavily upon the concern of the colonists that they were being taxed by the British government without representation. His whole argument, Backus affirmed, for religious liberty turned upon the point "whether our *civil* legislatures are in truth our representatives in *religious* affairs, or not." [41]

In religion, Backus said, "each one has a right to judge for himself." The area of religious judgment is an area in which the state has no right to interpose its authority. Backus's conclusion was a home thrust. "You do not deny the right of the British parliament to impose taxes within her own realm; only complain that she extends her taxing power beyond her proper limits. And have we not as good right to say you do the *same thing*?" [42]

Backus's long life allowed him to see many victories for the cause of religious liberty, but his death in 1806 prevented his witnessing its full consummation. Full religious liberty was not won in Massachusetts until 1833.

The dynamic thrust of the Separate Baptists was not confined in New England to Connecticut, Massachusetts, and Rhode Island. C. C. Goen has been able to identify Separate Baptist congregations in southern Maine, in southern and central New Hampshire, in southern Vermont, as well as in eastern New York and in northern New Jersey.

When the Revival began, most of the small community of Baptist churches adopted an "Old Light" stand, quite generally opposing the Revival. The older, pre-Awakening Baptist churches therefore gave little encouragement to the "New Light" or Separate Baptists and for a time refused to have fellowship with them. The Separate Baptists carried into the Baptist communion the revivalistic type of piety which was inspired by the Great Awakening. While this element rescued the Baptists from slow and sure decay, it at first increased the tension within the Baptist family.

Other points of tension also became apparent. Because of their English heritage, the "Old Light" Baptists were accustomed to adopting confessions of faith for their churches. The Separate Baptists insisted that the Bible alone should serve as the platform of belief. The Separate Baptists were also critical of the "Old Lights" for not requiring new church members to give clear evidence of a conversion experience before admission to the church. More than the "Old Light" Baptists, they emphasized the possibility of individual inspiration and the direct leadership of the Holy Spirit.

As the "Old Light" Baptists themselves gradually became permeated with a revivalistic piety, their distinctions from the Separate Baptists became less sharp and tended to disappear. The struggle for religious liberty and the American Revolution brought the two groups closer together. By the beginning of the nineteenth century they had become virtually one denomination.

It should not be supposed, however, that the trends in the Baptist denomination were all in the direction of unity. There were countervailing trends, also. William McLoughlin has called attention to the fact that in the last quarter of the eighteenth century there were three major forces which affected the mood and life of Americans. The first was the experimental and pietistic religion of the Great Awakening. The second was the new science and philosophy of the Enlightenment. The third was the new politics of the Revolution. The Separate Baptists were deeply affected by all of these forces.

A striking effect of the working of these influences was an erosion of the old Calvinist consensus which had obtained since the Puritan era. The rejection of the Puritan system opened the way for the growth of dynamic new movements. It was to be expected that the Separate Baptists would be caught in the fragmenting tendencies of these movements.

Isaac Backus sought to restrain the pietism of the Separate Baptists to the confines of a Calvinistic theology and a revivalistic type of worship. Here his influence was strongly conservative. After 1770 he directed more and more of his writing and evangelistic efforts to the task of combating alien movements which preyed upon the fringes of the Separate Baptist denomination. But he was not able to stop the egress of sizable elements of his people into sects and movements which he considered to be heretical. The loose polity of the Separate Baptists in New England, the lack of sophistication of their ministers and laymen, and their volatile pietism rendered them peculiarly vulnerable to the inroads of schismatic new ideologies.

The Separate Baptists lost a considerable number of adherents to the Freewill Baptist movement, which began in New Hampshire and eventually swept away many Separate Baptists on the northern frontier. The Freewill Baptists were an Arminian sect. The Universalist denomination garnered fewer proselytes from the Separate Baptist fellowship, although Separate Baptist ministers of some distinction, such as Elhanan Winchester, Hosea Ballou, and Caleb Rich, joined the Universalist ranks. The Shaker movement drew off many Separate Baptists, particularly in Massachusetts. On the other hand, a new version of hyper-Calvinism, stimulated by the "New Divinity" pupils of Jonathan Edwards, won converts among the Separate Baptists, including a few Separate Baptist ministers.[43]

THE SEPARATE BAPTISTS IN THE SOUTH

The movement of the Separate Baptists into the South has little direct connection with Isaac Backus. The scope of the Separate Baptist influence cannot be depicted, however, without at least a brief account of its southern progress.

The work of the Separate Baptists in the South received its initial impetus from two New England evangelists, Shubal Stearns (1706–1771) and Daniel Marshall (1706–1784). Converted in the Whitefield revivals, they became Separate Congregationalist itinerants, and later Baptist preachers. In 1755 Stearns led a small company of fifteen persons to Sandy Creek, North Carolina, near the Virginia border. This small group founded the Sandy Creek Baptist Church. Soon Marshall and his family (he had married Stearns's sister in 1747) joined them in the Sandy Creek community.

In their area of settlement, Stearns and his company found a fertile field for their evangelistic labors among the newly arrived English immigrants. Seventeen years after settling at Sandy Creek, the Separate Baptists numbered forty-two churches in the South, and one hundred twenty-five ministers. The wide-ranging itinerary of Daniel Marshall was especially effective. The Separate Baptist churches extended from the Chesapeake Bay southward to beyond Savannah, Georgia. The Sandy Creek Association was organized in 1758, and during the next twelve years it comprised all of the Separate Baptist churches in Virginia and the Carolinas. The yearly meetings of the Association were marked by large crowds and great evangelistic fervor.

The Separate Baptists continued for a long time to manifest much of the ebullient zeal of the Whitefield revivals. Belonging at first largely to the disinherited classes, they, in the course of time, gained social status, threw off many of their odd mannerisms, paid increasing attention to education, and gained converts from the well-to-do classes.[44] From the first, they were prominent in the battle for religious liberty. When the American Revolution came on, they identified themselves with the patriot cause.

In the South, the Separate Baptists began with a disposition toward a closer connectionalism than that which characterized the Separate Baptists of New England. It appears that the secret of this centralizing tendency lay within the magnetic personality of Shubal Stearns, who was something of a benevolent autocrat in church polity. The tendency of the Association to interfere in the internal affairs of the churches led in 1770 to the division of the body into three associations. After this division, and particularly after the death of Stearns the next year, the inclination toward centralization seems to have slackened.

For some years considerable tension was manifested between the hyper-zealous Separate Baptist churches and neighboring "Regular" Baptist churches which had been formed by the itin-erant labors of the Philadelphia Baptist Association. Gradually, however, the crucial points at issue between them were eased, and widespread unions occurred between 1787 and 1801. For some years thereafter, the groups so joined were known by the title "United Baptists." [45]

CONCLUSION

In the period of the Great Awakening, says John M. Mecklin, dissent in America became "revivalistic." [46]

> . . . the dissenting tradition, strong in the Separatist movement from the start and reënforced by his boyhood faith, carried Backus into the Baptist group, the most typical of all the dissenting sects. But in making this mo-mentous decision Backus, together with the host of Separatists who followed him, carried over into the Baptist group the revivalistic type of piety in-spired by the Great Awakening.[47]

The coming of the Separate Baptists into the Baptist family marked an incursion of a revivalistic type of piety, which had a lasting influence. The Separate Baptists also brought a new em-phasis upon the individual. The institutional church became secondary, while the individual soul stood alone before God. The individual, it was held, might be unlettered, untutored, of lowly origin, of small ability, and of little worldly standing. This made no difference. Each person must have his own experience with God in an experience of regeneration. Each could receive the immediate, direct leadership of the Holy Spirit. Each might receive personally a direct call from God to preach the unsearch-able riches of Christ.

In keeping with the emphasis of the Revival and of revivalism, the Separate Baptists emphasized the conversion experience. "The New England Separates," said one writer, "originally Congregationalists who generally turned Baptist, heightened the mood of Evangelicalism to its highest degree, making conversion everything, and finally stereotyping and institutionalizing this conception of Christian experience." [48]

The emphasis upon conversion was needed. Yet, in bringing the experience of conversion to the forefront of consideration, the Separate Baptists sadly neglected the larger body of Christian doctrine. As a group they were theologically weak. As a consequence, they came in time to have a doctrinal instability which made them a prey to other movements. Some Separate Baptists embraced universalism. Some became hyper-Calvinist. Others became more Arminian than the Arminians. When Alexander Campbell swept through Kentucky and Tennessee, it was the Baptists of Separate Baptist background who furnished him his most ready hearing.

The Separate Baptist emphasis upon a divine call to the ministry is one which has remained a vital emphasis in Baptist concepts of the ministry. Unfortunately, with this emphasis, there crept into Separate Baptist life a note of disparagement for an *educated* ministry. The Separate Baptists may be partly responsible for an anti-intellectualism which lingers on in the Baptist denomination and proves to be a deadly handicap when intellectual and moral leadership is demanded.

With the recovery of an intense evangelistic outreach attained during the Revival, the Separate Baptists identified themselves with great and earnest commitment. They conceived their business to be the saving of souls, and they gave themselves to this endeavor, in many cases, with heroic abandon. The fact that they defined evangelism in highly individualistic terms evoked the following comment by one student of the movement:

> Their concentration on "this one thing" was at once the secret of their greatest strength—the harvesting of converts and the planting of churches—and of their greatest weakness—the refusal to work out the full implications of personal religious experience in the context of the total Christian tradition and its larger social concerns.[49]

It was the remarkable growth of the Separate Baptists in the South which became responsible for the fact that the Baptists are the most numerous and perhaps the most generally dispersed religious group in the South up to the present time. Indeed, the life of the Separate Baptists has entered deeply into the Southern Baptist heritage. In the intense evangelistic and missionary outreach of Southern Baptists, it is not too much to say that the Separate Baptists live on. Revivalism remains alive among Southern Baptists as in no other large denomination. The tendency to interpret evangelism in terms of the conversion of individual souls, without consideration of the application of the gospel to grave issues obtaining in the social order, may be an inheritance from the Separate Baptists which needs drastic reassessment and revision.

William L. Lumpkin sees a distinct possibility that the centralizing tendencies of Separate Baptist associations, which stood in such marked contrast with the congregationalist extremism of the New England Separate Baptists, showed up in the more centralized structure of the Southern Baptist Convention.[50] However this may be, he is probably correct in thinking that the popular hymnody of Southern Baptists is more like the vernacular religious songs of the Separates than like the more formal hymns of the Regular Baptists. In addition, he says, "The attitudes of self-consciousness and self-sufficiency, of uniqueness and religious detachment, which are sometimes found among Southern Baptists, are not mere provincialisms but are traceable to antecedent attitudes of the Separates." [51]

There was an intense sectarian strain in the convictions of the Separates, which led them out of corrupt churches and church establishments supported by the state. The persecution which they endured for their faith would have been intolerable if they had not believed themselves to be a people set apart, with a unique message and mission. This sectarianism, however, caused them to think of the church as a local fellowship of believers rather than, first of all, a worldwide fellowship of faith. To them, the larger fellowship of God's people came to be defined by the bounds of the Baptist denomination, rather than by the bounds of the whole church. This conviction also was passed on to Southern Baptists, and it has become one of the demanding problems which face Southern Baptists at the present time.

4-ANDREW FULLER-
Theologian of Baptist Missionary Advance

Andrew Fuller had a significant role in the founding of the missionary society which sent William Carey to India in the vanguard of the modern mission movement. However, Fuller's work in the organization of the society was probably not as important to the mission enterprise as the work which he did to provide a theological climate conducive to the development of the mission movement which became so strong in the nineteenth century.

THE RELIGIOUS CLIMATE

Religious life in England during a large part of the eighteenth century was at a low ebb. In the established church, there was much apathy, skepticism, and worldliness. Nepotism, pluralities, and other kindred evils were all too prevalent within the church.

It was the Age of Reason. Deism gave an interpretation of religion which reduced the supernatural to a bare minimum. Under the influence of Hume and Locke, philosophy became skeptical. Arianism was a viewpoint extensively held in the Christian churches, especially among the Presbyterians. Both Arianism and Socinianism had penetrated deeply into the General Baptist fellowship. Indeed, the dissenting churches as a whole, far from escaping the religious decline, shared the general stagnation and retreat.[1]

By the middle of the century, the Evangelical Revival, led by John and Charles Wesley and George Whitefield, was in full swing. This revival had a profound and indeed a decisive influence upon the life of England. Unfortunately, Baptists at first looked upon the movement with suspicion. Although it might have been expected that the Arminianism of John Wesley would appeal to the General Baptists, it did not do so. The Socinianism of many of the General Baptists greatly reduced Wesley's influence among them, and his advocacy of infant baptism constituted a barrier.

Eventually, as a consequence of the Revival, a virile new group of churches did arise in the General Baptist fellowship. Dan Taylor, a Yorkshire miner who had been drawn to the Methodists by the Wesleys and Whitefield, embraced Baptist convictions and gathered together a number of churches which had been quickened by the Revival. A segment of this new alignment consisted of revitalized General Baptist churches. In 1770 the group formed a new body of General Baptists, called the "New Connexion," declaring that their design was "to revive experimental religion or primitive Christianity in faith and practice." [2] The "New Connexion" quickly became the dominant group of General Baptists. They were, says A. C. Underwood, "a child of the Methodist Revival, and manifested two Methodist characteristics: strong evangelical zeal and strong corporate feeling." While they were Arminian in theology, they chose the title "New Connexion of General Baptists," in order to differentiate themselves from the old General Baptists, who, by and large, had become Unitarian.[3]

Upon the Particular Baptists, too, the Evangelical Revival at first had small effect. This stronger wing of the Baptist family in England had little to do with the General Baptists because of the latter's Arminianism. The Arminianism of Wesley also made them suspicious and even hostile to him. Although Whitefield was a Calvinist, his open evangelistic invitations caused the Particular Baptists to complain that he spoke with an "Arminian dialect." [4]

The serious problem of the Particular Baptists was that, during the half century before the Revival, their Calvinism had hardened and atrophied. Hyper-Calvinism had become all but universal among the Particular Baptist churches. The hyper-Calvinist emphasis upon a rigid predestinarianism, and upon the "non-invitation, non-application scheme," as the Baptist historian Joseph Ivimey called it, had sapped the vitality of the churches.

This influence of hyper-Calvinism became marked through the work of John Skepp, who in 1710 became the minister of Curriers' Hall Church in London. The chief figures in the development of hyper-Calvinism among the Particular Baptists were, however, two other men. One was John Brine (1703–1765), who succeeded Skepp at Curriers' Hall, and the other was John Gill (1697–1771). These men were so afraid of Arminianism and Pelagianism that they refused to extend evangelistic invitations to the unconverted, lest they seem to rob God of the sole glory of converting the lost.[5]

The enervating effect of hyper-Calvinism stemmed from a rigid view of the doctrine of election. This view held that God had decreed before the world began who would be saved and who would be lost. Therefore, it was conceived to be both useless and highly presumptuous to invite men to repent and believe. Election, said John Gill, "is free and sovereign; God was not obliged to choose any; and as it is, he chooses whom he will, . . . and the difference in choosing one and not another is purely owing to his will." [6] Further, Gill said:

> [Election] is of particular persons; it does not merely respect events, characters, and actions; but the persons of men; as they are persons who are chosen in Christ, and appointed, not to wrath, but to obtain salvation by him; so they are persons who are foreordained to condemnation, whose names are left out of the book of life, whilst others are written in it.[7]

Not all of the excesses of popular hyper-Calvinism can be charged directly to perceptive minds, such as Brine and Gill, who were men of learning and of blameless life. However, other views belonging to the system of hyper-Calvinism became closely correlated with the doctrine of particular election in the minds of many who held hyper-Calvinist convictions.

One of these views was that nothing spiritually good could be the duty of the unregenerate. It was not their duty, therefore, to repent, to have faith, to pray, or to do anything else which was spiritually good. It was not their duty, because these were gifts of divine grace, not human attainments. All that the unregenerate could do was to wait for the moving of divine grace.

Closely related to the belief that faith was not a duty was the belief that a *warrant* was necessary to believe. A warrant was an evidence or a sign of a work of divine favor in the soul. Conviction of sin, with its accompanying mental distress, was such a sign, or warrant. A person with a warrant might regard himself as one of the elect and therefore go forward to saving faith. Yet such a warrant and the faith which followed were implanted in the heart at the initiative of divine grace, and they could not be initiated by the sinner.

Hyper-Calvinism frequently set the law and the gospel in the sharpest contrast and opposition to each other. The unregenerate were considered to be under the covenant of works, in which covenant the law obtained. Faith and spiritual exercises could not be required of them, since these were marks of the covenant of grace. Conversely, believers who were under the covenant of grace were exempt from the claims and requirements of the law. This dichotomy of law and grace defined the essence of antinomianism which frequently was associated with hyper-Calvinism. It should be said that the advocates of this notion were seldom grossly immoral. The view more commonly bred a spiritual lethargy which effectively nullified any evangelistic outreach on the part of the church.

The doctrine of eternal justification was a consistent derivative from the doctrine of election as held by hyper-Calvinists. According to this tenet, justification, like election, occurred in the secret counsels of God from all eternity. Elect sinners were therefore justified before they had experienced regeneration. This position separated justification from regeneration and, it was felt by many opponents of hyper-Calvinism, removed personal responsibility from the sinner's hands.

One of the salient doctrines of hyper-Calvinism was that of particular redemption. It was held that Christ died, not for the whole world, but for the elect only. A consequence of this teaching was that God, in his atoning work through Christ, had made no provision at all for the salvation of the nonelect. Besides, the atonement was frequently interpreted in rather crudely conceived substitutionary terms. Atonement was the payment of the debt which the elect incurred by sin. Christ incurred the wrath of God, and thus paid the debt of sin for the elect only.

One other feature of the hyper-Calvinist system should be mentioned here, the doctrine of imputation. Many hyper-Calvinists interpreted imputation to mean that Christ's righteousness is literally transferred to the sinner, while the sin of the sinner is literally transferred to Christ. Christ, it was held, not only took upon himself the sin of the sinner; he also "became sin for us." The punishment of Christ in the sinner's stead, therefore, was a punishment of him for the sins which were imputed to him. On the other hand, those who felt themselves to be elect and righteous by imputation, adjudged that they were entitled to *claim* salvation as their *right*, since the merits of Christ were attributed to them.

That an evangelistic spirit could not grow in such a climate would appear to be obvious. Yet it was out of this specific background that the modern missionary movement sprang, led by the great missionary William Carey. This background is graphically described by one of Carey's biographers, S. Pearce Carey:

> The pulpit doctrine of his [Carey's] denomination was extravagantly predestinarian. God's sovereignty was stressed till our responsibilities vanished.

Man was declared to have no power for penitence or faith, save through the super-enabling of God's selective grace. Here was no driving force for Missions. Faith ossified into fatalism. With the occult divine Will omnipotent and the human will judged helpless, even the godly grew passive. They who could think themselves the privileged exulted in their fortune, but remained unconscious of owing the good tidings to others. The favour was for the few. They left to God the ingathering of His own selected guests.[8]

After what A. C. Underwood calls "the winter of hyper-Calvinism," the "first stirrings of new life" appeared in the Midlands. In 1770 the Northamptonshire Association, comprising Baptist churches in several counties, published a circular letter. This letter contained the following passage: "Every soul that comes to Christ to be saved from hell and sin by him, is to be encouraged. . . . The coming soul need not fear that he is not elected, for none but such would be willing to come and submit to Christ." [9]

Nine years later Robert Hall (1728–1791), of Arnsby, father of a young man who was to become one of England's greatest preachers, preached a famous sermon for the Northamptonshire Association. His text was "Cast ye up, cast ye up, prepare the way, take up the stumblingblock out of the way of my people." At the urgent request of many persons, Hall expanded his address into a small book, which he entitled *Help to Zion's Travellers*. This book, published in 1781, was, in the words of Hall, "an attempt to remove various stumbling-blocks out of the way, relating to doctrinal, experimental and practical religion." The book's thesis was succinctly stated in Hall's own words: "The way to Jesus is graciously laid open for everyone who chooses to come to him." [10]

Hall's book became a classic among evangelical Baptists in England and America. To hyper-Calvinists, it was, in the words of Pearce Carey, "rank poison." To William Carey, who occasionally walked twenty-two miles on Sundays to hear Hall of Arnsby preach, it was like "sweetest wine." "He never read a book with such rapture. He drank it eagerly to the bottom of the cup." [11]

It is significant that the historian Ivimey thought that a new era in the Baptist fellowship began with the preaching of Hall's sermon to the Northamptonshire Association. The year 1779, he said, was "the commencement of a new era in the history of our denomination." [12] It was the beginning of a new era because Hall boldly advocated extending an open invitation to the lost.

Hall's forthright challenge found a ready response among able young men of kindred spirit, among whom may be named, besides Carey, Robert Hall, Jr.; John Ryland, the younger; John Sutcliff; Samuel Pearce; and Andrew Fuller. All of these men played significant parts in breaking out of the iron shackles of hyper-Calvinism and in launching the missionary movement of which William Carey was the most brilliant early representative.

In the founding of the missionary society which sent Carey to India, and in its valiant support for many years, Andrew Fuller played an indispensable part. He remained the society's secretary at home until his death in 1815, leading the fight for missions on the home base, and in this way he furnished the sinews of war for the overseas mission.

> I know not whether more to admire the self-denial which led Carey to Bengal, or the indefatigable labours of Fuller, in which there was, perhaps, as much self-denial, to procure the necessary funds. Think of the man who in his work on Deism could produce such a chapter as that with which it closes—on the consistency of redemption with the magnitude of creation—toiling through London to solicit contributions from reluctant givers, and often retiring from the more public streets into the back lanes, that he might not be seen by others to weep for his little success. Such men need no spices to embalm, no monument to perpetuate their memory.[13]

However, Fuller's distinguished work as secretary of the Baptist Missionary Society will not be the primary subject of this chapter. Rather, the focus will be upon his contribution as a theologian whose influence among the Particular Baptists of his day was crucial and decisive. As a theologian, he, more than anyone else, was the spokesman of the evangelical Calvinism which launched the enterprise of modern missions. "He was the man," says A. C. Underwood, "who dealt the mortal blow to the system which held that it was impossible for any but the elect to embrace the Gospel and that it was therefore useless to invite the unconverted to put their trust in Christ." [14] While Carey became the center of the new missionary effort, he found in Fuller's thought the theological undergirding for the launching of his great venture. From the work of Fuller he inferred that if it was the duty of all men to receive the gospel offer, it was the duty of those who were trustees of the gospel to carry it to the ends of the earth.[15]

A BIOGRAPHICAL SKETCH OF ANDREW FULLER

Andrew Fuller (1754–1815) was born in Wicken, Cambridgeshire. As a lad of sixteen, he became a Baptist at Soham. In 1775 he was called to the pastorate of that small church and stayed there until called to the Baptist church at Kettering, Northamptonshire, in 1782. He remained as pastor of this church until his death.

There was a strong element of hyper-Calvinism in the church

at Soham, and practical problems in the church relating thereto caused Fuller to give searching study to the hyper-Calvinist system. He was, however, very reluctant to make public his views on the subject, and he did not do so until he had been at Kettering for several years. At last, in 1785, his views were published in a small work which he called *The Gospel Worthy of All Acceptation.* This work became at once a hammer stroke against hyper-Calvinism and a bugle call to an open evangelistic and missionary effort. Fuller wrote copiously on many subjects in subsequent years; yet no other work attained the fame of this early writing. Also his main ideas, many of which found subsequent elaboration, received effective expression here. It will be appropriate to examine this book now with some care.[16]

THE GOSPEL WORTHY OF ALL ACCEPTATION

Throughout this book and, for that matter, throughout his preaching and writing career, Fuller was careful to guard the main points of a strict Calvinism. A primary assumption of this position was that salvation comes to the individual person as a gift from God, without merit on the part of the creature. Assuming the initiative of divine grace, the problem with which Fuller tried to deal was twofold: First, is it the *duty* of the sinner to believe in Christ? Second, is it the duty of the church to proclaim the gospel to every creature?

> The problem . . . of determining exactly the relation between the grace of God and the responsibility of man in the salvation of the race is at the heart of the Calvinist controversy. Andrew Fuller saw clearly what had not been seen in his denomination for a long time, that it was necessary to say something about *both*. To emphasize the first at the expense of the second is to create the stiff hyper-Calvinism which paralysed the Particular Baptists in the latter part of the eighteenth century. To emphasize human responsibility only is to veer towards Arminianism or humanism. Because he does emphasize both, balancing them over against one another, Fuller may rightly be given the name of Evangelical Calvinist.[17]

In searching the pages of the New Testament, Fuller noticed that the gospel was addressed to men freely and that all to whom it was addressed were invited freely to respond. God, he said, "has abundantly promised that all who believe in him, love him, and obey him shall be saved." [18] "The gospel is a feast, freely provided, and sinners of mankind are freely invited to partake of it." [19] This great invitation, Fuller thought, was and is a primary revelation of the Scriptures. It is therefore the duty of unconverted sinners to believe in Christ, for "it is the duty of every man to believe what God reveals." [20]

Arguing that faith in Christ is the duty of all men who hear or who have the opportunity to hear the gospel, Fuller amplified this conclusion by urging the following six points.

1. "Unconverted sinners are commanded, exhorted, and invited to believe in Christ for salvation." [21]

By detailed examination of biblical passages from both the Old and New Testaments, Fuller found it to be the duty of the unconverted to accept the salvation of God. "Divine invitation," he said, "implies an obligation to accept it." [22] The hyper-Calvinists enjoined upon the unregenerate a mere attendance upon the means of grace, in the hope that the initiative of God might accomplish their salvation. Fuller's warning concerning this kind of temporizing is stern. "The preaching . . . which exhorts them [sinners] to mere outward duties, and tells them that their only concern is, in this manner, to wait at the pool, helps forward their delusion, and, should they perish, will prove accessory to their destruction." The promises of God in the Scriptures are given not to those who wait at the pool for the moving of the water, but to those who *hearken, hear,* and *seek* after God. [23]

The warrant for trust in the divine mercy, Fuller said, was not the quickening of an emotional interest in Christ, as though the claims of God were dependent upon a subjective state in the sinner's private soul. The warrant is rather the divine promise, "that whosoever, relinquishing every false ground of hope, shall come to Jesus as a perishing sinner, and rely on him alone for salvation, shall not be disappointed." [24] The warrant is God's promise, not a subjective feeling.

2. "Every man is bound cordially to receive and approve whatever God reveals." [25]

"It is allowed by all, except the grossest Antinomians," said Fuller, "that every man is obliged to love God with all his heart, soul, mind, and strength; and this notwithstanding the depravity of his nature." This obligation extends to the revelation which God makes in every relationship. Adam was obliged to love God in all God's perfections, as these were revealed in the works of creation. Moses was obliged to love God as God displayed himself in his wonderful works of providence. So we are obliged to love him in the more glorious displays of himself as a Savior of sinners through the death of his Son. "To suppose that we are obliged to love God as manifesting himself in the works of creation and providence, but not in the work of redemption, is to suppose that in the highest and most glorious display of himself he deserves no regard." [26]

Fuller's argument here, though somewhat elusive, was quite profound. God's revelation of his power and glory in creation and providence excites the wonder and even veneration of the natural man. But response to natural revelation is not enough. The natural man is also obligated to approve and embrace God in God's supreme disclosure of himself — in Jesus Christ.

3. "Though the gospel, strictly speaking, is not a law, but a message of pure grace; yet it virtually requires obedience, and such an obedience as includes saving faith." [27]

The gospel message, Fuller urged, thrusts an obligation upon men to hear it and believe it, because of the dignity of its author and the importance of its subject-matter. "We are ambassadors for Christ," says the apostle, "as though God did beseech you by us: we pray you in Christ's stead, be ye *reconciled* to God" (2 Corinthians 5:20, KJV, italics added). Reconciliation to God involves everything that belongs to true conversion. It means that the sinner justifies God's government, condemns his own rebellion against God, and accepts the terms of peace. In substance, this is the same thing as to repent and believe the gospel.

Fuller's attack here upon both the Antinomians and the Arminians, who held that all the sinner could do was to attend passively upon the means of grace, was unconcealed. "To speak," he said, "of an embassy from the God of heaven and earth to his rebellious creatures being entitled to nothing more than an *audience*, or a decent *attention*, must itself be highly offensive to the honour of his majesty. . . ." [28]

4. "The want of faith in Christ is ascribed in the Scriptures to men's depravity, and is itself represented as a heinous sin." [29]

Fuller observed that if faith were no more a sinner's duty than *election* or *redemption*, which are acts belonging peculiarly to God, unbelief could not be charged to the evil disposition of the sinner's heart. But it is so charged in the Scriptures. "No man is reproved for not doing that which is naturally impossible; but sinners are reproved for not believing, and given to understand that it is solely owing to their criminal ignorance, pride, dishonesty of heart, and aversion from God." [30] If unbelief is a sin, said Fuller, then faith is a duty.

5. "God has threatened and inflicted the most awful punishments on sinners for their not believing on the Lord Jesus Christ." [31]

On this point, Fuller buttressed his argument by appeal to

a series of New Testament passages: Luke 19:27, John 3:18, and 2 Thessalonians 2:10-12. It is true, he says, that salvation is the *gift* of God. Yet it is also true that unbelief is the "procuring cause" of damnation. Eternal death is the "proper wages" of sin. "He that believeth on him is not condemned; but he that believeth not is condemned already, *because* he hath not believed in the name of the only begotten Son of God." [32]

6. "Other spiritual exercises, which sustain an inseparable connexion with faith in Christ, are represented as the duty of men in general." [33]

Examples of such spiritual exercises are the love of God, the love of Christ, the fear of God, repentance, and humility or lowliness of mind. These, being integrally connected with faith, God requires of all men. They are component elements of all men's duty to God.

His constructive argument made through these six points, Fuller turned to answer objections, most of which, he observed, emanate in the Arminian camp. The way in which he dealt with objections shows that Fuller remained a staunch Calvinist.

The first objection was concerned with the "decrees of God." The question was this: How can a general invitation to sinners to accept the gospel be consistent with the election of some to eternal life, and a consequent rejection of others? [34] Fuller's reply began with an admission that this question cannot be answered with entire satisfaction. Both a general invitation, and a particular election, however, are taught in the Scriptures.

> The truth is, there are but two ways for us to take: one is to reject them *both*, and the Bible with them, on account of its inconsistencies; the other is to embrace them both, concluding that, as they are both revealed in the Scriptures, they are both consistent, and that it is owing to the darkness of our understandings that they do not appear so to us.[35]

Fuller called to his side the support of Paul, the apostle. "After all that he had written upon God's electing some, and rejecting others, he, in the same chapter, assigns the failure of those that failed to their 'not seeking justification by faith in Christ; but as it were by the works of the law. . . .' " [36] Fuller also observed that other advocates of predestination, such as Augustine, the Reformers, the Puritans of the sixteenth century, the "divines" of the Synod of Dort, and the nonconformists of the seventeenth century, all believed it the duty of every sinner who heard the gospel to repent and believe in Christ.[37]

Following John Owen, a seventeenth-century theologian whom

he frequently quoted, Fuller distinguished between man's duty and God's purpose. God's purpose for the destiny of any individual cannot be certainly known for it has not been revealed. On the other hand, that it is the duty of the church to preach the gospel to every creature, and the duty of every person who hears to repent and believe, has been openly declared in the scriptural revelation. The Scriptures, said Dr. Owen, "command and invite all to *repent* and *believe;* but they know not in particular on whom God will bestow repentance unto salvation, nor in whom he will effect the work of faith with power." [38]

Another objection, closely connected with the doctrine of election, concerned the problem of "Particular Redemption." If the atonement of Christ excludes a part of mankind, on what ground can *all* men be invited to accept it?

Fuller answered carefully in accordance with his Calvinistic presuppositions. "Christ, by his death, opened a door of hope to sinners of the human race as *sinners;* affording a ground for their being invited, without distinction, to believe and be saved." [39] The invitation, Fuller was saying, was to be extended to all men without distinction. The heralds of the gospel are so commanded to declare it.

But human duty does not affect the secret purpose of God. "As God might send his Son into the World to save men, rather than angels, so he may *apply* his sacrifice to the salvation of some men, and not of others." [40] The preacher of the gospel is charged with the task of inviting all men to believe and be saved, and he is no more concerned with particular redemption than he is with election, "both being secret things, which belong to the Lord our God, and which, however they be a rule to him, are none to us." [41]

Fuller next addressed his attention to the supposition that the unregenerate live under the covenant of works, not under the covenant of grace. As shown in another part of this discussion, if it were true that sinners live under the covenant of works, then they have no obligation to believe the gospel, except the obligation of waiting for the saving fiat of God.

Fuller thought this argument to be highly specious. Sinners are not under the covenant of works, although they are under the *curse* of having broken the law of God. The point to be emphasized is not the claim of the law upon them, but the claim of the gospel upon them. "It is enough for us that the revealed will of God to sinners says, *Believe;* while the gospel graciously adds the promise of *salvation.*" [42]

Another objection to extending a free invitation to the lost concerned "the inability of sinners to believe in Christ, and to do things spiritually good." [43] Fuller's discussion is intended to be an answer to those who argued that, since God's enabling grace was necessary to bring the unregenerate to faith, the sinner in his natural state is unable to believe. Since the sinner lives under this inability, he has no obligation to believe. One is not obliged to do what he cannot do.

Fuller's answer was one which he derived essentially from his great theological mentor, Jonathan Edwards. However mystifying this answer may be to a modern mind, there is no doubt that Fuller and the evangelical Calvinistic Baptists of his day found it to be a very important help in their controversy with the hyper-Calvinists. The answer rested upon a distinction between natural and moral inability. No man, Fuller reasoned, was responsible to do what he was naturally unable to do. He is, however, responsible for what he is morally unable to do. Blind Bartimeus suffered a natural inability — he was blind. No man could hold him responsible for not being able to see. On the other hand, the unbelieving Jews suffered a moral inability. They "closed their eyes, lest they should see, and be converted, and be healed." [44] They could not see because they *would* not see. Their blindness involved culpability and guilt.

> It is just as impossible . . . for any person to do that which he has no mind to do, as to perform that which surpasses his natural powers. . . . Those who were under the dominion of envy and malignity "could not speak peaceably"; and those who have "eyes full of adultery *cannot* cease from sin." Hence, also, the following language, "How *can* ye, being evil, speak good things?"—"The natural man receiveth not the things of the Spirit of God, neither *can* he know them." [45]

To the evidence of Scripture, Fuller added an *ad hominem* argument. "If any person imagine it possible," he said, "of his own accord, to choose that from which he is utterly averse, let him make the trial." [46]

What Fuller was attempting to do by the distinction between natural and moral inability was to conserve the Calvinist conviction that man was powerless to turn to God except through the initiative of God's grace, while affirming at the same time that this powerlessness was the result of man's own sin; moreover, that this incapacity to turn to God left the sinner responsible and guilty. Men could not believe because they would not believe. This moral inability is the situation of all men, except those to whom the condescending grace of God is extended. Yet those who proclaim the gospel have no right to make prior judgments as to whether the grace of God will be extended to any given individual or not. God's enabling grace is in the hands of God alone, but the invitation of the gospel is to be proclaimed to all men.

Very closely related is the next objection which Fuller answered. This concerns the work of the Holy Spirit in the fulfillment of spiritual duty. The Arminians and Socinians held, said Fuller, that if faith and conversion are acts of obedience, "they cannot be wrought of God." Hyper-Calvinists, on the other hand, urged that, since faith and conversion are wrought of God, they cannot be acts of obedience. Fuller's understanding of the mysteries of grace and of human duty could envision them only in paradoxical union: Faith is the gift of God; faith is the duty of man. ". . . the Scriptures uniformly teach us that all our sufficiency to do good or abstain from evil is from above; repentance and faith, therefore, may be duties, notwithstanding their being the gifts of God." [47]

In his conclusion, Fuller cautioned that the character of his discussion, which had urged faith as a duty, should not be taken to indicate that this duty derived from the mere *authority* of God. The command to faith does indeed derive from the authority of God, but it must be understood that the purpose of God, in making overtures to men, is to extend mercy to the perishing. It should also be emphasized, Fuller thought, that although faith is a duty, the response of faith is not therefore a meritorious act or work on the part of the believer. If it were a meritorious work, it could claim a proper reward. Faith indeed is rewarded, but its reward is not a recognition of merit; it is a gift of divine grace.[48]

The justification of God which comes by grace through faith has its counterpart in the most solemn and awful warnings to those who reject the offer of mercy. Those who reject the entreaties of the gospel will receive the ruin of eternal death.[49]

The duty of ministers, Fuller said, is "not only to exhort their carnal auditors to believe in Jesus Christ for the salvation of their souls; but it is at our peril to exhort them to anything short of it, or which does not involve or imply it." With pointed reference to the lethargic indifference which had gripped the Particular Baptist fellowship under the influence of hyper-Calvinism, Fuller observed, "We have sunk into such a compromising way of dealing with the unconverted as to have well nigh lost the spirit of the primitive preachers, and hence it is that sinners of every description can sit so quietly as they do, year after year, in our places of worship." [50] He charged his fellow ministers to lay upon the hearts of sinners the word from God, "Repent ye, therefore, and be converted, that your sins may be blotted out." [51] "We need not fear," he said, "exhorting sinners to holy exercises of heart, nor holding up the promises of mercy to all who thus return to God by Jesus Christ." [52]

FULLER'S LEADING IDEAS

While nearly all of Fuller's leading ideas are set forth in *The Gospel Worthy of All Acceptation,* some of these received more careful elaboration in the writings with which he was busily occupied for the remainder of his life. Circumstances determined that his writings would be principally of a controversial nature. At one time or another he entered the lists against Arminianism, Antinomianism, Socinianism, Sandemanianism, and Deism. His writings attest to the fact that, although this unschooled clergyman never became a technically qualified scholar, he was well read in the theological literature of his time; that he was a cool and fair, but relentless, antagonist in debate; that he wrote in a trenchant and clear, if unadorned, style of English prose; and that his best efforts show the workings of a powerful, if not a scintillating, mind. In order to convey some idea of the system which came to be called "Fullerism" among Baptists of the late eighteenth and early nineteenth centuries, several of Fuller's principal convictions will be further examined.

GOD'S SECRET WILL AND REVEALED WILL

In a hard-hitting work designed to show the evils of Antinomianism, Fuller undertook to show that the antinomian perniciously substitutes the "secret for the revealed will of God." [53] The antinomian becomes more concerned for the electing decree of God, which no man can know, than for the revelation of His will which God has plainly made in the Scriptures.

> It is thus that men stumble upon the dark mountains, and fall into many dangerous errors, besides those on justification. . . . To what is it owing, but to the substituting of the secret for the revealed will of God, that Christians should be afraid to pray for the salvation of their neighbors, ministers for that of their hearers, and parents for that of their children, lest they should not prove to be of the elect? [54]

A better example is that of the apostle Paul, whose heroic endeavors for the salvation of mankind were motivated by his hearty grasp of God's *revealed* will. "God he well knew would regulate *his own conduct* by his wise and righteous decrees, but they could be no rule to him, inasmuch as they were utterly beyond his knowledge." [55]

The dark shadow of doubt which lingers in the mind of the thoughtful person over the concession that there might be a disparity between the secret and the revealed will of God posed a problem which Fuller never solved. Indeed, this problem is indigenous to Calvinism. But by putting revelation in the forefront of the consideration of the gospel, Fuller cleared the ground for an open evangelistic and missionary invitation. The gospel, on the authority of God's revealed will, was to be proclaimed to all men, on the supposition that they could believe it. The recovery of this emphasis was a great boon for the Baptists in Fuller's day. Indeed the names of Carey, Marshman, and Ward testify that it was a boon for the world.

REVELATION

Fuller urged repeatedly that the revealed will of God discloses that all men bear a responsibility for hearing and for doing that will. He acknowledged that there are degrees of responsibility, depending upon the opportunity which different persons have of hearing the gospel. He believed in a general revelation of God through the created order. Following the discussion of the apostle Paul's presentation in the first chapter of Romans, Fuller thought that this revelation was sufficient to establish the fact that God's eternal power and Godhead may be clearly seen in the things which he has created. This revelation is also adequate to impress upon the mind of man that God ought to be worshiped, so that all men are without excuse for denying God the veneration which properly belongs to him.

> When I consider the heavens and the earth, with their vast variety, it gives me reason to believe the existence of a God of infinite wisdom, power, and goodness, that made and upholds them all. Had there been no written revelation of God given to us, I should have been without excuse, if I had denied a God, or refused to glorify him as God.[56]

The human reason, however, has been corrupted by sin and distorts the knowledge of God which is received through the light of nature. For a "competent knowledge of God, and of his will for us," a more complete revelation is necessary. This revelation, Fuller believed, comes to us through the Scriptures.

It is not surprising to find Fuller to be a biblicist. The Scriptures of both the Old and New Testaments are "a perfect rule of faith and practice." The Bible is of "divine inspiration and infallibility." The knowledge of God which comes through the light of nature must be supplemented by that which comes through God's word, the Holy Scriptures. God's works in nature show us God's being and creative power; the Scriptures disclose God's character and his will for us. Human reason alone could not discover what God reveals. Yet the truth of God disclosed in the Scriptures is not contrary to reason. Reason, aided by the Holy Spirit, can discover the truth of God revealed in the Scriptures.[57]

In a brief study of Fuller's use of the Bible, Norman H. Maring has shown that, although Fuller believed the Bible to be infallible in all its statements, he made little use of this concept. Rather, he found the essential witness of the Bible to be located in its saving truth which it discloses. Fuller said,

> A true believer, so far as he understands it, *does* believe all Scripture truth; and to discredit any one truth of the Bible, knowing it to be such, is a damning sin; but yet it is not the credit of a chronological or historical fact, for instance, that denominates one a true believer. The peculiar truth, by embracing of which we become believers in Christ, is the *gospel*, or the *good news* of salvation through his name. The belief of this *implies* the belief of other truths; such as the goodness of God's government, as the Lawgiver of the world; the evil of our sin; our lost and ruined condition by it; our utter insufficiency to help ourselves, etc.; but it is the soul's embracing, or falling in with, the way of salvation by Jesus Christ, that peculiarly denominates us true believers.[58]

It speaks well for Fuller's Christian insight, as well as for his stature as a theologian, that although in a real sense he was a biblicist, he was not a bibliolater. He searched for the answer to the question: What is it that the Scriptures reveal which is of more ultimate authority than the Scriptures themselves? He was led by the Scriptures to the supreme revelation which God had made of himself in Christ.

> The only display of the Divine perfections which can be denominated perfect is in the salvation of sinners, through the obedience and death of his beloved Son. After all the preceding manifestations of his glory, it may be said, "no one has seen God at any time; the only begotten Son, who is in the bosom of the Father, he hath declared him." In this undertaking, every Divine perfection meets and harmonizes.[59]

A non-Calvinist would likely feel a keen regret that Fuller held throughout his life to the view that the secret will of God, which will no man can know, determined human destiny for reasons beyond human understanding. Yet his emphasis upon revelation, upon God's revealed will disclosed in the Scriptures, came to the fore, and consideration of the secret will receded. This matter of emphasis made a considerable difference in the tone and outlook of Fuller's theology and in that theology's beneficial effects in the area of its influence.

The revelation of the Scriptures, Fuller believed, disclosed God to be engaged in the great enterprise of human redemption. In this enterprise his grand agent is Jesus Christ. No appraisal of Fuller's theology would be complete without calling attention to the place which he gave to the redeeming work of Christ.

ATONEMENT

On the whole, Fuller's view of the atonement fits in quite well with the orthodoxy of his time. Christ, the eternal Son of God, the second person of the Godhead, was in possession of the powers and qualities required for the reconciliation of God and man. As man, Christ assumed the human nature which qualified him to identify with the race of fallen human beings, although he himself was without sin. Fuller was careful to say that Christ was one person, the God-Man, preserving in his person a hypostatical union of divine and human qualities without an intermixture of properties. This was good Chalcedonian Christology.[60]

Fuller reacted strongly to deistic writers who conceived that the Christian doctrine of atonement represented God the Father as an implacable, vengeful tyrant, demanding full satisfaction against those who had broken his law, while Christ the Son was represented as being full of compassion, and, at the cost of extreme suffering, as interposing himself as a sacrificial offering to save men from the Father's wrath.[61] On the contrary, said Fuller, divine love is the first cause of our salvation. "The love of God wrought in a way of righteousness; first giving his only begotten Son to become a sacrifice, and then pouring forth all the fulness of his heart through that appointed medium." [62]

The specific theory of atonement to which Fuller principally subscribed, it appears, was what is known as the governmental theory. He may have derived this view through his study of Jonathan Edwards, although he does not credit Edwards for it. In any case, he did not conceive the sacrifice of Christ to be a payment, in quantitative terms, of the *debt* which men have accumulated by their sins. Rather, said Fuller,

The incapacity of God to show mercy without an atonement, is no other than that of a righteous governor, who, whatever goodwill he may bear to an offender, cannot admit the thought of passing by the offence, without some public expression of his displeasure against it; that, while mercy triumphs, it may not be at the expense of law and equity, and of the general good. . . .[63]

No considerate citizen, who values the public weal, could blame a magistrate for putting the penal laws of his country so far in execution as should be necessary for the true honor of good government, the support of good order, and the terror of wicked men.[64]

The atoning sacrifice of Christ, in the sinner's place, enabled God to show mercy, while at the same time upholding the majesty of his righteous justice.

Fuller did not hesitate to assert that Christ, by stepping into the place of sinful man in his atoning sacrifice, became a substitute for sinners. Yet he was careful to say that God was not personally angry with his Son. Fuller dissociated himself from the view that the guilt of the sinner was so transferred to Christ that Christ *became* guilty, or that the sin of the sinner was so transferred to Christ that Christ *became* sin.

As all that is transferred in the imputation of righteousness is its beneficial effects, so all that is transferred in the imputation of sin is its penal effects. To say that Christ was *reckoned* or *counted* in the Divine administration *as if he* were the sinner, and came under an *obligation* to endure the curse for us, is one thing; but to say that he *deserved* the curse is another. To speak of his being guilty by imputation is the same thing, in my ear, as to say he was criminal or wicked by imputation; which, if taken properly, for his being reckoned *as if he were so*, is just; but if properly, for his *being so*, is inadmissable. Guilt is the inseparable attendant of transgression.[65]

The imputation of sin to Christ was meant to be taken figuratively, said Fuller, not literally. "For Christ to die as a substitute, if I understand the term, is the same thing as his dying *for us*, or *in our stead*, or that *we should not die.*" [66]

It was characteristic of Fuller to insist that, although the sufferings and death of Christ were offered in such a way as to render them consistent with God's justice, this offering was at the same time an act of pure grace. It was in no sense required by justice, and there was no way in which the sinner could demand it as a claim arising from his own deserts.

By grace we are to understand the exercise of free favour, and consequently the bestowment of good where evil is deserved and may in justice be inflicted. . . . Grace, therefore, always implies that the subject of it is unworthy; and that he would have no reason to complain if all the evil to which he is exposed were inflicted on him.[67]

Although he tended to play down his Calvinistic conviction that the atonement was limited in its application, it appears that this conviction was lifelong. It surfaced clearly in his debate with the Arminian Baptist leader Dan Taylor. The question was not, said Fuller, whether Christ's atonement was sufficient for the salvation of the whole world. If the number of human beings, and the multitude of their offenses, had been multiplied a thousand times beyond their actual limits, Christ's sufferings would have been sufficient for the salvation of all men, *provided* God had been pleased to make them effectual to that end. The real question, said Fuller, was the design of God in his extension of the efficacy of the atonement. Fuller thought that the atonement was extended only to the elect.

> All I contend for is that Christ, in his death, absolutely designed the salvation of all those who are finally saved; and that, besides the objects of such absolute design, such is the universal depravity of human nature, not one soul will ever believe and be saved.[68]

CREATION AND REDEMPTION

Attention should be called, however briefly, to Fuller's sustained and generally consistent championship of the theme of redemption in his concept of God's relationship to the world, and, indeed, to the whole created order. Fuller's most mature and most impressive work is perhaps *The Gospel Its Own Witness*, in which he engages in debate with the deists. While this writing does not command complete assent from the modern Christian mind with respect to the arguments which Fuller uses, or with respect to the apologetic method employed, its scope of thought and its imaginative sweep make it a powerful piece of theological writing.

One of Fuller's principal charges against the deists was that, although deism acknowledged a God, it denied or overlooked his moral character. Our thought of God, Fuller replied, must always be Christologically centered. When we think of the vastness of the created order and of the God who created it, we must think of Christ as the agent of creation. We must not think of God as a being of naked power. Rather, we must think of his power in its Christlike character. So, we must not measure the tiny stature of man in quantitative terms against the vastness of the universe. For the importance of man is to be gauged in the scale of God's redemptive purpose, which makes the earth the theater of redemption and unites creation, providence, and salvation within the will of one God whose sovereignty is the sovereignty of goodness and mercy.

The habitable earth, Fuller said, by the interposition of the Mediator, was divinely appointed to become the abode of righteousness.

> Here a trophy was to be raised to the glory of sovereign grace; and millions of souls, delivered from everlasting destruction, were to present an offering to Him "that loved them and washed them from their sins in his own blood." Here, in a word, the peculiar glory of the Godhead was to be displayed in such a manner as to afford a lesson of joyful amazement to the whole creation "throughout all ages" of time, yea, "world without end." [69]

CONCLUSION

The two roles in which Andrew Fuller rendered his most distinguished service to Baptists were as secretary of the Baptist Missionary Society and as a theological writer. From 1792 until his death in 1815, his labors for the mission were indefatigable and heroic. "Fuller lived and died a martyr to the Mission," says one of his biographers. On behalf of this cause, he wrote hundreds of letters in his own hand, made frequent trips to solicit funds for its support, and did battle on its behalf against powerful antagonists. Besides numberless trips in England for the mission, he made one trip to Ireland and five journeys to Scotland. At the end of one tour he wrote, "I have been enabled to collect as much as 2,000 pounds in the course of six weeks, after a journey of 1,200 miles." During all this time, he had the care of the church at Kettering, was in demand as a denominational leader and speaker, and was incessantly busy writing letters, articles, and books. When he died at the age of sixty-one, his physician said that the resources of his once powerful frame were as exhausted as those of a person whose body was in the last stages of consumption.

Fuller was a courageous and independent intellect, combining balance, perspicuity, candor, and strength. The cast of his mind was conservative.

As a theologian of considerable capacity and power, Fuller's most signal service was rendered to his own denomination in furnishing his brethren with the weapons for freeing the denomination from the imprisonment of hyper-Calvinism, and for launching out upon a new era of evangelism and missions. W. T. Whitley said: "The influence of Fuller told steadily on the larger body of Particular Baptists, and the foundation of the Baptist Missionary Society blazed the new path destined to be trodden by all who counted." [70] Fuller well deserves the tribute paid to him by another historian of English Baptists, A. C. Underwood. "It may be said," writes Underwood, "that he was the soundest and most creatively useful theologian the Particular Baptists have ever had." [71]   *175101*

The influence of Fuller upon the life of American Baptists is more difficult to assess. Writing in the year 1859, American Baptist historian David Benedict (1779–1874) remarked that forty years earlier many Baptists in the United States had been in a "state of ferment and agitation" over the modifications of the old Calvinistic creed which had been made in the writings of Fuller. The followers of Fuller, denominated "Fullerites," set themselves in opposition to the "Gillites," followers of John Gill, who were preaching a rigid application of the doctrine of a limited atonement. Not surprisingly, the "Gillites" accused the "Fullerites" of Arminianism, while the latter accused the former of hyper-Calvinism. The Gill party, Benedict observed, were most strongly represented among the Baptists of New York, Philadelphia, and farther south, while the Baptists of New England emphasized the Calvinist doctrines somewhat less strongly, and the "New Light" Baptists were Calvinists of a still milder type.

Benedict further observed that for a number of years the asperity of feeling between the two parties had been considerably diminished but that the trend in Baptist preaching had told heavily in the direction of an open invitation to sinners. Indeed, said Benedict, perhaps with a tinge of sadness, most Baptists seemed to care little for doctrinal preaching any more, and generally they had lost interest in the points at issue between the "Gillites" and the "Fullerites." [72]

Fuller's influence upon a more vital evangelism among the Baptists of America was certainly real, though of an undetermined extent. The rise of a missionary spirit among American Baptists between the turn of the century and 1859 had developed markedly through the agency of many factors, of which the weight of Fuller's theology was only one consideration. The effect of the Carey mission in India, of the work of Adoniram Judson in Burma, of the heroic labors of Luther Rice in America, of the missionary outreach sponsored by the Triennial Convention and by numerous other missionary societies, the intense evangelism of the Separate Baptists — these were all additional factors which must be taken into account.

Like other Calvinists, Fuller emphasized the initiative of God's grace in salvation. God's grace is sovereign. However, Fuller turned from speculation about the decrees of God in eternity, to God's offer of salvation in history.

To orthodox Calvinists, salvation or reprobation were determined in eternity. Fuller did not deny this. But he did claim that God has offered salvation in Jesus Christ; that it is the duty of the church to make Christ known by the proclamation of the gospel; and that it is the duty of the sinner to *believe*.

Here was a turning from speculation about what God may have decided in eternity, to an emphasis upon God's offer in Christ, to an emphasis upon responsible decision by each person who hears the gospel proclamation.

This theology was deeply evangelical and practical, and had at the same time intellectual depth. Considering the time and place at which he came upon the scene, and the crucial historical situation to which his message spoke, Andrew Fuller played a distinguished and an invaluable part in leading the Baptists to embrace a vital evangelical interpretation of the gospel.

5 - ALEXANDER CAMPBELL -
Advocate of Reformation

Alexander Campbell was one of the most influential religious leaders on the American frontier in the first half of the nineteenth century. Although he was within the Baptist fellowship for only a relatively brief period of time, his influence upon Baptist life and thought, as well as his contribution to the American religious scene as a whole, is worthy of consideration.

RELIGION ON THE AMERICAN FRONTIER

The treaty closing the Revolutionary War set the western boundary of the United States at the Mississippi River. The territory of the western areas was vastly extended by the Louisiana Purchase in 1803. The first general census in the new nation, taken in 1790, revealed that the population of the country was 4,000,000, of which about 200,000 persons were already living west of the Allegheny Mountains. The economic slump along the Atlantic seaboard following the Revolution gave a decided impetus to population movements westward. The migration continued at a high rate until the return of good times, about 1820.

The throngs which spilled into the frontier sections of the Great West included many Baptists. Most of the Baptists were, in varying degrees, Calvinists. The Baptist ministers were farmer-preachers. Educational prerequisites for admission to the ministry were nonexistent. The scattered Baptist churches were self-governing. Baptist polity was suited to the frontier.

In this vast area, the struggle for existence was a leveler which tended to erase inherited privilege and the social distinctions common to an older culture. The intense, emotional nature of religious experience was accentuated by the isolation of frontier life, the craving for companionship, and the uncertainties of the wilderness existence.

The revivalistic type of piety which made a powerful incursion into Baptist life during the Great Awakening became more pervasive on the frontier. The Great Revival which shook the western frontier between 1801 and 1804 was a phenomenon unique in American history. The Great Revival in the West found its principal exponents in the Presbyterians, the Methodists, and the Baptists.

In the West, the Baptists found themselves in competition with representatives of few other denominations. The Anglican or Protestant Episcopal Church lost its border population in Virginia to the Baptists, Methodists, and Presbyterians. After the Revolution, the Episcopal Church gained in vitality, but it remained a church of the upper middle classes of the East.[1] For more than a century following the Great Awakening, the Congregational Church continued to be a provincial New England denomination which appealed mostly to the middle classes in established eastern communities.[2]

The Presbyterians were somewhat more effective. The pattern of Presbyterian growth followed the migrations of the Scotch-Irish, the second great wave of which began about 1760, and lasted until about the time of the Revolutionary War. These immigrants penetrated particularly to western Pennsylvania, to the Valley of Virginia, to the hill country of the Carolinas, and to Kentucky and Tennessee. The Scotch-Irish migrations made the Presbyterian Church, during the latter half of the eighteenth century, preeminently the church of the frontier. However, the rigid constitutional system of Presbyterianism made it unable to adapt to frontier conditions without fracturing its unity. Even more important to its decline of influence on the frontier was its loss of members to the Methodists, to the Baptists, and, at a later time, to the Disciples of Christ.[3]

In the nineteenth century the Methodist Church assumed a leading position in the West. The centralization of control in this church, while incompatible with the individualistic tastes of the frontier people, gave it cohesion and direction. The aristocratic features of Methodism were softened by the democratic spirit of its circuit-riding preachers. Its fondness for emotional demonstrations and for an Arminian theology put it in tune with the spirit of the frontier.[4]

Religious partisanship was more active and virulent on the frontier than in the East. In the western areas the isolation of many settlements, as well as the individualism and low educational level of the settlers, made them peculiarly susceptible to religious controversy. "In isolated frontier districts," said Peter G. Mode, "the unsectarian mind would have been a monstrosity." [5]

Many of these strands of frontier religion are evident in the life and work of Alexander Campbell. During his sojourn in the Baptist fellowship, Alexander Campbell became one of the most controversial figures in Baptist history. Most Baptist accounts of his notable career deal largely with the points of controversy, thereby neglecting the objectives which Campbell had in mind, and the religious convictions which motivated his actions. Therefore, after a brief biographical sketch of Campbell, this chapter will first set forth the most important points of his theology, without any special notice of the Baptist reaction. Subsequently, the debate which arose within the Baptist ranks will be depicted in the context of Campbell's efforts to implement his views. Finally, a brief assessment of Campbell's influence upon the life and thought of the Baptists will be attempted.

A BIOGRAPHICAL SKETCH OF ALEXANDER CAMPBELL

Alexander Campbell was born in Antrim, Ireland, in 1788, and he died in Bethany, West Virginia, in 1866. On his father's side, he descended from a Scotch family long resident in Ireland. His early education was received at home under the tutelage of his father, Thomas Campbell. When Alexander was sixteen years of age, Thomas Campbell moved with his family to Rich Hill and established an academy, in which Alexander became his assistant.

Thomas Campbell and his immediate family belonged to the Old Light Antiburgher division of the Seceder branch of the Presbyterian Church. In 1807 Thomas Campbell migrated to southwestern Pennsylvania because of ill health, and he became the pastor of several small Presbyterian churches on the Pennsylvania frontier. His family soon left Ireland to follow him, but the wreck of their ship delayed their arrival in America for a year. During this year Alexander studied in the University of Glasgow.

In America, Thomas Campbell soon found himself out of favor with the Presbyterians because of his pronounced opposition to sectarianism. He therefore renounced the authority of the synod to which he belonged, surrendered his status as a Presbyterian minister, and led in the formation of an independent congregation called "The Christian Association of Washington" (Pennsylvania). He had no intention of founding a new denomination.

When the family arrived in America to join Thomas Campbell,

Alexander found himself heartily in accord with his father's aims and course of action, as set forth in Thomas Campbell's recently written *Declaration and Address.* In 1809 the Christian Association became the Brush Run Church, and Alexander Campbell became the pastor. Soon the leadership of the Campbell movement passed to this gifted son of Thomas Campbell.

In 1811 Alexander married a Presbyterian woman. When their first child was born, Campbell made a searching study of infant baptism to determine whether his child should be christened. He was led by this study to conclude that the New Testament gave no sanction to infant baptism and to affirm that baptism should be administered by immersion only to Christian believers. Shortly thereafter, he, his wife, and his parents were all immersed by a Baptist minister.

Under Campbell's leadership, the Brush Run Church adopted immersion, and the church was received into the Redstone Baptist Association of Pennsylvania in 1813. In the meantime, Campbell engaged in a program of study and of frequent preaching. Soon it became apparent that he was a man of considerable charm and persuasiveness, that he was a preacher of power, and that the scope of his learning was virtually unmatched in the frontier society in which he elected to exert his influence. He became, in short, a leader.

In 1816 Campbell preached his famous "Sermon on the Law" before the Redstone Baptist Association. In this message, he exalted the authority of the New Testament over that of the Old. The sermon enhanced his fame, but it also aroused suspicion among some of the ministers of the association concerning the orthodoxy of the brilliant young preacher.

In 1823 he began the publication of a monthly periodical which he called *The Christian Baptist.* In its pages Campbell zealously advocated his views, some of which caused consternation and heated debate in the Baptist community far and wide. *The Christian Baptist* was discontinued in 1829, but Campbell then began the publication of a larger periodical, *The Millennial Harbinger,* which furnished him an organ of expression for the remainder of his life.

In addition to his other gifts, Campbell was an extremely skillful debater. In an era when religious controversy was prevalent and when religious debates excited great public interest, Campbell's famous debates put him in the forefront of public attention. His principal debates were held in 1820, 1823, 1829, 1837, and 1843.

The debate in 1829 pitted him against Robert Owen, the noted British social reformer, philanthropist, and skeptic, concerning the validity of the claims of Christianity. His debates of 1820 and 1823 gave him opportunity to contest the validity of infant baptism with Presbyterian opponents and cast him in the role of a Baptist champion.

Serious differences, however, between Campbell and many of his fellow Baptists arose very early in his public career. From the beginning of his affiliation with the Baptists, Campbell's opposition to the Philadelphia Confession of Faith, his hostility to other ministers, and his dissatisfaction with the institutional forms of Christianity generated tension in the Baptist fellowship. In the early 1820's this tension increased when, in debating the subject of baptism with Presbyterian ministers, Campbell began to advocate what seemed to be a doctrine of baptismal regeneration. Finally, between 1825 and 1830, widespread defections occurred from Baptist ranks to the Campbell movement, and many others were excluded from Baptist churches and associations. These separations continued sporadically until about 1833.

In 1832 Campbell's followers united with the New Lights of Kentucky and Ohio, led by Barton W. Stone, and the union came to be known as the "Disciples of Christ."

This chapter is not primarily concerned with Campbell and his movement after the separation from the Baptists. Yet it should be noted that in 1840 he founded Bethany College in Bethany, Virginia (later West Virginia), becoming president of the institution and a member of its faculty. For a description of the rest of his busy life, the following compact summary must suffice. After the separation,

> Alexander Campbell found himself no longer a free-lance reformer within the Baptist denomination but the most influential figure in an unorganized movement embracing scores of churches with some thousands of members in half a dozen states. From 1830 he was increasingly occupied with wide interests—an extensive correspondence, many visitors, long tours for preaching, lecturing, and visiting the churches, the editing of a monthly magazine, the management of a printing plant and a publishing business, the administration of a post office, and the operation of a large farm. There was no abatement of his zeal for the restoration of the primitive pattern of the church in all its essentials, but he viewed with a more friendly eye the supplementary devices and "expedients" that might be useful under modern conditions. He ceased to denounce the societies and organizations through which the denominations carried on their wider work and he gained a new interest in constructive policies which would bind the reforming churches into a brotherhood and promote their effective operation.[6]

In his last years, the mind of "the Sage of Bethany" became

somewhat impaired, but he lived to old age with the satisfaction of knowing that his movement had achieved a striking success and that the convictions for which he had contended were still steadily winning adherents.

CAMPBELL'S THEOLOGY —
A CONSTRUCTIVE STATEMENT

To achieve the union of all Christians, to rediscover the "ancient Gospel," to restore "the ancient order of things," to revitalize the church by a new vision of essential Christianity — these were the grand objectives to which Alexander Campbell dedicated his life. What he meant by these objectives cannot be understood, however, unless they are examined in the context of his general intellectual outlook. Hence, it is appropriate to begin with Campbell's concept of religious knowledge and how such knowledge is acquired.[7]

RELIGIOUS KNOWLEDGE

Campbell followed John Locke in believing that all knowledge is acquired by means of sensory experience. Out of sensory impressions are constructed "ideas," and these in turn must be referred to sensory observations for test and verification. Campbell also believed in the validity of Francis Bacon's inductive method of reasoning. The mind starts with a minute observation of facts. It heaps fact upon fact until it builds up a generalization therefrom.

Knowledge of the past must be gained by depending upon the "reports" of persons who were observers of facts which they had apprehended by sensory experience. In order to judge the truth of a report then, we must ask whether it is based upon "sensible facts." We must ask whether these facts were "public," i.e., subject to verification by more than one witness. We must ascertain whether "monumental" and "commemorative" institutions arose from the historical facts or events under consideration, which institutions evinced the sensory happenings from which they derived. We must determine whether these monumental proofs came into being simultaneously with the events which they were intended to commemorate. Baptism and the Lord's Supper, for example, are monumental proofs for factual events which transpired in the apostolic age.

If sensory experience is required for a knowledge of mundane realities, it is required also for a knowledge of spiritual realities.

Yet it is important for the student of Campbell to remember that Campbell did not believe that God and spiritual reality can be discovered by the investigations of the natural reason. They are known only by revelation.

> To constitute a divine revelation, in our sense of the terms, it is not only necessary that God be the author of it, but that the things exhibited be supernatural, and beyond the reach of our five senses. For example; that God is a Spirit, is beyond the reach of our reasoning powers to discover, and could not be known by any human means. That a Spirit created matter, or that God made the earth, is a truth which no man could, from his five senses or his reasoning powers, discover. It is therefore a revealed truth. That man has a spirit in him capable of surviving his mortal frame, is also a supernatural truth.[8]

For Campbell, the repository of supernatural truth which God has communicated to man is the Bible. Indeed, the Bible is the sole source of our knowledge of such truth. Campbell had a low opinion of the Deists, who thought that the unaided reason can gain a knowledge of God by surveying the created order. It is not by reason, but by revelation alone, Campbell thought, that we know that "the heavens declare the glory of God."

Campbell believed that the Bible is the divinely authenticated record of the experiences which the inspired writers had with God. The facts which are there recorded, the precepts and mandates there prescribed, were received from the Spirit of God directly by the writers.

Campbell was sure that the revelationary content of the Bible was communicated to the biblical writers through the *senses* of those who set it down in writing. God, he thought, *spoke* to the writers, and "dictated," or "indited," the Book. The revelation came by means of spoken words. The Bible is therefore itself a concrete object deriving from sensory experience, to be received upon the reliable testimony of witnesses.

So far, it would appear that Campbell subscribed wholly to a dictation theory of the Scriptures. Actually, his position was much more complex. For, concerning the question as to just how far the biblical writers were dependent upon the Holy Spirit for the exact words they used, Campbell's answer was that only supernatural truths were spoken directly by God. Insofar as the Scriptures contain records of natural, historical occurrences, the Spirit strengthened the memory of the writers, directed the choice of sources, and protected the writers from error.

On the basis of his premise that all knowledge comes through the senses, Campbell should have explained how God could have exercised any oversight of the biblical writers without *speaking* to them. He did not seem to be aware of this inconsistency.

Campbell's views of the biblical revelation had other refinements. A very important belief pertained to the relative authority of the two testaments. He did not believe that the authority of the Old Testament was equal to that of the New. In the "Sermon on the Law," delivered before the Redstone Baptist Association in 1816, Campbell first brought his views on this subject to public notice. In the Campbell-Walker debate in 1820 he developed his views extensively.

Campbell believed that God had dealt with man in biblical history in terms of nine progressive stages, dispensations, or covenants, the last and most authoritative of which comprised the Christian dispensation. The Jewish dispensation, beginning with Moses, terminated with the giving of the new covenant.

With the coming of the Christian dispensation, the Law of the Mosaic covenant was ended. This did not mean that the moral principles embodied in the Law were abrogated, for these existed before the Mosaic covenant, and were independent of it. They had been declared by the Mosaic Law, not created by it.

The claim that the Law had been abrogated had sweeping implications. It meant that the way of salvation as described in the New Testament completely superseded that set forth in the Old. Therefore, the nature, form, and government of the church are defined by the New Testament alone. No Christian duties or institutions could be validated by drawing analogies between them and the requirements of the Mosaic Law. For example, the pedobaptist effort to validate the institution of infant baptism by drawing an analogy between it and the institution of circumcision in the Old Testament could not be sustained.

Campbell thought that the laws of the kingdom in the Christian dispensation were given at Pentecost. The effect of this view was that he did not find the New Testament writings themselves to be all of equal authority. The book of Acts was exalted to a place of preeminence, even above the Gospels, the content of which related, he thought, to the period just before the giving of the laws of the Christian era. Just behind the book of Acts were ranked the New Testament Epistles.

In accord with his own presuppositions, Campbell undertook to be a faithful interpreter of the Scriptures, particularly of the New Testament. He was acquainted with the new scholarly approach to the Bible as literature, and he undertook to employ this approach. Since ideas are related to words, he thought that a responsible study of the Scriptures must be conducted in the original languages, and a careful exegesis should be made with these as tools of investigation. Due attention should be directed, he thought, to whether a given passage or book should be interpreted as history, poetry, allegory, or parable. Particular interest, he believed, should be given to miracles, prophecies, and spiritual gifts, in both the Old Testament and the New, for these were "facts" which evidenced the validity of the writings in which they were embodied, facts capable of being apprehended by the senses, and attested by witnesses, who did so apprehend them.

By following the empirical method of observing the use of each word and the time, place, circumstance, and purpose of each utterance, a mass of particular instances and facts would, Campbell thought, yield the general truths of Christianity and the laws for the government of the church.

The utter seriousness with which Campbell regarded the text of the New Testament, and the confidence which he accorded to the method which he used in its study, yielded an estimate of the Word which should occasion no surprise to the student of Campbell. For the New Testament became a law book, presenting the revelation of God and the will of Christ in a written Word which is to be received as completely and finally authoritative.

Essential Christianity

Many have remarked that the driving motivation of Campbell was Christian unity on the basis of a restoration of the "ancient gospel." His concern for unity and restoration cannot be denied. Yet his earnest study of the New Testament reveals that he was grasped by a deeply evangelical concern. To him the message of the Scriptures was a message of salvation. The restoration of the ancient gospel must be accomplished so that God's redemptive plan and purpose might be clearly and luminously disclosed. The church must be united because without this unity its missionary task in the world was crippled and nullified.

An appraisal of Campbell's interpretation of Christianity must take account of the fact that he was not concerned with the whole body of divinity in the way in which a professional theologian would have been concerned. He was not occupied in setting forth the teaching of the Bible on every point of doctrine. He grappled rather with the problem of what the Bible disclosed to be the terms of salvation. These terms were the "ancient gospel" because they disclose the way of salvation. The church is to be united as a strategic move to make it an effective agency of evangelism and Christian nurture.

The conclusion which he reached in his quest for essential Christianity is best stated in his own words in his book *The Christian System*.

> But the grandeur, sublimity, and beauty of the foundation of hope, and of ecclesiastical or social union, established by the author and founder of Christianity, consisted in this . . . that the belief of one fact, and that upon the best evidence in the world, is all that is requisite, as far as faith goes, to salvation. The belief of this one fact, and submission to one institution expressive of it, is all that is required of Heaven to admission into the church. . . . The one fact is expressed in a single proposition—that Jesus the Nazarene is the Messiah. The evidence upon which it is to be believed is the testimony of twelve men, confirmed by prophecy, miracles, and spiritual gifts. The one institution is baptism into the name of the Father, and of the Son, and the Holy Spirit.[9]

The belief of one fact, that Jesus is the Christ; submission to one institution, immersion — here is essential Christianity in a nutshell, as Campbell saw it.

However, to many persons to say that Jesus is the Christ was a confession so bare, so devoid of interpretation, that it was of little value. Indeed, it was suspected that Campbell concealed Arian or even Unitarian assumptions underneath it.

Actually, Campbell's Christology was quite orthodox. He believed that the divine Son was coeternal and coequal (although he did not like these terms) with the Father and the Spirit. Before the incarnation, however, the Son was the eternal Word. It was only when he became flesh that he became the Messiah. As Messiah, the eternal Word assumed human form in order to seek the salvation of men.[10]

FAITH

A distinctive element in Campbell's concept of salvation was his understanding of faith. In the scheme of salvation, he placed faith before repentance. He did this for good reason.

Faith is the belief of testimony. "Where testimony begins," said Campbell, "faith begins; and where testimony ends, faith ends." To have faith in Christ is to believe the testimony of the New Testament writers that Jesus is the Messiah. Saving faith is historical faith, for it is acceptance of the historical record in which the apostolic witnesses give their testimony. This testimony is subject to perennial verification in the experience of every Christian believer.

> Evidence alone produces faith, or testimony is all that is necessary to faith.
> . . . To exhort men to believe, or to try to scare them into faith . . . by
> effusions of natural or mechanical tears, without submitting evidence, is as
> absurd as to try to build a house or plant a tree in a cloud.[11]

Campbell thought that it is useless to pray for faith. If one desires faith, let him look at the testimony and the evidence, and then *believe*.

It is obvious that Campbell was seeking to be true to his empiricist presuppositions in his concept of faith. But if faith is a mere belief in testimony, what results is an intellectualistic understanding of faith. This tendency toward intellectualism was modified in Campbell's case by his conviction that faith includes trust and confidence. To believe the testimony about Jesus means that we come to trust *him*. Trust, based on evidence, yet transcends evidence in personal devotion and adoration.

REPENTANCE

After faith comes repentance. Campbell did not define repentance as godly sorrow for sin. Sorrow may indeed be an element in it. The decisive quality of repentance, however, is a change of view and a change of behavior. It is obedience. To the Jews, repentance meant:

> Change your views of the person and character of the Messiah and change
> your behavior toward him; put yourselves under his government and guid-
> ance, and obey him. [To the Gentiles it meant] Change your views of the
> character of God and of his government, and receive his Son as his am-
> bassador; and yield him the required homage by receiving his favor and
> honoring his institutions. This is reformation towards God and faith in
> the Lord Jesus Christ.[12]

Separation of faith and repentance for purposes of definition and study did not mean that Campbell thought that faith and repentance were separable in experience. They were, rather, complementary elements of one experience, which might be called conversion, or regeneration.

THE AGENCY OF THE HOLY SPIRIT

What does the Holy Spirit have to do with the conversion experience? Campbell's answer to this question was one of the most controversial features of his theology.

Far from believing that the Holy Spirit has direct encounter with the soul of an unregenerate person, Campbell believed that the divine Spirit operates upon the mind and conscience of the unbeliever only through the written Word. This means that the unregenerate man does not have personal traffic with the Holy Spirit before conversion, but only with the written Word which the Holy Spirit inspired. Campbell claimed, "that all the converting power of the Holy Spirit is exhibited in the Divine word." [13] Again, "As the spirit of man puts forth all its moral power in words which it fills with its ideas, so the Spirit of God puts forth all its converting and sanctifying power in the words which it fills with its ideas." [14]

Campbell was seeking to be consistent with his empirical assumptions. The Holy Spirit, exerting its influence only through the written Word, operates in a manner consistent with the only way in which man can really know — by means of sensory apprehension. Occasionally, however, Campbell found it necessary to depart from the empirical framework of his thought in order to be true to the realities of the spiritual life. This he did in his understanding of the Holy Spirit's role in the life of a person after conversion, and in the life of the church. For the Holy Spirit inhabits the life of the believer, and indwells the body of Christ.

> As the glory of the Lord equally filled all the tabernacle and the temple, so the Spirit of God animates, consoles, and refreshes the whole body of Christ. . . . He that enjoys the favor of Jesus Christ, the love of God, and the communion of the Holy Spirit, has all the fulness of God, and is as blessed as mortal man can be.[15]

BAPTISM

If faith was the belief in one fact, that Jesus is the Messiah, it was closely tied also to one "institution," baptism. What Alexander Campbell believed about baptism has puzzled most of his keenest interpreters and has given offense to many persons — most of all, quite likely, to the Baptists. For it began to appear that Campbell was adding a term to the Baptist understanding of the "plan of salvation." Besides repentance and faith, it seemed, he added a third factor, as in the following order: (1) Faith, (2) Repentance, (3) Immersion.

Very evidently, Campbell was seriously impressed by New Testament declarations that baptism was "for the remission of sins." In his debate with W. L. Maccalla in 1823, he began to make public statements which seemed to indicate that he believed baptism to be necessary for salvation.

> The water of baptism, then, *formally* washes away our sins. The blood of Christ *really* washes away our sins. Paul's sins were *really pardoned* when he believed. Yet he had no solemn *pledge* of the fact, no *formal* acquittal, no *formal purgation* of his sins until he washed them away in the water of baptism.[16]

The following statement, made in 1827, seems even more explicit:

> . . . we have the most explicit proof that God forgives sins for the name's sake of his Son, or when the name of Jesus Christ is named upon us in immersion:—that in, and by, the act of immersion, so soon as our bodies are put under water, at that very instant our former, or "old sins," are washed away, provided only that we are true believers.[17]

An authoritative interpreter of Campbell, W. E. Garrison, pointed out that the position of Campbell was not that of baptismal regeneration, for Campbell did not believe that baptism in itself carried redemptive power. Man is not saved by baptism alone. Campbell, Garrison said, distinguishes between

> the state of a man and the character of a man, and between *real* and *formal* remission of sins. These two distinctions are closely connected. Real remission expresses God's attitude toward the past sins of a man who has changed his character through faith and repentance. Formal remission expresses God's attitude toward those sins when the man has changed also his state; i.e., has entered the state of sonship or of citizenship in the kingdom of God, through fulfilment of the positive requirements which are the conditions of entrance.[18]

The distinction which Garrison explicated seems overly subtle. There is little wonder that multitudes of persons have thought that Campbell believed immersion to be a requirement for salvation. The impression is hardly diminished when a favorite illustration of Campbell is considered. A foreigner, he said, who comes to the United States cannot realize the privileges of citizenship until he has changed his state from being an alien to becoming a citizen through due process of law. Baptism, like naturalization, is an oath of allegiance by which an alien becomes a citizen. Although the formal oath does not effect a change in the disposition of the person, it does change his state. It is the culmination of the process of assuming citizenship.[19]

On the other side of the ledger must be placed Campbell's famous reply to a pious lady from Lunenburg, Virginia, in 1837. In this reply, Campbell said, "There is no occasion . . . for making immersion, on a profession of faith, absolutely essential to a Christian — though it may be greatly essential to his sanctification and comfort." [20]

Did this reply concede that the terms of salvation might not include immersion in *extraordinary* circumstances, while preserving immersion as the means by which salvation is *ordinarily* completed? Campbell's intent is still not clear. Possibly, the precise meaning of baptism was never clear in his own mind.

In any case, Campbell believed that the gift of the Holy Spirit to the individual believer coincided with immersion. "For so soon as any person, through faith and immersion, is adopted into the family of God, and becomes one of the sons of God, then he receives the Spirit of Christ. . . ." [21] Campbell remembered the scriptural injunction and promise, "Be immersed for the remission of your sins, and you shall receive the gift of the Holy Spirit." [22]

CHRISTIAN UNION

One of Alexander Campbell's most passionate convictions was that all sects and sectarianism among Christian believers should be done away and that a grand union of all Christians should be effected on the basis of essential Christianity.

This interest in Christian unity Campbell had derived from his father. In his prophetic and statesmanlike "Declaration and Address" of 1809, Thomas Campbell had shown Christian unity to be the pulsebeat of his own life. He said:

> To prepare the way for a permanent Scriptural unity among Christians, by calling up to their consideration fundamental truths, directing their attention to first principles, clearing the way before them by removing the stumbling blocks—the rubbish of the ages, which has been thrown upon it, and fencing it on each side, that in advancing toward the desired object they may not miss the way through mistake or inadvertency, by turning aside to the right hand or to the left, is, at least, the sincere intention of the above propositions. It remains with our brethren now to say, how far they go toward answering this intention. . . . [23]

By the advocacy of the simple terms of the "ancient gospel," which terms were faith in Jesus as the Christ, and immersion, Alexander Campbell conceived that he had directed the attention of the Christian community to the "fundamental truths" and "first principles" upon which Christian union could be accomplished. For the terms of union, he believed, were precisely the same as the terms of salvation. [24]

As a young man, Alexander Campbell also took very seriously another of his father's insights, namely, that the way to Christian union involved "clearing the way . . . by removing the stumbling blocks — the rubbish of the ages. . . ." In the early part of his career, Campbell devoted a great deal of his attention to the task of removing the "stumbling blocks," the "rubbish of the ages." His zealous devotion to this task put him on a collision course with many of his fellow Baptists.

When the larger Baptist community first saw the face of Alexander Campbell, it was the face of an iconoclast. This face clearly appeared in the issues of his widely read journal, *The Christian Baptist*. In his role as an aggressive reformer, Campbell seemed to aspire to undermine all established religion. He believed that, with the foundations of ecclesiasticism destroyed, primitive Christianity would be given a cleared field. "The stream of Christianity," he said, "has become polluted, and it is useless to temporize and try experiments. All the reformations that have occurred and all the religious chymistry (sic) of the schools have failed to purify it." [25] He therefore conceived the first order of business in the task of restoring primitive Christianity to be that of razing the "foundation of the Pedo-baptist system."

Until 1830 he considered the Baptists capable of being reformed, although he had in general a rather low opinion of the Baptist ministry.[26] Before and after that date, however, he was unsparing in his denunciation of what he considered to be the distortions of the gospel among the Baptists themselves. In the belief that it would be easier to restore primitive Christianity than to reform any part of contemporary Christendom, he said, "We turn from the stream . . . and seek the fountain."

Campbell possessed great powers of sarcasm and invective. Dismay and consternation and not a little misunderstanding and resentment were aroused when this most brilliant member of the American Baptist community made his scathing attacks upon Baptist practices and institutions which allegedly obstructed Christian unity and a restoration of primitive and pristine Christianity.

No feature of Campbell's attacks engendered more turbulence than his involvement in the antimission movement which was proceeding as a damaging controversy among Baptists on the frontier. The return of Luther Rice from Asia and his heroic exertions among the Baptists to win support for the mission of Adoniram Judson in Burma had crystallized a backlash of antimissionism, particularly among Baptist hyper-Calvinists in the vast American frontier areas.

Campbell did not intend to oppose missions *per se,* nor did he intend to give aid and comfort to the hyper-Calvinists. He opposed missionary societies, Bible societies, Sunday schools, and tract societies, because he found no biblical authority for them. He thought also that the sectarian nature of the various missionary schemes demonstrated the invalidity of their claims to be in the service of the gospel. He asked, "Are they not evidently mere sectarian speculations, for enlarging their sects, and finding appointment for their supernumerary clergy?" [27] The various societal organizations, missionary and otherwise, he thought to be "great religious engines" designed for the preeminence of those leaders by whom they were created, and "ultimately tending to a national creed and establishment." [28]

Finding in the New Testament no sanction for the institutional propagation of the gospel except by the local church, Campbell thought that missionary and other societies were backed by no divine authority. The societal effort transferred the glory of the church "to a human corporation." Missionary enterprises must be conducted by the local church, under local church authority, and in a local church capacity.

Campbell insisted that a prerequisite to missionary endeavor was Christian unity. A sectarian missionism sets itself against the "wisdom and plans of heaven."

After the separation of the Campbell party from the Baptists, Campbell changed his views on the subject of cooperative missionary endeavor, and he sought to unite his followers in an effective plan of cooperation. This change could not undo the damage which his attacks had caused to missionary and other benevolent causes, especially in frontier areas.[29]

Underneath these flamboyant attacks, Campbell was deeply in earnest. He was making a plea for a fundamental reconsideration of the nature and claims of the gospel. Campbell addressed a question of perennial validity to his Baptist brethren: namely, are you sure that the message which you are taking to the "heathen" is the *real* gospel?

Campbell discerned other stumbling blocks which obstructed the pathway to a restoration of the ancient order of things. One was the clericalism of the clergy. The clergy had covered over simple Christianity with so much ecclesiastical machinery and theological verbiage that they had made themselves indispensable for managing the one and understanding the other. The clergy were "hireling priests" who, instead of opening up for their people the treasures of the Scriptures, rather stood between them and any genuine biblical understanding. The special, divine "call" to the ministry, which the clergy claimed as their own birthright, set them apart from and above their people as a special privileged class. They did not preach the good news of a biblical, simple gospel. They preached the sectarian tenets of their own parties, thereby tearing apart the body of Christ, instead of effecting its healing union.[30]

The Baptists caught their share of Campbell's fire. It may

have been some consolation to them that he was not partial in the dispatch of his strictures and censures. He attacked synods, presbyteries, conferences, assemblies, and hierarchies, all of which he believed had no sanction in the New Testament, and which assumed legislative and administrative control over local churches. He also attacked Baptist associations for the same reason. The fact that associations were not biblically endorsed was only a small part of the evil which they caused. They were to be condemned also because they became instruments of coercion over individuals and churches.[31]

With regard to creeds and confessions of faith, Campbell's attitude was that of a thoroughgoing iconoclast. He believed that creeds usurped the place of the Bible as the touchstone of religious authority, that they were an abridgment of that liberty of opinion which belonged to every Christian, and that they were used by a designing clergy to forge the shackles of clerical and ecclesiastical despotism. They were artificial religious constructs, the effect of which was to cut off contact with the vital facts of religion and to substitute false and deceptive theories in the place of those facts.[32]

Creeds substituted an artificial and therefore a false terminology for biblical language. Campbell strongly advocated the use of "Bible names for Bible things."

> Now as all correct ideas of God and things invisible are supernatural ideas, no other terms can so suitably express them as the terms adopted by the Holy Spirit, in adapting those supernatural truths to our apprehension. He that taught men to speak, would, doubtless adopt the most suitable terms in his language to reveal himself to his understanding. To disparage these terms, adopting others in preference, is presumptuous and insolent on the part of man. . . . From this source spring most of our doctrinal controversies. Men's opinions, expressed in their own terms, are often called bible truths. In order then to a full restoration of the ancient order of things there must be a "pure speech" restored.[33]

Campbell gave a long list of "those Babylonish terms and phrases" which had formed, so to say, a murky screen which shut out the light of biblical truth. A few of his examples may be cited: the "Trinity," "The Son is eternally begotten by the Father," "the Holy Ghost eternally proceeding from the Father and the Son," "The divinity of Jesus Christ," "the humanity of Jesus Christ," "This he said as man, and that as God," "Original sin, and original righteousness," "General and particular atonement," "Legal and evangelical repentance," etc.[34] "Let it be remembered," Campbell said, "that, as these terms were not to be heard in the primitive church, in restoring the ancient order of things they must be sent home to the regions of darkness whence they arose." [35]

THE BAPTIST REACTION

As early as his "Sermon on the Law" in 1816, Alexander Campbell became an irritant in the Baptist fellowship. This does not mean, of course, that he or his opinions were universally disliked by the Baptist people. Indeed, his personal charm and persuasiveness, the plausibility of many of his "reforms," and the authentic evangelical note which rang through much of his preaching and writing gave him a potent influence among the Baptists.

As previously noted, a widespread separation between the Baptists and the "Reformers" eventually occurred. The Redstone Baptist Association was the first body to take formal action. In 1825 they excluded thirteen churches for holding the tenets and practices of Campbell. Tate's Creek Association in Kentucky soon followed the example of Redstone when ten orthodox churches excluded a reforming majority of sixteen churches. In 1828 the Beaver Association in western Pennsylvania disfellowshiped the Mahoning Association, which had adopted the sentiments of Campbell. The next year the Mahoning Association dissolved.

The instances cited above are but early examples of a conflict which assumed great proportions. Between 1825 and 1830, large defections to the Campbell movement occurred from the Baptist churches in Kentucky, western Pennsylvania, Ohio, Tennessee, and Virginia. Among those who defected to Campbell were reputable Baptist ministers of ability and influence, who propagated the Campbell version of the gospel with zeal and with telling effect.

A sampling of Baptist reactions from different areas may indicate the points of tension. In 1825 Campbell received a letter from R. B. Semple, the early historian of Virginia Baptists and one of the leading Baptist ministers in Virginia. In retrospect, Semple's letter seems to possess a quality of prescience.

Semple, Andrew Broaddus, and other Virginia Baptist leaders were friendly to Campbell when the latter first went to Virginia in 1825. They invited Campbell into their homes and pulpits, patronized his paper, and professed admiration for his learning, his various talents, and his sincerity of purpose.

Semple's letter contained the following estimate of Campbell: "As a man, in private circles, mild, pleasant, and affectionate;

as a writer, rigid and satirical, beyond all the bounds of scripture allowance." Semple complained that *The Christian Baptist,* though edited with ability, was deficient in "a New Testament spirit." He said to Campbell:

> Your opinions on some other points are, I think, dangerous, unless you are misunderstood, such as casting off the Old Testament, exploding experimental religion in its common acceptation, denying the existence of gifts in the present day, commonly believed to exist among all spiritual christians, such as preaching, etc. Some other of your opinions, though true, are pushed to extremes, such as those upon the use of creeds, confessions, etc., etc. Your views of ministerial support, directed against abuses on that head, would be useful; but levelled against all support of ministers (unless by way of alms) is so palpably contrary to scripture and common justice, that I persuade myself there must be some misunderstanding. In short, your views are generally so contrary to those of the Baptists in general, that if a party was to go fully into the practice of your principles, I should say a new sect had sprung up, radically different from the baptists. . . .[36]

Many Baptist associations adopted resolutions specifying and condemning the supposed errors of the Reformers. An instructive example is the resolution of the Beaver Association in 1829, referred to later as the "Beaver anathema." The resolution charged that the Reformers taught:

> That there is no promise of salvation without baptism; that baptism should be administered on belief that Jesus Christ is the Son of God, without examination on any other point; that there is no direct operation of the Holy Spirit on the mind before baptism; that baptism procures the remission of sins and the gift of the Holy Spirit; that man's obedience places it in God's power to elect to salvation; that no creed is necessary for the church; that all baptized persons have a right to administer the ordinance of baptism.[37]

All features of the Campbell system came under searching and critical review by the Baptists. Needless to say, the Baptist reactions contained varying degrees of insight, as well as of misunderstanding and prejudice. The Baptist opposition to "Campbellism," however, was focused upon three crucial points which should be given brief consideration.

RELIGIOUS AUTHORITY

Many of the Baptists of the period taught the equal authority of the Old and New Testaments, while, as shown above, Campbell placed the authority of the Old Testament in an inferior position to that of the New. This difference, however, does not seem to have been a main point of consideration. Spencer Clack, a Baptist editor, pointed out in 1827 the main area of disagreement with regard to biblical interpretation: "We cannot agree as to what the Bible teaches. The Baptists think the Bible teaches the doctrine in their creeds; you think it teaches what you have written and published. . . ." [38]

The use of and subscription to confessions of faith became the storm center of the Baptist contention with Campbell respecting the question of religious authority. Baptist reactions to Campbell's slashing attacks upon creeds were divided. Two large associations of Kentucky Baptist churches had been constituted on "the Bible alone" by the time Campbell began his career. These churches were of a Separate Baptist background. The first association in Kentucky to adopt the views of Campbell was the North District Association, a group of churches of identifiable Separate Baptist composition.

On the other hand, the first associations in Kentucky to take action against "Campbellism" were the Elkhorn and the Franklin, associations of Regular (Particular) Baptist background.[39] At its annual session of 1830 the Franklin Association warned:

> We wish it to be distinctly understood that all persons aiming to prostrate our constitutions and the union, by declaring against creeds, or by sapping and mining the pillars of our constitutions, by innovations on our faith, customs and usages, ought to find no place in our pulpits, or at our communion tables.[40]

That the Baptists were as staunch biblicists as was Campbell himself there can be little doubt. They would have agreed that confessions of faith were harmful if they distorted the meaning and message of the Scriptures. The point of contention was stated by Virginia Baptists' greatest preacher, Andrew Broaddus. To hold, said Broaddus, that the great principles of evangelical truth are contained in the Scriptures "is only saying what many who differ from us may say. Indeed, this is not saying what are our views of these principles." Broaddus believed that

> . . . our churches stand in need of a *summary* of leading principles, such as have generally been recognized by the great body of United Baptists, to be incorporated in the Church Covenant, or in the Constitution, and to be resorted to as occasion may require, to be the test of fellowship, and to enable the churches, with more facility, to clear themselves of radical and injurious errors.[41]

It is ironic that Campbell's bold attack upon creeds and confessions had the opposite effect upon orthodox Baptists from what Campbell had intended. For it induced these Baptists to place a strong emphasis upon confessions as a bulwark of defense against the "reformation." This tendency is shown in the action of the Russells Creek Association of Kentucky in 1830:

This Association, as well as all others with which we correspond, knowing that heretical and contradictory tenets are maintained by many who *profess* to believe the Scriptures to be the word of God, and the only rule of faith and practice, have deemed it necessary to adopt certain principles of union, expressing their views of the fundamental doctrines of the Scriptures. Therefore, should any member of the Association discard said principles of union, and maintain the propriety and expediency of uniting upon a bare profession of a belief in the Scriptures, that such an individual is at war not only with the Association, but with the whole connection. . . .[42]

The Terms of Christian Union

As noted earlier in this chapter, Campbell thought the basic terms of Christian union to be: (1) belief in Jesus as the Messiah, and (2) immersion in the name of the Father, Son, and Holy Spirit.

This plan of union appeared plausible to a great number of people and seemed to furnish the only relief from the evils appearing in the sectarianism which afflicted the era. However, the sectarian attitudes which the Baptists claimed to see in Campbell and his followers themselves furnished from the first a stone of stumbling. W. E. Hatcher, a shrewd observer of "Campbellism" of a generation later, remarked that Campbell "seemed to have the essence of discontent and revolt in his constitution." His "showy oratory, his adroitness as a debater and his slashing and denunciatory style as a writer," were poor equipment for one whose primary purpose was to build rather than to destroy.[43]

Campbell communicated to his followers his penchant for contention and debate. Young John L. Waller, a keen Kentucky Baptist critic of "Campbellism," wrote in 1835:

Let me fall in company with one of you upon the highway—he may be a stranger—let the subject of religion be introduced; and ere he utters five sentences I will know who he is. His phraseology is peculiar. He talks of reformation—the ancient order of things—of entering the kingdom by immersion, etc. Let me enter a meeting-house. A man is speaking from the pulpit. He is describing scrap preachers, ridiculing a call to the ministry, and the operations of the spirit, he sports with the idea of being pardoned or regenerated before immersion; he tells us that God has done all he intends to do in giving us the scriptures; that in order to the remission of sins a person must believe, reform, and be immersed into the name of the Lord. Need I hear any more to ascertain to what sect he belongs? [44]

While the reaction to the Campbell movement varied widely, in very few places in the Baptist community was the cause of Christian union promoted thereby. In Kentucky, especially, the reaction was disruptive and divisive. Despite the efforts of Campbell himself to stay the excitement, "Campbellism" became, according to Kentucky Baptist historian J. H. Spencer, "a raging epidemic." The spirit of worship, said Spencer, declined in the churches, while church meetings were scenes of bitter controversy concerning

> creeds, confessions of faith, and church constitutions; the minister was constantly interrupted by impertinent questions and pointed contradictions, while preaching, and the old songs, sung so often, with joyous praise, for a whole generation, were made the butt of ridicule.[45]

The social circle and even the home were invaded by wrangling and heated controversy.

There is no doubt that Campbell's interpretation of faith as a belief in testimony had a powerful appeal to many persons, including many Baptists. Baptists, Methodists, and Presbyterians had preached that the way to salvation led through a long period of conviction, of agonized seeking for the Lord, of a radical rebirth through the agency of the Holy Spirit, and of a public profession of faith before the church, including a narration to the assembled congregation of one's Christian experience.

In the case of strongly Calvinistic churches, the whole matter of conversion depended upon whether one was a member of the elect. But Campbell's interpretation put the question of election in the realm of the individual's free and personal decision. This removed the need for a long period of mourning for one's sins and of agonizing with God for salvation. Rather, it was incumbent upon the sinner to believe the testimony that Jesus is the Christ and to obey the scriptural command to be baptized for the remission of sins. All this the sinner could do, and he could do it at once.

Baptists argued that Campbell's version of the gospel underestimated the depth of sin, undercut the initiative of God in salvation, and made the attainment of salvation a human achievement.[46]

Baptists also believed that a mere acknowledgment of Jesus as the Christ was a foundation too insubstantial to support the construction of a united church. There is danger in any union, said Andrew Broaddus, which requires simply the confession of Jesus as the Messiah. It is possible to hold radically wrong views concerning the person of Christ, while making this acknowledgment at the same time. "Is it of no importance as to Christian fellowship, what one thinks of Christ, whether he is truly divine, or only an angel or even a mere man?" It is possible to make the confession that Jesus is the Christ and still to deny, Broaddus observed, the divinity of Christ, atonement by his blood, the influence of the spirit, and justification by faith. The Campbell confession permitted a Christology so vague and indefinite as to mean either very much or very little. Can the church be reunited upon so shadowy a term? [47]

The Baptists were even more antagonized by the meaning which Campbell appeared to assign to immersion. In 1830 the "learned and godly" Silas M. Noel, of Frankfort, Kentucky, warned in his circular letter to the Franklin Association that Campbell was advocating the doctrine of baptismal remission of sins. Only a little while later, the Concord Association stated baldly their view of the "Campbellite" theory of baptism: ". . . when they speak of regeneration, they only mean immersion in water." [48]

The traditional Baptist conception of baptism was stated by J. B. Jeter in his criticism of Campbell's doctrine of baptism. Baptism, said Jeter, "is the *means of declaring*, or *confessing*, the remission of sins, previously obtained by faith." [49] As soon, however, as the water of baptism is regarded as of equal importance with the cleansing blood of Christ, the sign, by degrees, comes to be substituted for the thing signified, and the ceremonial is preferred to the vital. Thus, the error of Campbell is identical in nature with the error of infant baptism.[50]

Considering the difference in the meaning of baptism as held by the Reformers and the Baptists, it is not surprising that an agreement between them concerning the *mode* of baptism was not basic enough to furnish a platform for Christian union. Indeed, to the Baptists, the meaning which the Reformers assigned to baptism struck at the very foundations of the church.

THE AGENCY OF THE SPIRIT IN CONVERSION

The Baptists were perhaps more alarmed by what they considered to be Alexander Campbell's attacks upon the principles of evangelical Christianity than by his too facile prescriptions for Christian union. For this reason, none of the features of "Campbellism" aroused more contention among the Baptists than Campbell's interpretation of the influence of the Holy Spirit in conversion.

In 1830 the Concord Association of Kentucky advised that "when they [the Campbellites] are talking about the Spirit, we believe they only mean the written word. . . ." [51] In the same year, Noel, warning Baptists of the heresies of Campbell, mentioned Campbell's advocacy of "the operation of the Spirit through the word of Scripture alone," his denial of "the agency of the Holy

Spirit in regeneration," his rejection of an "inward call" in the soul, and his contempt for "Christian experience." [52]

Some years later, A. M. Poindexter charged that the Reformers believed that "the whole converting power of the Holy Spirit is in the truths revealed in the Holy Scriptures." [53] Baptism therefore precedes the coming of the Spirit to take up his abode in the believer's heart. Until baptism, the Spirit operates abstractly and by proxy through the media of word and water, in order to effect an entrance into the heart. The whole process of faith and repentance, and so of regeneration and remission of sins, Poindexter thought, has been a human process, accomplished through the external agencies of word and water, the Holy Spirit not being personally present.

The Baptists, reading the human situation with Calvinistic eyes, thought that the optimism of the Campbell scheme was a "deadly hostility to experimental religion." [54] It denied God's prevenient grace. It meant that conversion involves no change of heart. It cut off the personal agency of the Holy Spirit in convicting and regenerating the sinner. It left beyond the possibility of salvation all gross sinners whose wills cannot be moved by the unaided truth alone. "I do not wonder," said A. P. Williams, of Missouri, rather harshly, "that Campbellites have no one to tell a 'Christian experience' before the church. He who has nothing to tell should tell nothing." [55]

CONCLUSION

Perhaps the most able study of "Campbellism" ever done by a Baptist was written by J. B. Jeter, whose *Campbellism Examined* (published in 1855) was considered by many Baptists to be an unanswerable refutation of "Campbellism." Jeter, a Virginia Baptist, knew Campbell personally and was a student of the Campbell movement from an early period. His personal estimate of Campbell is worth quoting.

Mr. Campbell was a man of learning, of much miscellaneous information, and of great readiness and fecundity of mind. His learning . . . was various rather than profound, and his imaginative far exceeded his rationative power. There was, in my humble judgment, a screw loose in his mental machinery, which became more obvious as he grew older, and terminated in downright monomania. No writer within my knowledge ever repeated his thoughts so frequently, wrote so much that needed explanation, or so glaringly and often contradicted himself, as he did. This is all explicable on the supposition that he labored under an idiosyncrasy which was gradually developed into mental derangement. This supposition, too, vindicates him in making statements which could hardly have been made by a sound and well-balanced mind without guilt. With this ground of defense, I have no hesitation in expressing the opinion that he was a good man. His life was devoted to an earnest and fearless advocacy of principles which, in the main, were right. The supreme and exclusive authority of the Scriptures in religion, immersion the only baptism, and believers the only subjects of the ordinance, and church independence, are important doctrines which he held in common with the Baptists, and most zealously defended. He wrote, too, many valuable articles on matters of faith, and practice, along, we must think, with much that was visionary and erratic.[56]

No contemporary in the Baptist denomination in America was the equal of Campbell in versatility and ability. While there were men like Broaddus and Jeter who were perhaps his equal in native intelligence, they lacked his range of interest and his scope of thought. Younger contemporaries, such as Jeter and A. P. Williams, sensed some of the philosophical elements in Campbell's views. Yet they were not prepared to trace out the sources of his thought and to show the influence of eighteenth-century Enlightenment concepts upon his theological methodology and upon his theological conclusions. There is substantiation for saying that much of Campbell's thought was beyond the range of the great mass of the comparatively unsophisticated Baptists. No doubt the same observation might be made of the great majority of his own followers.

The leaders among the Baptists who opposed Campbell reverted to their most strongly held position, their knowledge of the Scriptures, as interpreted from their definite, if moderating, Calvinism. From this position, they were able to give his proposals rather searching examination, however unfortunate it may have been that the scrutiny seldom penetrated to the presuppositional level.

In retrospect the potential value of Campbell's thought was that it presented viable alternatives to religious tenets and practices which had settled into unquestioned conventional patterns. To Baptists, Campbell thus furnished a great opportunity for a fresh reconsideration of the vital substance of the gospel. Campbell's emphasis upon free human decision in matters of faith was a fresh breeze blowing through a religious community which was infiltrated with predestinarian hyper-Calvinism. Even the more healthy elements of this community had tended to stereotype the mold of religious experience and therefore had, in many cases, stultified its meaning.

Campbell had many of the superlative gifts which would have made him a great teacher, as well as a great leader, among the Baptists if the times for this role had been more propitious and if Campbell himself had followed a more temperate and winsome strategy. Unfortunately he appeared to many Baptists to be smitten with a messianic complex which polarized his opposition and cut off communication. Discussion assumed rigid defensive postures on each side and made difficult a meeting of minds. If the Baptists, and especially the Baptist leaders, had been able to understand Campbell fully, perhaps the tragic separation and division would not have occurred.

For this division, Campbell himself was partly to blame. The spirit of contention, evident in his own attitude, was transferred to many of his followers and was abundantly returned by many of the Baptists. Differences of opinion degenerated, in many cases, into wrangling. The harvest of bitterness was long continued. The spirit of contention penetrated the Baptist fellowship perhaps more than ever before.

For whatever reason, the appeal for unity which Campbell made seemed to many Baptists to be presented with damaging sectarian overtones. There was among the Baptists less interest in the unity of the church after the Campbell movement than there was before it. The Baptists apparently felt so profoundly threatened that they reinforced their own denominational defenses and became, as a denomination, more exclusive than they had been before.

It is to be noted that, after Campbell, the use of "creeds" and confessions of faith declined in Baptist usage. Also, the superior authority of the New Testament over the Old became a common tenet among Baptists. Just how much Campbell's influence is to be seen in these developments is, however, difficult to measure.

Campbell's insistence upon the limitation of the agency of the Holy Spirit in the conversion experience was a corrective to the view of many Calvinistic Baptists to the effect that the individual person was compelled to wait in supine helplessness for the moving of the Spirit. The belief in the freedom of the individual to exercise faith as a matter of personal decision has been more prevalent among Baptists since Campbell's day. Other factors, however, demand caution in assigning the credit for this development to Campbell.

Even so, it is difficult to see that the Baptists would have gained overall in limiting the agency of the Spirit to the written Word. The Baptists were also right in refusing to concede that baptism is in any sense necessary for salvation. It may be that they misunderstood Campbell on this point. If they did understand him aright, they could not have gone over to his personal position without fatally compromising their own convictions concerning the nature of faith and the nature of the church.

The Baptist fear of what they thought to be a sacramental interpretation of baptism, however, led to an impoverishing of their own understanding of the baptismal rite. "Campbellism" strengthened by reaction the Baptist tendency to interpret baptism as a "mere symbol," thus further robbing baptism of its biblical meaning as a profoundly significant symbol and experience.

One result of Campbell's efforts for Christian unity was the birth of several great new denominations, one of which, the Disciples of Christ, has been at the forefront of the ecumenical movement. In the ecumenical movement, many Disciples and many Baptists have to some extent found that unity in Christ which Alexander Campbell worked for with passionate and laborious dedication.

6 - J. R. GRAVES -
Champion of Baptist High Churchism

The Landmark Movement, called by its early advocates "Old Landmarkism," arose in the Southern Baptist denomination near the middle of the nineteenth century. The name of the movement was suggested by two Old Testament passages: "Remove not the ancient landmark, which thy fathers have set" (Proverbs 22:28), and "Some remove the landmarks . . ." (Job 24:2, KJV).[1]

The movement was intended to defend and preserve what its leaders thought to be the historic, distinctive principles of the Baptists. Particular attention was directed to those Baptist tenets which were thought to be under attack from outside the Baptist community, or which were believed to be threatened by the neglect of misguided Baptists themselves.

THE LIFE OF J. R. GRAVES

The author and prophet of the movement was James Robinson Graves (1820–1893), who was born in Chester, Vermont. Due to the death of his father when Graves was only two weeks old, the family was impoverished and Graves was able to secure little formal schooling. He undertook to make up this deficiency by diligent private study.

In early manhood, Graves taught school in Ohio and Kentucky. In 1845 he secured a teaching position in Nashville, Tennessee. Soon thereafter, he became the pastor of a small church in Nashville, and in 1846 he became the assistant editor of *The Baptist*, a weekly periodical with about one thousand subscribers. In 1848 he became the sole editor of this paper, the title of which in the meantime had been changed to *The Tennessee Baptist. The Tennessee Baptist*, under the leadership of the young editor, became a primary organ of Landmarkism. By 1859 the subscription list had risen to over twelve thousand, and the paper had become the principal Baptist voice in the Mississippi Valley.

From the beginning of his association with *The Baptist,* Graves wrote polemical articles against non-Baptist denominations, and he undertook to challenge his fellow Baptists to be true to the old landmarks of their faith. Some of these writings won the attention of the Baptist public over an extensive area.

Graves's leadership role was considerably enhanced when in 1851 he called a mass meeting of interested Baptists. The meeting was held at Cotton Grove, Tennessee, on June 24. At this meeting, Graves submitted five "queries." They read as follows:

> 1st. Can Baptists, consistently with their principles or the Scriptures, recognize those societies not organized according to the pattern of the Jerusalem Church, but possessing different governments, different officers, a different class of members, different ordinances, doctrines, and practices, as churches of Christ?
>
> 2nd. Ought they to be called gospel churches, or churches in a religious sense?
>
> 3rd. Can we consistently recognize the ministers of such irregular and unscriptural bodies as gospel ministers?
>
> 4th. Is it not virtually recognizing them as official ministers to invite them into our pulpits, or by any other act that would or could be construed into such a recognition?
>
> 5th. Can we consistently address as brethren those professing Christianity who not only have not the doctrines of Christ and walk not according to his commandments, but are arrayed in direct and bitter opposition to them?[2]

The resolutions which derived from these queries are known in the history of the movement as "The Cotton Grove Resolutions."

Early in his campaign for Baptist orthodoxy, Graves was fortunate in securing the support of two men whose ability and dedication were of superior quality. J. M. Pendleton (1813–1891), pastor of the Baptist church of Bowling Green, Kentucky, formed a personal acquaintance with Graves in 1852, and he soon became a convert to many of Graves's controversial views. Pendleton wrote extensively in Landmark periodicals, and he published several books which came to be well known. His chief contribution to the Landmark cause was a pamphlet in 1852 entitled *An Old Landmark Re-set.* In this composition Pendleton took a decided stand against any Baptist recognition of pedobaptist preachers as Christian ministers. The pamphlet excited attention throughout the Southern Baptist denomination and put the Landmark issue for the first time at the forefront of denominational consideration.

The second of Graves's very important converts was Amos Cooper Dayton (1811–1865). Dayton, a dentist by profession, was converted to Baptist views from Presbyterianism in 1852. Shortly thereafter he met Graves and soon became a Landmarker of the strictest sort.

Dayton was a polemical writer of some skill. He was also a writer of fiction. His main contribution was a novel in two volumes entitled *Theodosia Ernest,* which popularized the characteristic tenets of Landmarkism. In the late 1850's, and for three or four decades thereafter, many thousands of Baptists all over the South read *Theodosia Ernest.*

Graves, Pendleton, and Dayton were known by their followers as the "Great Triumvirate" of Landmarkism. They composed a formidable team in the advancement of the Landmark cause. Graves and Dayton became particularly active in denominational organizational life and thereby widened both their personal influence and the influence of Landmarkism. Graves entered the publishing business, and by the early 1850's, the books from his presses were reaching a large Baptist audience. His editorial work expanded beyond *The Tennessee Baptist* to include a monthly, a quarterly, and an annual.[3]

In the year 1855 Graves republished G. H. Orchard's *A Concise History of Foreign Baptists,* which originally had received publication in London in 1838. Very soon after Graves's publication of this work, Landmarkism became, in the words of W. W. Barnes, "a fiercely fighting force." [4] Graves's enthusiasm concerning this work is understandable, for he believed that Orchard had given irrefutable historical proof that Baptist churches had existed in continuous succession since the apostolic era.

In 1856 Graves published his powerful attack upon Methodism, *The Great Iron Wheel.* This was followed closely in 1857 by *The Little Iron Wheel,* another stinging attack upon the Methodist system. In 1858 *Trials and Sufferings for Religious Liberty in New England* was sent to the press from Graves's productive pen. This book was an absorbing account of the persecutions which the Baptists had endured in colonial New England at the hands of the Puritans. In 1860 Graves's work entitled *The Trilemma,* a vigorously argued refutation of Presbyterianism, came from the press.

When Graves became assistant editor of *The Baptist* in 1846, he was an obscure, though talented, young man of twenty-six years. Ten years later he had become the most powerful figure among Baptists in the Southwest and indeed one of the most commanding personalities in the Southern Baptist Convention.

Before giving some attention to the principal Landmark doctrines, perhaps a brief preliminary estimate should be given of this unusual man.

In making Nashville the base of operations for the formative stage of his career, Graves could hardly have made a more fortunate selection of a place in which to develop the great influence which he came to possess. Surrounding Nashville was a vast territory which had scarcely emerged from the conditions of a frontier culture. During the two decades which immediately preceded the advent of Landmarkism, Baptist ranks in Tennessee, as well as in neighboring Kentucky, Alabama, and Virginia, had been torn by one controversy after another. Controversies arising in Baptist circles over hyper-Calvinism, antimissionism, and "Campbellism" were aggravated by continuing battles with other denominations, particularly with the Methodists, the Presbyterians, and the "Campbellites."

To such an environment the particular talents which Graves possessed were admirably adapted. He possessed the facile pen and the rough-and-ready temperament which an editorial career on the frontier demanded. He was a man of obvious personal courage, a vigorous, forceful writer, and a leader of tremendous energy and drive.

Graves's followers considered him to be a preacher of great power. No less discerning a critic than John A. Broadus acknowledged him to be a public speaker of extraordinary ability. The spellbinding quality of his platform address achieved in his own time an almost legendary reputation. A testimony from his biographer on this point may be cited:

> He was equally at home in the city or before the rural throngs that hung on his words. Time lost its measure. . . . For two or three hours they would hang upon his words. And his reserve powers were apparently exhaustless. In the mighty sweep of his eloquence, he would mention with candor so many relevant things that his hearers felt there was no limit to the great things he could tell. And his exhilaration was so great that he seemed tireless. So when he would assay to close, clamors rang out from many parts of his audience, "Go on! Go on!" The writer has seen and heard it on many occasions.[5]

This platform skill was of great advantage to Graves in public debates. In the whole Southwest, he became the acknowledged Baptist champion. One historian observes that he had about a dozen oral discussions with debaters representing other denominations, proving himself to be a "fearless, peerless and successful champion of Baptist and New Testament orthodoxy." [6] The great

West had not seen such a resourceful debater since Alexander Campbell had traveled through the area a quarter of a century before.

Graves's personal motivations are naturally difficult to assess. In a revealing personal statement, however, he acknowledged himself to be the recipient of a divine call, not only to preach the gospel, but also to make war upon "errors and erroneous systems," thus following the example of Jesus and Paul. "These words," said J. R. Graves, "burned upon my eye, and rung (sic) with weighty import in my ear, 'Every plant which my Father hath not planted shall be rooted up!' " [7]

The decade preceding the outbreak of the Civil War was the formative stage of Landmarkism. This decade witnessed the movement's greatest surge of power, determined its direction, and nailed the planks of its doctrinal system rather securely into place. The war interposed a profound interruption of its advance. What came after the war, although important, was the development and extension of Landmarkism, the tenets of which received their definition in the prewar era. It therefore seems fitting at this point to discuss some of the main features of the movement's peculiar ideology.

THE LANDMARK DOCTRINAL SYSTEM

According to his biographer, J. R. Graves could endure no doubts in matters pertaining to faith. "To him there was nothing in mere theories. He wanted facts, not painted mists and carefully woven cobwebs. All is real, present, visible." [8]

The strict and rigid biblicism which characterized the thought of Graves and of the other members of the "Great Triumvirate" was calculated to leave no doubts. The Landmark leaders made a forthright appeal to Christ as the only lawgiver, and to the Bible as the only law, in all matters of faith and practice. They believed that Christ not only founded the church and perpetuated it, but that he also gave, in specific, biblical commandment, all the principles of its structure, government, and life.[9]

THE NATURE OF THE CHURCH

The heart of Graves's doctrinal system was his belief concerning the church. Central to an understanding of his view of the nature of the church is a grasp of his thought about the local church, the relationship of the church to the kingdom, and church succession.

The Church a Local, Visible Institution

The founding of the church by Christ himself, Graves believed, made the church a "divine institution." This opinion in itself was not signal. But Graves also contended that Christ specified that the church is to be a visible, local, organized institution *only*.

Graves noted that the word *ecclesia* in New Testament Greek, the word which "the Holy Spirit selected," had but one possible literal meaning — a local organization. The word is so used one hundred times in the New Testament. In the remaining ten instances of its use, it is used figuratively, "by synechdoche — where a part is put for the whole, the singular for the plural, one for all." [10] Today, said A. C. Dayton, the church is exclusively what it has always been: *". . . a local assembly of baptized believers, meeting by his [Christ's] authority to administer his ordinances, and transact the business of his kingdom in his name."* [11]

If the church is local only, then strict local self-government is one of its cardinal features. A local church, said Graves, is "complete in itself, independent of all other bodies, civil or religious, and the highest and only source of ecclesiastical authority on earth, amenable only to Christ, whose laws alone it receives and executes." [12]

Since the Landmarkers conceived the church to be local only, they explicitly denied such conceptions as the invisible church, the universal church, the church militant, or the church triumphant. Christ "has no invisible kingdom or church, and such a thing has no real existence in heaven or earth. It is only an invention employed to bolster up erroneous theories of ecclesiology." [13] Ideas of an invisible, universal church, said Graves, are "invisible nonsense." [14] Dayton thought that the alternative to visible, local churches is all too clearly indicated by the developments of history. This alternative is that of man-made, central ecclesiastical establishments which embrace all local congregations within themselves, "in a state of dependence and subjection." [15]

The Church and the Kingdom

The kingdom of God, Graves believed, is composed of local, visible churches. Kingdom and church, he said,

were used as synonymous terms by the evangelists so long as Christ had but one organized church, for they were then one and the same body. So soon as "churches were multiplied," a distinction arose. The kingdom embraced the first church, and it now embraces all the churches. [16]

The analogies which Graves used for this notion are revealing. As the twelve tribes of Israel, he said, together composed the kingdom of Israel, as the various states together compose the United States of America, so the churches together compose the kingdom of God.[17]

The kingdom, Graves believed, has been in existence since the time of John the Baptist. Further, since the kingdom cannot exist without one or more of its component units, there was one church in existence in the days of John. This church originated when John made ready a people for Christ, and the Lord received this little body as his disciples. The disciples became the church because they were "called out of the world by conversion and baptism" and "associated in a visible body according to the direction of Christ their only Head and King. . . ." [18] As long as there was only one church, this church was coextensive with the kingdom. As authentic churches increased in number, they became, collectively, the kingdom.

Church Succession

The main doctrine of the Landmark faith was the doctrine of church succession. This doctrine derives its principal importance from the fact that it held in ingenious, compact summary all of the characteristic elements of the Landmark system.

The claims of the true church, Graves thought, rested upon three biblically based, fundamental principles: First, the true church was founded by Christ. Second, the true church has enjoyed a perpetual existence since its founding. Third, the true church has possessed the same essential structure throughout its history.[19] Every religious society which lays claim to being a church

> must establish the fact of the existence of a similar people to themselves, holding and teaching similar doctrines and principles of Church polity, during the Apostolic period (A.D. 100) and by the apostles recognized as Christians; and also from this period down through succeeding centuries, until the present. . . .[20]

The gist of the church succession theory was that all true churches have been interlocked in visible, definable, continuous, unbroken, historical succession from the days of Christ, who founded the church, to the present time. The theory did not of course require that any particular church, founded, for example, in apostolic times, has had a perpetual existence since its founding. It meant, rather, that

> Those first Churches were not extinct till others were in being, descended

from themselves, and having the same Lord, the same faith, the same baptism, the same objects, the same offices, the same character of members, and, like themselves, executing the laws and observing the ordinances of the kingdom.[21]

For any group to establish its claim of being a gospel church, it must have been integrated into this chain of gospel churches, and it must have preserved an identical "structural organism" with that of all others of "this illustrious family of gospel churches." [22]

The church succession concept furnished a rule-of-thumb criterion by which the claims to church status of all ecclesiastical groups may be evaluated. Every church should hold within its life and polity all the elements which Christ prescribed for the composition of a church. The lack of any one element must be accounted grounds for total disqualification.

The sweeping application of this criterion becomes apparent when Graves enumerates the constituent elements of a true church. If a "religious society" was not founded by Christ;[23] if it is not structurally constituted according to Christ's commandment;[24] if it is combinative and anti-republican in its government (this was Graves's most frequently used argument in *The Great Iron Wheel*) ; if, specifically, it is not organized on the principle of local church autonomy;[25] if it does not practice a membership of believers only, a practice of believer's baptism only, and a practice of immersion as the only form of baptism;[26] if it has apostatized;[27] if it has persecuted;[28] if it is guilty of all of these charges, or of any one of them, it is not a church.

Graves set forth three types of proof for the doctrine of church succession. Graves made his principal appeal to the Scriptures. The main proof text was Matthew 16:18 (KJV), ". . . upon this rock I will build my church; and the gates of hell shall not prevail against it." [29] This sure word of Christ, said Graves, foretold that his church would never be destroyed, but should stand and be perpetuated through successive and multiplied churches until it filled the world.[30]

Graves simply assumed that the church which was meant in this passage and in other passages was a local, institutional church and that it was perpetuated by propagating other churches of undeviating character.

The second type of proof which Graves employed was an appeal to the vindication of history. Since Graves's use of the Scriptures in supporting the church succession view was filled with *a priori* judgments, historical research became useful only as an appurtenance to dogmatic positions, which were quite impervious to refutation by historical inquiry. The appeal to history was designed to be confirmatory to, and corroborative of, the basic foundations of biblical promise.

Graves was aware that an accurate chronicle which traced the history of the Baptists from the apostolic era to modern times would immeasurably strengthen the Landmark claim that only Baptist churches were true churches, and such a chronicle would triumphantly demonstrate their organic succession. This feat he believed G. H. Orchard's *A Concise History of Foreign Baptists* to have accomplished for the first time. His reception and use of this unreliable work was as enthusiastic as it was uncritical.

Orchard identified the history of the Baptists with the history of dissent. To him the following dissenting groups were certainly Baptists: the Cathari, the Novatianists, the Donatists, the Paulicians, the Henricians, the Albigensians, the Waldensians, the Anabaptists, and others. Graves accepted this genealogy without question. These groups, he believed, sustained the chain of Baptist witness back across the ages to the time when all Christian societies were Baptist churches.

The final refinement by which the Landmarkers supported the church succession theory was to show that the theory did not need to be proved. If a congregation bears the unmistakable marks of a New Testament church, its succession in the line of apostolic churches may be accepted without further inquiry or proof. This point was especially emphasized by Dayton.

> When we find a body of professed believers which has the ordinances and the doctrines of Christ, we are justified in the absence of proof to the contrary in taking it for granted that it came honestly by them. If it looks like a true church, and acts like a true church, to me, it is, and must be a true church, until the contrary has been established.[31]

Certain implications of the Landmark view of the church become unmistakably clear from an examination of the theory of church succession. One implication is that only Baptist churches are true churches. Another is that the church which Jesus founded was a Baptist church. A third inference which may be drawn is that, in Graves's view, the name "Baptist" may be written before even the kingdom of God, for the kingdom is composed of Baptist churches.

THE AUTHORITY OF THE CHURCH

Graves was able to compress the Landmark conclusion with

respect to the authority of the church into one inclusive principle, namely, the sole and exclusive jurisdiction of the local Baptist church over all "gospel acts." By "gospel acts," Graves appears to have meant the essential and legitimate tasks of the church. These acts were: (1) the preaching of the gospel, (2) the observance of baptism, and (3) the celebration of the Lord's Supper.

This positive conception of the church's business had negative, polemical implications which were given pointed statement, for the performance of these acts by non-Baptist ministers and societies were denominated by the Landmarkers "alien preaching," "alien immersion," and "alien communion." Baptist recognition of the validity of these "gospel acts" when performed by non-Baptists was titled "affiliationism." "Affiliationism" was roundly condemned by the Landmarkers.

Preaching

Since preaching is one of the "gospel acts" which the church is divinely charged to fulfill, and since only a Baptist church is a valid church, it follows that none but Baptist churches are authorized to confer a commission to preach the gospel. This assumption by the Landmarkers was soon widened to deny that non-Baptist ministers are validly ordained to perform any "ministerial act" — that is, to preach, to baptize, or to administer the Lord's Supper. The question then boiled down to whether the ordinations of non-Baptist ministers are in any sense valid.

In Landmarkism, interest centered again and again upon the role of the ministry. However, the Landmarkers were not primarily interested in the authority of the minister to perform or administer "gospel acts," but in the authority of the church to do so. For example, Graves said that baptism is to be administered by "a specific body." [32] ". . . It is the church that administers the rite and not the officer, *per se* — he is but the hand, the servant of the church." [33]

The principal work produced by the Landmarkers on the subject of pulpit "affiliation" was the celebrated tract by J. M. Pendleton entitled *An Old Landmark Re-set*. Answering in the negative the question "Ought Baptists to recognize Pedo-Baptist preachers as gospel ministers?" Pendleton urged two points: first, baptism is essential to the constitution of the church; second, church authority is essential to the commission of the gospel ministry. Pendleton summarized his conclusions as follows: "Where there is no baptism, there are no visible churches. . . . Pedobaptist Societies are not gospel churches . . . Baptists should not therefore recognize Pedobaptist preachers as gospel ministers." [34]

The rather astonishing conclusions which Pendleton voiced above were based on the assumption that proper baptism is essential to the existence of a church. There is no baptism without the observance of the proper mode, immersion, with respect to a proper subject, a believer, for a proper design, the declaration of a faith already possessed, under a proper administration, that is, under the authority of a Baptist church.[35] The statement that regular baptism as above defined is necessary to the very existence of a church was a specifically Landmark assertion.

The Landmarkers were in earnest in their denunciation of pulpit affiliation. Graves declared that Baptists should no more think of inviting other Protestant ministers to preach in Baptist pulpits than they would think of inviting Roman Catholic priests to do so. To recognize the ordinations of non-Baptist ministers or priests as valid is to recognize as valid the "societies" which commissioned them; to sanction the latters' infant membership, their sprinkling for baptism; and, indeed, to endorse all that these "societies" believe and teach.[36]

Baptism

The Landmarkers directed polemical attention to "alien" immersions, because valid baptism belonged, they believed, exclusively to the authority of the local Baptist church. Since Baptists in America universally rejected sprinkling and pouring as valid modes of baptism, the Landmarkers simply joined all other Baptists in rejecting the validity of these modes.

"Alien" immersions, however, were immersions performed by Methodist, Presbyterian, Episcopalian, Disciples, or other ministers. The question which Landmarkism asked was whether Baptist churches should (or had any right to) recognize these immersions as valid baptisms. The question was as practical as this: If a person who has been immersed by (for example) a Methodist minister presents himself for membership in a Baptist church, should this church recognize the previous immersion as a valid baptism, or should the church require the candidate for membership to be re-immersed under the authorization of a Baptist church, as a condition of membership?

The real question which Landmarkism then raised was whether administration by a Baptist church is necessary for valid baptism. The Landmark case against "alien" immersions rested upon two foundations which were a simple modification of Pendleton's premises cited above: first, to be valid, baptism must be under the administration of a true church. Second, valid baptism is necessary to the constitution of a true church.

That the Landmark reasoning here was circular is obvious. Yet the position assumed was not meaningless, however audacious it might have been. Only a true church could have valid baptism; only true baptism could produce a valid church. Only that baptism is valid, said Graves, which is "scripturally administered by a gospel church." [37] Since non-Baptist societies were not gospel churches, their immersions could not be "scripturally administered." "Alien" immersions were therefore not valid baptisms and could be accorded no recognition by Baptist churches.

This position, however, was conclusively vindicated in Landmark opinion by the assertion that valid baptism is necessary to the constitution of a true church. So-called baptismal acts, said Dayton, whether involving immersion or not, if performed by unbaptized ministers under the authority of unbaptized churches, are null and void. Such rites are invalid because they are administered by unbaptized administrators; they are invalid also because they are performed under the false authority of counterfeit churches. Graves and Pendleton fully agreed with Dayton's argument on this point.[38]

Graves took the "alien" immersion question with great seriousness. Pedobaptist immersions, he believed, are polluted by the doctrine of baptismal regeneration. Their subjects are "confessedly unpardoned and unregenerate when they come to the water." The design of their candidates is not to confess faith in Christ, but to obtain salvation in the act. Their ministers who baptize have received false commissions from false churches. To endorse such immersions, Graves believed, is to endorse all the errors of the false churches which sponsor them.

Communion

By the time Landmarkism originated, the Baptists of America were almost universally close communionists. The assumptions underlying the close communionist stand were usually twofold: (1) Immersion is essential to valid baptism. (2) Baptism is prerequisite to Communion. Another assumption should be mentioned, the assumption that the Lord's Supper is an ordinance which Christ placed under the exclusive administration of the local church.

The Landmarkers accepted these traditional Baptist positions wholeheartedly. Even here, however, they took a further step which was fully consistent with their premises. They affirmed that pedo-baptists were ineligible for the Supper, not only because they had not been baptized, but also because they were not members of *any* church. They were only members of "religious societies" and had no more right to the Supper than had members of a craftsmen's guild or a masonic lodge. The addition of this element — exclusion of non-Baptists because they were members of *no* churches — was simon-pure Landmarkism. The Landmarkers believed that what passed as an observance of the Lord's Supper in non-Baptist churches was at best a meaningless imitation of the *real* ordi-nance, and at worst a presumptuous seizing of the prerogatives of the true church.

In his latter years, Graves worked vigorously to impress upon the Baptists that the Lord's Supper is an ordinance which be-longs strictly to the jurisdiction of the local Baptist church. Strict local Communion, as Graves envisioned it, prescribed Communion for the assembled members of the local church only, with no Communion privileges extended to anyone who did not belong to the particular church which was celebrating the ordinance. This requirement denied Communion privileges not only to visit-ing pedobaptists, but also to visiting Baptists as well.

By insisting upon strict local Communion, Graves hoped to cut off such "loose" practices of "intercommunion" as prevailed among Baptists of his time. Intercommunion involved the cele-bration of the Lord's Supper at associational meetings and con-ventions, in which representatives of a number of churches par-took of the Supper together.

Graves believed that open Communion was the inevitable tendency of all affiliationism, and its most shameful expression. Here not only paganism entered the church, but something worse — Antichrist himself, in the persons of pedobaptists who repre-sented all the pretensions and falsehoods by which the true gospel through the centuries had been corrupted and subverted.

The way to stop this profanation, Graves thought, was for each Baptist church to practice strict local church Communion. He argued that adherence to local Communion was the only way to halt the slide "into the slough of open communion." [39]

A CRITIQUE OF THE LANDMARK DOCTRINAL SYSTEM

Graves's appeal to the Baptist community was to stand by the old landmarks of the Baptist faith. He said,

I was the first man in Tennessee, and the first editor on this continent, who publicly advocated the policy of strictly and consistently carrying out in our practices those principles which all true Baptists, in all ages, have professed to believe.[40]

However, one of the features of Landmarkism which arrested the attention of many Baptists contemporary with the movement's origin was not its appeal to the Baptist denomination's historic landmarks, but rather what seemed to be its elements of innovation. In 1877, J. B. Jeter, editor of the *Religious Herald* of Virginia, and a longtime opponent of Landmarkism, made the following ringing indictment:

We must not conclude that an opinion is sound because it is old, or false because it is new. Still, the presumption is in favor of the truth of the old rather than of new opinions. Old Landmarkism is about twenty years old. . . . The denomination has certainly practiced an interchange of pulpits for a hundred years, and we have seen no resolution of any convention, association, or church condemning the practice, that dates back more than about twenty years; and all such resolutions have indicated, not the views of the denomination, but of certain earnest brethren in a comparatively small portion of the country. We do not question their right to hold these sentiments, or their sincerity in embracing them, or the purity of their motives in defending them; but we wish it to be distinctly understood that they took a new "departure"; and are contending, not for old and settled principles, but against a denominational custom coeval with its origins in this country. . . . Our fathers were earnest Baptists, equally ready to toil or suffer for their principles, but they were not Landmarkers. They opposed Pedo-baptism, by sound and scriptural arguments; but accorded to its advocates due credit for their learning, piety and usefulness, and cooperated with them, so far as they could without sacrificing their distinctive principles.[41]

This brief critique of Landmark views will, therefore, evaluate the movement's claims by setting them in historical context. In this context, many of the Landmark claims cannot be sustained.

THE NATURE OF THE CHURCH

The contrast between Landmark views and historic Baptist thought is readily apparent in regard to the doctrine of the nature of the church.

The Church as Local Only

In traditional Baptist thought, a twofold view had been held with respect to the nature of the church. The first concerned the universal, spiritual church; the second, the particular, local church. The universal church was conceived to be an unorganized, uninstitutionalized spiritual entity, composed of redeemed individuals of the past, the present, and the future. The particular church, on the other hand, was a visible, local congregation, the breaking into view of the universal church in a particular locality. The local church takes to itself certain institutional forms, but its nature is determined by the nature of the universal church. Its essence is spiritual. It was and is a fellowship of believers, a gathered community.[42]

The Landmark denial of the universal spiritual church negated any church status to all non-Baptists and undercut any possible ecumenical relationship between Baptist and non-Baptist churches. Many Baptists of the time in which this view was propounded thought Landmarkism betrayed an element of real and harmful innovation. The reaction of John Leadley Dagg (1794–1884) may be cited as an example. Dagg's *Manual of Theology: Second Part . . . Church Order,* published in 1859, contained an incisive critique of Landmarkism. At the time, Dagg was professor of theology and president of Mercer University in Macon, Georgia. In the following excerpt, Dagg refuted the Landmark contention that the church is local only.

> Who are the saints that constitute Christ's inheritance, among whom the Ephesians had been admitted as fellow-citizens? Unquestionably not the church at Ephesus. They can be no other than the whole redeemed people of Christ, the whole household of faith. Jews and Gentiles were united under the gospel; constituted one fold, under Christ, the one shepherd; one body, of which he is the head; one family, gathered together in him; one house, over which he, the Son, presides. This body was not the local church.[43]

The Church and the Kingdom

Traditionally, Baptists for the most part identified the kingdom of God with the universal spiritual church. However, Graves's identification of the kingdom with the aggregate of Baptist churches was a position for which it would be difficult to find precedent in Baptist thought. In 1880 J. Lansing Burrows expressed an opinion which was held by many intelligent Baptists. Burrows said:

> The position that the terms "Kingdom of God, of heaven, of Christ" are applied exclusively to local visible churches—or to the aggregate of local visible churches—is so utterly untenable, as to induce wonder how any man with the most superficial examination of the Scriptures, could bring himself to announce it.[44]

Church Succession

Grave's endorsement of G. H. Orchard's *A Concise History of Foreign Baptists* turned out to be quite specious. Orchard's identification of the history of the Baptists with the history of dissent, a lead followed uncritically by Graves, probably would not be endorsed by any serious student of church history today. The Paulicians, the Novatianists, the Donatists, and the like, all held beliefs and practices which preclude their being certified Baptists.[45]

Just where Graves obtained the theory of church succession is difficult to determine. Orchard does not seem to have been cognizant of the Landmark requirement that historical succession is necessary to the present existence of the church. To Orchard, the "bond of union" by which Baptists could be traced in all ages was not a link succession of Baptist churches, but rather a sharing in faith in Christ, which was publicly expressed through baptism.

Graves may have taken the idea of a link succession of churches from the hand of a fellow editor, John L. Waller, of Kentucky, whose article on "Reformation" in 1852 contained a brief statement of a link succession doctrine. Waller's statement was made with little emphasis and was not followed up subsequently with any particular interest or energy.

In Waller's article, too, was stated the thesis that Protestantism has no true churches because the Protestant sects are children of an apostate mother, the Roman Catholic church. Graves took this thesis and gave it elaborate and powerful treatment, particularly in his book *The Trilemma*. In this book Graves identified the Roman church as the "great whore," the "mother of harlots," the "man of sin," etc. The Protestant churches, he affirmed, are her illicit progeny, who partake of all her corruptions by direct inheritance. Over against the Catholic-Protestant monolith stands the Baptist kingdom of God in an implacable antagonism. The Protestant bodies must go back wholly to their mother, or cleansing themselves of all heresies and impurities, they must move resolutely forward to the Baptist fold.

Only a tiny fraction of Baptist writers prior to Graves were this sectarian, and many contemporary Baptists were disturbed by the novelty of Graves's exclusive claims under the guise of old and settled Baptist principles. W. W. Everts, pastor of a Baptist church in Louisville, speaking in direct reaction to *An Old Landmark Re-set*, aimed at Landmarkism the following general indictment: "It is a strange assumption that this new high church dogma should be claimed as an old land-mark of our denominational estate. We regard it rather as a new stake, which can be set down and maintained only in sectarian arrogance." [46]

THE AUTHORITY OF THE CHURCH

A similar contrast between historic Baptist views and Landmarkism may be seen in regard to the doctrine about the authority of the church.

Pulpit Affiliation

None of the great Baptist confessions of faith deny non-Baptist ministers the right to preach, or impugn their ministerial call. The argument from silence should not be overly pressed, but neither should the absence of evidence be ignored.

The debate which was caused in the denomination by the Landmark agitation brought two positions to light, both of which contradicted the Landmark position. The first was that the call to preach is a divine call, the authority of which transcends the authority of the local church.[47]

John Leadley Dagg raised the fundamental question: namely, does the commission to preach the gospel depend upon ordination by a local church? Dagg replied that the ordination by a church is indeed enjoined in the Scriptures, and a neglect of it obscures the evidence of a divine call. Nevertheless, the call to the ministry comes from the Holy Spirit and is "complete in itself, without the addition of outward ceremony."[48] Ministers, Dagg thought, are officers in the universal church. The authority to preach is an authority which belongs to the body of Christ, and this authority transcends denominational bounds.

The second position was less frequently expressed, although it was not unrelated to the first. This position involved the recognition of a ministerial authority which transcends all denominational bounds, and which comes to rest upon the sovereign right of the Holy Spirit to call whom he will to be his ministers, and upon the consequent right of ministers, as officers in the kingdom, or the universal church, to welcome one so commissioned into the ministerial fellowship. "Ministerial fellowship," said S. W. Lynd, associate editor of the *Western Recorder,* "is not, and cannot be, given by the churches. It can be given only by the eldership."[49]

"Alien" Immersions

The question of "alien" immersions was not an issue among early English Baptists and indeed has not become one to this day. Before 1800, the majority of the Baptist community in America had been willing to accept the validity of pedobaptist immersions.

The traditional Baptist conviction concerning baptismal validity was directed to two concerns, the mode of baptism and the subject of baptism. The mode must be immersion; the subject must be a believer. The reception of "alien" immersions was, however, a matter of discussion in the Baptist community for some years prior to the rise of Landmarkism. Such baptisms were considered "irregular" but not invalid. The customary procedure for dealing with them appears to have been somewhat as follows. When a person who had received immersion at the hands of a non-Baptist minister presented himself for membership in a Baptist church, the church was careful to inquire whether the candidate had been converted before his baptism, and whether he intended by his baptism to declare a faith already possessed, rather than to complete his salvation by baptism. If he had been immersed as a believer, his immersion usually was accepted as a valid baptism.

In any event, it was not true that, as Graves charged, the denomination had declined from a universal disapproval of non-Baptist immersions to a "looseness" upon the subject. The trend was rather in the opposite direction. The denomination had advanced from a long period in which the question was not even raised through a period in which there was a difference of opinion but a comparative lack of concern about the question, to a period in which differences of opinion were crystallized into bitter partisan alignment. This last was the Landmark phase.[50]

Communion

The close communionism of the denomination prior to Landmarkism, as indicated above, did not rest upon Landmark principles, because it did not include the assumption that only Baptist churches are churches at all. Indeed, most Southern Baptist leaders, during and after the Landmark controversy, continued to discuss the subject in its traditional bearings. P. H. Mell, many times president of the Southern Baptist Convention, exemplified this tendency. Writing in 1853, Mell expressed delight in the fellowship which Baptist ministers enjoyed with ministers of other evangelical denominations. With respect to the Lord's Supper, however, Mell was firm in holding that Baptists were not at liberty to extend the privileges of Communion to pedobaptists. "If baptism is a prerequisite, and we believe that nothing but immersion is baptism, how can we admit those who have been sprinkled in infancy or even in adult age?" [51]

LANDMARKISM AFTER THE CIVIL WAR

The rising tide of Landmarkism was arrested and subdued by

the Civil War. When the war was over, Landmarkism appeared for a time to have succumbed in the general devastation and the paralysis of southern life and culture. The giant task of rebuilding the denomination's institutions and agencies was carried on almost entirely by non-Landmarkers. The Domestic Board, the Foreign Board, and the Southern Baptist Theological Seminary were slowly reactivated and reinvigorated with little visible help from the Landmarkers.

But Landmarkism was only dormant; it was not dead. Succeeding years were to prove that it was still a virile, grassroots, people's movement.

The burden of Landmark leadership after the war rested heavily upon the shoulders of J. R. Graves. Dayton had died in 1865, worn out prematurely by tuberculosis. Pendleton, in spite of the fact that he was the only native southerner of the "Great Triumvirate," was also the only abolitionist and unionist among them. In 1862 he moved North to Upland, Pennsylvania, and he remained there for the rest of his active ministry.

The Graves who emerged from the war was less belligerent, more conciliatory in temperament, but he was still unquestionably the Landmarker *par excellence* and the undisputed leader of the Landmark movement. Into the task of reconstructing and reinspiriting the Baptist cause in the Mississippi Valley he threw himself with the contagious enthusiasm and the courageous determination which had characterized his whole career. He preached and lectured throughout Mississippi, Tennessee, Arkansas, Louisiana, and Texas. Sometimes he was absent from his home for extended periods while he exerted to the full his powerful platform abilities.

After the war, Graves settled in Memphis. With characteristic energy and imagination, he tried ambitiously to revive his publication ventures, but one after another of them decisively failed. One notable exception to these failures was his paper, which he began to republish in 1867 under the title *The Baptist*.

This periodical exerted a potent influence upon the Southern Baptist community, particularly in the Southwest, even though the paper fell two or three thousand subscriptions short of reaching the subscription total of the prewar *Tennessee Baptist*. Though less polemical than the prewar paper, *The Baptist* was more folksy and newsy, while at the same time Graves used its columns to keep up a steady drumfire advocacy of Landmark principles. By 1875 the paper had an Arkansas department, a Mississippi department, and a Louisiana department. When Baptist newspapers arose in these states later, they usually showed a Landmark coloration. The paper was read and widely commended also in Tennessee, Alabama, Texas, and Kentucky. Indeed, the correspondence columns of the paper showed that Landmarkism was penetrating to every geographical section of the convention.

Before Graves died, Landmarkism had become so prevalent in the Baptist community of the Southwest that a vast area with good reason might have been entitled "the Landmark Belt." In this area should be included Tennessee, part of Kentucky, northern Alabama, Arkansas, Mississippi, Texas, and Louisiana. Also, pockets of Landmarkism began to appear on the non-Landmark periphery — especially in southern Illinois, southern Missouri, northern Florida, South Carolina, and various parts of Georgia. Landmark adherents showed up also as far west as California and Oregon.

The pages of *The Baptist* clearly indicate that Graves's views had been formed in the prewar era. Thereafter, his great productivity was devoted mainly to the exposition and amplification of positions reached perhaps not later than 1859. He continued to make war upon pedobaptists and "Campbellites" and to insist upon other characteristic emphases of Landmarkism. In his latter years he gave more and more attention to the strict local church Communion theory and to a chiliastic interest which he had shown since his early life.

Graves continued to be the stormy petrel of denominational life after the war, but he ceased to be the disruptive influence which he had been in the late 1850's. He remained *persona non grata* in the leadership councils of the denomination, but few continued to think of him as really dangerous. Intelligent non-Landmark leaders respected his candor and pungency — and attempted to stay out of his range. Of his brother editors in the Southern Baptist denomination, only the redoubtable J. B. Jeter of Virginia's *Religious Herald* remained an adamant antagonist of Landmarkism. Graves had frequent occasion to complain about the "heavy cannonade" which Jeter directed against the positions of "strict Baptists." [52]

For ten years after the war, Graves's writing efforts were directed principally to the pages of *The Baptist*. Beginning in 1875, however, he began again to publish books, and some of these were among the most remarkable of his productions. There was little in them, however, that was really new. Only the most important will be mentioned here.

In 1875 Graves published *The Great Carrollton Debate,* 1184 pages of text embodying the discussion of Graves with Jacob Ditzler, a Methodist champion. The two men argued the principal tenets of pedobaptism. In 1880 Graves published *Old Landmarkism — What Is It?* This small book of 262 pages enabled Graves to give the clearest, most forceful, and most systematic exposition of Landmarkism which he ever attempted. In 1881 he published *Inter-communion of Churches Unscriptural, Deleterious, and Productive of Evil Only.* This volume was a forcefully argued discussion in support of strict local church Communion. In 1886 Graves published a revised edition of *The Great Iron Wheel.* The new edition was called *The New Great Iron Wheel.* In this volume Graves showed nowhere a softening of his attitude, which was evident in earlier works, toward Methodism or pedobaptism.

In 1883 Graves published his most ambitious literary effort, *The Work of Christ in the Covenant of Redemption: Developed in Seven Dispensations.* The great value of this work to the student is not in the ecclesiological positions represented, for these appear relatively unchanged, but in the fact that in this work the extreme chiliastic framework of Graves's thought appears with unwonted clarity.

Graves also published other books of smaller compass, but the *Seven Dispensations* was his *magnum opus,* and with it may appropriately be closed this discussion of his life and thought.

The long career of J. R. Graves was drawing toward its close. A paralytic stroke in 1884 made him a semi-invalid. Early in 1889 a fall in his yard crushed his side and put him in a wheelchair for the remainder of his life. Even then the indomitable spirit of the man enabled him to preach so persuasively that his "Chair Talks" became famous.

A second paralytic stroke in the early summer of 1893 came upon him while he was preaching in his pulpit in Memphis. Graves said to the deacons who rushed to his side to assist him, "Tell them [the congregation] to sing 'On Christ the Solid Rock I Stand!' " On June 26, J. R. Graves died, muttering at the last, "What a change! What a change!" So passed from the earthly scene one of the most remarkable figures in the history of the Baptists in America.

To trace the fortunes of Landmarkism into the twentieth century is beyond the scope of this chapter. However, in the Southern Baptist denomination Landmarkism gradually ceased to be an irritant and a challenger, and it became instead a domestic in the denominational household.

The influence of the movement widened until it infiltrated in varying degrees most of the agencies of the Southern Baptist Convention, and for many years Landmarkism made its appearance in much of the denominational literature. It also widened in geographical extent, as Southern Baptists who believed in its tenets migrated to the Midwest, the Far West, and the mountain states — and, for that matter, to Hawaii and Alaska.

Somewhat paradoxically, as its influence widened, its influence became less intense. The original synthesis of elements which J. R. Graves had welded into a compact system was unable to maintain itself. Graves's identification of the kingdom of God with the aggregate of Baptist churches was, for the most part, quietly dropped. Strict local church Communion remained strong only here and there in the Landmark belt. Church successionism, it would seem, was not widely held after the quarter century mark of the present century.

At present, Landmarkism seems muted and subdued. It remains identifiable in the virtual disappearance among Southern Baptists of the doctrine of the universal spiritual church, in a widespread negative attitude toward "alien" immersions in the mid-South, the Southwest, and the West, and in the hostility of Southern Baptists toward the ecumenical movement. In short, the Landmark movement, though still in being, is now undergoing a gradual decline.

CONCLUSION

J. R. Graves was a man of native genius. Unfortunately, his educational opportunities were pathetically inadequate for the best development of his extraordinary talent. He was an important figure because of his profound influence upon a great denomination, the Southern Baptists. His thought was pivotal because it was crucially influential in setting a direction for this denomination's history which the denomination would not otherwise have followed.

In his own time, Graves sounded a rallying cry to a dispirited Baptist community in the Southwest. His strident denominationalism put iron in the Baptist blood, shored up the Baptists' faltering ranks, and enabled him to march ahead of his multitudes of followers in the direction in which he thought that the "true" church should go.

Graves's life was a passionate quest for the purity of the church. The singlemindedness and the courage with which he pursued this aim deserve the greatest respect. Anyone who undertakes a sober estimate of his contribution, however, is likely to have serious misgivings concerning the benefit of his long-range influence.

Some decades ago, O. L. Hailey, Graves's son-in-law and biographer, acknowledged that it was a question for debate in the denomination whether the contribution of J. R. Graves was a bane or a blessing to Baptists. It is still a question for debate.

7 -
WILLIAM NEWTON CLARKE -
Representative of Theological Liberalism

The last decades of the nineteenth century posed many problems which a growing host of intelligent Christians felt could not be ignored. Signal advances in the natural sciences resulted in a growth of confidence in the scientific method as a guiding mode of approaching various kinds of human problems. New discoveries and new theories in biology, geology, and paleontology brought about a whole series of intellectual crises. New developments in psychological, sociological, historical, and philosophical study set the old creeds and systems of thought in new and challenging perspectives.[1]

William Newton Clarke was one of the leaders in Protestantism who attempted to work out a new understanding of the older creeds in the light of these great challenges. Before considering Clarke's specific contribution, we will look at the scope of the challenges and the responses that were made to them in the latter part of the nineteenth century.

THEOLOGICAL FERMENT

The Origin of Species (1859), by Charles Darwin, had little impact upon the intellectual life of America until some years after the Civil War. By 1870 it was receiving considerable attention, and a subsequent work by Darwin, *The Descent of Man* (1871), applied the evolutionary thesis to man himself. Through the writings of an English philosopher, Herbert Spencer, the evolutionary hypothesis was widely popularized.

By the 1870's there was evident a growing desire on the part of Christian evolutionists to show that evolution was consistent with the tenets of Christianity. John Fiske in 1874 argued that evolution "is God's way of doing things." Prominent churchmen, such as Henry Drummond, President James McCosh, of Princeton College, Henry Ward Beecher, and Lyman Abbott, acknowledged a cordial subscription to a belief in evolution.

By the end of the century, evolution was both popularly and learnedly discussed in Christian circles. Scientists and liberal theologians joined hands in affirming that the evolutionary doctrine had strengthened rather than weakened their faith. Needless to say, this friendly attitude toward evolutionary thought was not universally held among Christians. As a matter of fact, it was rejected by most of the clergy and by the rank and file of the laity. In the South, especially, opposition was intense.[2]

In looking at the elements which shaped the new challenge to orthodox Christianity, developing trends in biblical studies should be mentioned. Biblical higher criticism began to exert a strong influence in America in the post-Civil War era. This type of criticism, involving a scientific, literary-historical study of the Bible, received a strong impetus in the 1880's when the writings of Julius Wellhausen, a great German Old Testament scholar, began to be widely known in this country. Wellhausen believed that the Old Testament itself bore the marks of evolutionary development. He sought to show that the Old Testament religion began in primitive polytheism and progressed to an ethical monotheism.

In the field of New Testament studies, Ferdinand Christian Bauer of Tübingen made investigations fully as radical as those of Wellhausen in Old Testament studies. In 1881 a critical edition of the Greek New Testament appeared from the English scholars Westcott and Hort. This distinguished work served to focus attention upon New Testament criticism.[3]

Higher criticism brought the Bible and the whole history of the church under the scrutiny of critical research in which the disciplines of philology, paleography, comparative religion, and other related approaches were given free rein.

Because the Old Testament was more complex and less sensitive on doctrinal grounds, it was attacked first, but the New Testament was soon involved. Authorship questions arose: Did Moses write the Pentateuch? Did John write the Fourth Gospel? Did Paul write Ephesians? In their train were much larger questions of interpretation: Was the Creation story derived from Babylonian myth? Did St. Paul transform and distort "the religion of Jesus"? Could the "historical Jesus" be recovered? And beneath all of these searchings lay the real, the basic question: Was the Bible inspired? Could something so historically conditioned truly bear a revelation, and if so, how and in what sense?[4]

Evolutionary theory and higher criticism were only two factors in an intricate complex of forces which brought about a searching reappraisal of Christian faith on the American scene. After the Civil War the influence of the great German theologian Friedrich Schleiermacher (1768–1834) began to make inroads into American theological thought through men like Horace Bushnell. Schleiermacher shifted, to a considerable degree, the locus of religious authority from the Bible to religious experience. Philosophical idealism, whose preeminent exponent in Europe was Georg W. F. Hegel (1770–1831), and whose most persuasive American exponent was Josiah Royce (1855–1916), had a strong influence even in circles in which subscription to it was not explicit. Idealism was an optimistic philosophy which affirmed that the universe is essentially rational and that irrational elements will eventually be overcome by reason. The thought of Albrecht Ritschl (1822–1899) was another influence which served to shape the theological views of liberal American theologians of the latter nineteenth and the early twentieth centuries. Ritschlianism was especially hospitable to modern thought. Its emphasis upon practical Christianity and its concern for the Jesus of history gave it an unusual appeal to a certain class of American minds. The Ritschlian Christology, however, tended to exalt Jesus as an example to be followed rather than as a Lord to be worshiped.

The emergence of a new intellectual climate, some features of which have been sketched above, elicited various responses, as might be supposed, in the American Christian community. Three general types of response may be identified. The first was the reaction of the older orthodoxy. This group comprised wide differences of outlook within its own ranks but it was permeated by a heritage of Calvinism and revivalism. As new problems arose, the older orthodoxy unfortunately separated itself from demanding intellectual forces which were altering the world. Its obscurantism alienated many theologians and lay intellectuals. Believing the Bible to be the infallible source of religious truth, it resisted the challenges of science and biblical criticism in the name of a thoroughgoing supernaturalism. Its increasing defensiveness and other worldliness made it unable to grapple trenchantly with dynamic economic, social, and political problems which attended the vast industrial expansion and urban growth.

At the opposite end of the spectrum was a much smaller group of humanists. Humanism rejected explicitly any idea of a divine revelation and emphasized man's self-directed "quest for the good life." [5]

A third general grouping may be indicated by the term "liberalism." The effort of the liberals was to bring Christianity and contemporary culture into harmony, under the conditions imposed by the late nineteenth- and early twentieth-century world. When this basic outlook has been stated, however, it is necessary to identify two groups of liberals, whose differences were important. The division between them occurred at the point at which they attempted to relate the biblical faith to culture. One group may be referred to as "modernistic" liberals and the other as "evangelical" liberals.

Many modernistic liberals in the course of time found themselves fairly close to some of the positions of the humanists. However, the modernists were serious Christians who were called modernists because their views were basically determined by modern culture. They believed that the Christian heritage must be evaluated by the decisive standards of modern science, philosophy, psychology, and social thought. So seriously was modern thought taken by them that they gave up the belief in a normative authority to be found in the Bible, in the church, or in Christian tradition. They nevertheless felt that there were permanent elements in historic Christianity which should be retained, although these elements should be held under constant critical scrutiny.[6]

On the other hand, the evangelical liberals believed that the essence of the Christian faith could and should be preserved in adjustment with the demands of the modern era. So much did they cherish the Christian heritage that their position has sometimes been called "progressive orthodoxy." On the whole, they were committed Christians who were at the same time modern men. They desired to reevaluate the Christian message in the light of modern thought and to reestablish it in terms which would be relevant to a new time.

The determination of liberals to come to terms with modern knowledge in their interpretation of Christianity committed them to the following positions: They

(1) accepted the principle of organic evolution; (2) employed the historical-critical method in their study of the Bible; (3) utilized the findings of psychology and sociology; (4) appropriated the insights of modern philosophy, and especially those of philosophical idealism; (5) recognized vital moral values in a fully socialized democracy.[7]

Although the evangelical liberals differed markedly among themselves, it is possible to state in general terms some of their common convictions with respect to the Christian faith. At the center of their understanding of Christianity was an optimistic view of human nature, which involved a radical modification of the orthodox doctrines of sin and of human depravity. Man, having ascended from lower forms of life, was not believed to be a special act of creation. Moreover, sin was not the result of an historical "fall" from a state of innocence, but a failure of man to moralize his natural instinctual life in terms of the emergence of his spiritual life. Despite his failures and weaknesses, man, the liberals thought, has a natural tendency to progress toward the achievement of a noble spiritual destiny.

A striking common denominator of evangelical liberalism was its reverence for Jesus Christ. The liberals considered Jesus to be the clue to an understanding of the character of God, and to an understanding of human life and destiny. *"The methodological starting point for evangelical liberalism,"* says Lloyd J. Averill, *"was invariably the revelation of God in Jesus Christ."* [8] While the liberals considered Jesus to be a unique revelation of God, their emphasis was usually upon the "humanity" rather than upon the "deity" of Christ. They were therefore regarded by the orthodox as having an Arian tendency in their christological views. The exaltation of Jesus of Nazareth in distinction from the "Christ of faith" caused the liberals to think of Jesus as humanity's great teacher and great example, the ideal toward which the upward climb of man should be directed.

The evangelical liberals made little attempt to "prove the existence of God." The traditional proofs for God's existence were given small credence. Rather, the liberals' main concern was to think through the doctrine of God with principal attention to God's character. The character of God was interpreted in the light of Christ. God, it was believed, is preeminently the Christlike God.

God's "natural attributes" were given only secondary attention by the liberals. God's attributes and acts, the liberals believed, must always be considered in terms of his Christlike character. In view of this requirement, the atonement as a substitutionary offering to God was repudiated for various adaptations of the Moral Theory of atonement. God, the liberals believed, did not need to be appeased by a vicarious offering. Rather, we see in the work of Christ what God is always doing to redeem. In close connection with this insight, the liberals gave first priority to the paternal nature of God, rather than to his power or his "justice." God is the "holy Father."

The liberal acceptance of evolutionary thought called attention to the work of God in the cosmic process, rather than to his transcendence over it. God is the indwelling Spirit of the universe. A leading evangelical liberal, William Adams Brown, observed that God "is not a transcendent being living in a distant heaven whence from time to time he intervenes in the affairs of earth. He is an ever-present spirit guiding all that happens to a wise and holy end." [9] Also encouraging to the idea of the divine immanence was the liberal affinity for philosophical idealism, which conceived the divine Spirit to be somehow resident in the spirit of man. And since God indwells both the cosmos and the human spirit, the world was thought to be a rationally ordered system, consonant with the reason of man.

The immanence of God was readily interpreted to be preeminently the presence and movement of God in human life and experience. So important did this concept become in liberalism that experience became for some liberals the prime locus of religious authority, rather than the Bible, tradition, or the church.

WILLIAM NEWTON CLARKE — BIOGRAPHICAL SKETCH

William Newton Clarke (1841–1912) has been chosen as a Baptist representative of theological liberalism. His theological position indicates a very definite alignment with the evangelical liberals, a group in whose ranks were to be found Baptists of considerable stature and influence. After setting forth a few biographical details concerning Clarke, this discussion will address itself first to an exposition of his theological views, and second, to an inquiry concerning his particular place among the Baptists.

Clarke was born in a Baptist parsonage in Cazenovia, New York. He graduated from the Oneida Conference (Cazenovia) Seminary in 1858. In 1861 he received the A.B. degree from Madison University, and two years later he graduated from the Theological Seminary of this school.

Clarke was called to be pastor of the First Baptist Church of Newton Centre, Massachusetts, in May, 1869. Many of the faculty and students of Newton Theological Institution were members of his congregation. He remained in this pastorate for eleven years. On September 1, 1869, he married Emily A. Smith of Waverly, Pennsylvania.

The next church of which Clarke became pastor was the Olivet Baptist Church of Montreal. While here he published his *Commentary on Mark* (1881), a volume in the *American Commentary* series.

In 1883 he accepted the chair of New Testament Interpretation at the Baptist Theological School in Toronto. His duties in this school also involved the teaching of homiletics.

Four years after going to Toronto, Clarke accepted the pastorate of the Baptist church at Hamilton, New York. When President Ebenezer Dodge, of Hamilton Theological School, died suddenly in January, 1890, Clarke was asked to fill in at Hamilton in the teaching of Dodge's class in theology. A few months later, in June, 1890, he accepted the position of J. J. Joslin Professor of Christian Theology, at Hamilton. In 1908 he resigned his professorship, but he was given a lectureship in Christian Ethics at the seminary. He died suddenly after a fall at his winter home in De Land, Florida, on January 14, 1912.

Not all of Clarke's scholarly productions can be mentioned here. His most famous and most widely useful book was *An Outline of Christian Theology*, published in 1898. Other works are listed as follows: *Can I Believe in God the Father?* (1899); *What Shall We Think of Christianity?* (1899); *A Study of Christian Missions* (1900); *The Use of the Scriptures in Theology* (1905); *The Christian Doctrine of God* (1909, written for the *International Theological Library* series); *Sixty Years with the Bible* (1909, a kind of spiritual autobiography); and *The Ideal of Jesus* (1911).

THE THEOLOGY OF WILLIAM NEWTON CLARKE

The theological views of Clarke were set forth most comprehensively in *An Outline of Christian Theology*, published in 1898. This book will furnish the principal guide for this essay on Clarke's theology. The book grew out of his lectures to his classes over a period of years, appearing first in printed but unpublished form for the use of his students, Sydney Ahlstrom says of this work:

> [The *Outline*] is unquestionably Clarke's most memorable accomplishment. Lucid and fervently written, conceived against the broad background of evolutionary theory and in full cognizance of the historical criticism, it became virtually the *Dogmatik* of American Liberalism. Published first in 1898, it had passed through twenty editions by 1914.[10]

Harry Emerson Fosdick, one of Clarke's pupils, remarked in later years that the *Outline* "brought down upon him [Clarke] the invectives of the orthodox," but attained immediate favor among men of more liberal bent both in America and in Britain. The following appreciative comment about the book came from Marcus Dods:

> Has it ever happened to any of our readers to take up a work on systematic theology with the familiar divisions, God, Man, Christ, the Holy Spirit, the Church, the Last Things, and open it with a sigh of weariness and dread, and find himself fascinated and enthralled and compelled to read on to the last word? Let any one who craves a new experience of this kind procure Doctor Clarke's *Outline.*[11]

Clarke discussed the main topics of theology in traditional order. There are chapters on God, Man, Sin, Christ, The Holy Spirit and the Divine Life in Man, and Things to Come. A separate treatment of a doctrine of the church was, significantly, omitted. A friend and theological benefactor of Clarke, William Adams Brown, attributed the wide popularity of the *Outline* to its timeliness, its reverent, Christian spirit, its "clear and simple style," and its "singular serenity."

> The author approached the vexed questions of theology with a quiet confidence which at once disarmed criticism and allayed fear. He contemplated the changes wrought in our view of the world by modern science with calmness, as if they were a matter of course. He was untroubled by Biblical criticism. The theory of evolution was accepted without question; the traditional eschatology so courteously dismissed that one scarcely realized that it was gone. . . . He seemed as much at home spiritually in the modern world as he had been when a boy in his father's house.[12]

Clarke resembled Schleiermacher in believing that the main task of theology is a study of and exposition of the religious life. "Theology," he said, "is preceded by religion, as botany by the life of plants. Religion is the reality of which theology is the study." [13] There is a strong echo of Schleiermacher, also, in his belief that man has a religious nature. This nature makes religion universal among all men.[14]

Clarke's belief in the divine immanence caused him to believe that God seeks to disclose himself to all men; that, therefore, there is some truth in all religions because of this divine self-impartation; and that Christianity should be hospitable to truth wherever it is found.[15]

The Christian religion differs from other religions in that its concept of God and its impulse and power are derived from God's self-revelation in human history which culminated in Jesus Christ. On the other hand, Christian theology attempts to present the Christian view of the great, perennial themes which are the problems and questions of all the great religions.[16]

> The inestimable advantage of Christian theology is that it walks in the light. Its first fact is that God has willed to make himself known. Hence its office is not to "seek after God, if haply it may feel after him and find him," but to receive his self-manifestation made in Christ, and view the

field of truth and religion in the light of it. Upon the basis of the Christian revelation it builds a structure into which it works all the proper materials of theology. To other religions it says, with Paul, "What therefore ye worship in ignorance, this set I forth unto you." It declares that where men have groped after a God, a God exists, a real and living God, the Father of Jesus Christ, a Saviour to men.[17]

CHRISTIAN THEOLOGY — ITS SOURCES

When Clarke asked where Christian theology finds the materials with which it works, his answer, granted his liberal presuppositions, is not surprising. These materials, he said, may be found anywhere. "Christianity claims to set forth the one living God, to whose realm all things belong. Its field for materials is therefore as wide as his creation." [18] The two great sources for Christian theology, he added, are the Christian revelation and the universe (including man and nature).

Believing that revelation is God's self-disclosure to man, Clarke said that this self-disclosure occurred first, not in a book, but in experience. Prior to the record of the disclosure was the disclosure itself, in life and history, and preeminently, authoritatively, in Christ.

Clarke's position was an exaltation of Christian experience as a primary locus of revelation. Though God reveals himself in Christ, this revelation has to be carried to the inner life and made real in experience. "The agent in this work is the Holy Spirit, and the results are the Christian experience and the spiritual church." [19]

The Christian revelation has continued in the world, said Clarke, in the Christian life from which it sprang, and in the Scriptures. The first Christian revelation lived on in the lives of Christ's disciples. It continued to live in the church. The value of the Scriptures, Clarke said in another reminder of Schleiermacher, is its record of, and embodying of, experience.

> The Bible itself is an expression of experience. If this experience had not continued the Bible would have become only the record of an ancient and forgotten life, powerless to preserve Christianity in the world. This experience, on the contrary, would have preserved Christ's gift to man if there had been no Bible. The value of the Scriptures in keeping the experience true is beyond all estimation; and yet to think that Christianity would have perished from the world if there had been no Scriptures is to overlook its living power, as well as the teaching of its early history.[20]

Believing that Christian experience is a mediator between Christian theology and its principal source, the Christian revelation, Clarke was quite prepared to concede that the Christian theology of any age is an expression of the Christian experience of that particular period. Consequently, theology varies to some extent from age to age, since it is modified and limited by the intellectual and spiritual outlook of the environment in which it is written. "To theologize outside the Christian consciousness of one's age," said Clarke, "is as impossible as to live outside the atmosphere." [21]

The position which Clarke took on Christian experience means that the Scriptures are related to revelation in a derivative position. "Christianity is not a book-religion, but a life-religion. It centers in a person, and consists in a life, and Scriptures are its servant, not its source." [22]

However, Clarke's understanding of the Bible cannot be seen without measured consideration. Indeed, his understanding of the Bible was quite crucial to his conception of the Christian religion.

THE BIBLE AND THE CHRISTIAN REVELATION

Clarke grew up in a religious environment in which it was believed that the Bible was equally inspired in all its parts. The Scriptures were regarded as having complete authority for Christian faith and practice. Even after his views of the Bible changed, he was always a reverent, devout, scholarly student of it. Throughout his life, a study of the Scriptures always occupied a primary place in both his professional and his devotional life. What he said about himself in the 1870's could be applied to his whole career. "I can truly claim," he said, "that in interpreting the Bible I was profoundly conscientious." [23]

By the 1870's Clarke was beginning to have serious questions about the doctrine of biblical inerrancy.[24] In the 1880's, however, he made what seems to have been a fairly thorough study of higher criticism and came gradually to embrace the validity of this method of biblical study. Higher criticism helped him particularly both in coming to terms with factual errors which he found in the Bible, and with moral difficulties which were not in accordance with the spirit of Christ. In 1900 he could write:

> The higher criticism removes the cause of the deepest of those moral difficulties, for it shows us that Christians need not attribute to the God of Christ all the acts and passions that Israelites attributed to the God of Israel, or approve the moral judgments that were recorded in days of inferior moral light. . . . I have found the new light making much intelligible that was once confused, and much credible that was once hard to believe. Thus the modern method has come to me not mainly as a perplexing thing, though of course it has brought perplexity now and then, but far more as a means of light and help.[25]

In coming to his new views, Clarke found doctrines of the inspiration of the Scriptures troublesome and, he believed, unnecessary. He repudiated entirely the doctrine of plenary verbal inspiration, and he found the "dynamical" theory (which affirmed that the thought of the Bible was divinely inspired, but not the actual words) to be little more satisfactory.

Clarke was restive even with the term "inspiration" as applied to the Bible. In keeping with his view that the revelation of God occurs in life and action, Clarke preferred to say that men were inspired, not books.[26] How the book was written, he said, was a matter of indifference to him. The test of the book is not its certification by outward authority, but what it contains. "Theories of inspiration have always been dictating the contents of the Bible, telling us what we must find." [27] Anything that is true depends for its certification, not upon some theory about how it came to be true, but upon its own validity.[28] The Christian element in the Bible carries the power of self-authentication, in that it speaks with convincing truth to the condition and the hearts of men. If it does not do this, no amount of certification of its inspiration is any good, anyhow.[29]

The critical attitude to which Clarke held involved not only the literary and historical criticism which had been called "higher criticism," but also what may be called a religious criticism as well.[30] Since God revealed himself preeminently in Christ, Christ becomes the criterion by which all spiritual truth is judged, and thereby the criterion in the light of which all Scripture is evaluated for its revelational quality. The principle to be observed, said Clarke, is that only the Christian element in the Scripture is for Christian theology the formative and indispensable element.

> A system of Christian theology has God for its centre, the Spirit of Jesus for its organizing principle, and congenial truth from within the Bible and from without for its material. As for the Bible, I am not bound to work all its statements into my system: nay, I am bound not to work them all in, for some of them are not congenial to the spirit of Jesus which dominates Christian theology, and some express truth in forms that cannot be of permanent validity.[31]

The Bible is the "reporter" of Christ, and the "bearer" of his revelation of God. It is therefore worthy of reverent honor and diligent study, but it does not have an independent authority of its own. It is to be honored because the sovereign voice of God sounds through its pages.

The Bible, Clarke believed, is not a collection of divinely inspired, propositional truths; it is a history of God's self-manifestation.[32] Moreover, if God, as Clarke believed, continues to disclose himself, revelation continues. It is found wherever God discloses himself, at any time in history, and in any part of the human race.

Although Clarke did not develop this larger concept of revelation at length, Christ remained in his thought as the undisputed criterion and fulfillment of all revelation.[33] In addition, Clarke conceived that the agent of continuing revelation is the Holy Spirit.

> God is our Father, and the Bible is his servant, to make him known. Christ is our Saviour, and the Bible is his servant, that he may save us. The Holy Spirit is our teacher, and the Bible is his servant, to show us Christ. We are God's children, and the Bible is our servant, to show us our Saviour and Father, and to guide our feet into the way of peace.[34]

SOURCES FOR THEOLOGY OUTSIDE THE CHRISTIAN REVELATION

Clarke believed that the immanence of God in the world process enables the reverent mind to discover what God is doing therein. This attitude made him view affirmatively the disciplines of science and philosophy which concerned themselves with a study of various aspects of the world's ongoing process. He valued especially the various disciplines related to the study of man, for "he [man] is the chief creature of God in the world, and in him God must be manifested more fully than in any other of his works that are known to us." [35]

Clarke was convinced, however, that the Christian theologian uses the various disciplines of learning and the various experiences of mankind by taking his (the theologian's) stand first at the basic Christian insight that God can rightly be interpreted only in the character which he has revealed in Christ. Everything is to be looked at from this standpoint.

> There are many who feel on scientific grounds that they must search the universe for God without having personality and moral significance first in mind. . . . But [we] may be thankful that when we go forth searching for knowledge of God in the regions beyond, the Founder of Christianity leads us out from the Father's house, where we have begun to be acquainted with him for whom we seek.[36]

THE CHRISTIAN DOCTRINE OF GOD

It was characteristic of Clarke as a Christian liberal that he began his consideration of the doctrine of God, not with a discussion of God as First Cause or as Creator, but as personal Spirit. Because God is Spirit he can be apprehended by the spirit of man, and because God is personal he can have communion with finite personal spirits which bear his image.

It is also significant that the personal revelation by which God discloses himself to man centers in Jesus Christ. For in Jesus Christ the moral nature of God is revealed. Clarke said:

> By the Christian doctrine of God is meant, in the present discussion, the conception of God which Christian faith and thought propose for the present time, in view of the Bible, and of history, and of all sound knowledge and experience, interpreted in the light of Jesus Christ the Revealer.[37]

Clarke thought it much more important to discern clearly and accurately the character of God than to prove the existence of God, or to set forth his "metaphysical attributes." Consequently, a discussion of God's existence and metaphysical attributes was for Clarke a definitely secondary consideration. With his eye upon the revelation of God in Christ, Clarke defined God as "THE PERSONAL SPIRIT, PERFECTLY GOOD, WHO IN HOLY LOVE CREATES, SUSTAINS, AND ORDERS ALL." [38]

> In the character of Christ, and hence in the Christian character, we possess a true and trustworthy view of the character of God. Christ is given us as the expression of God, and as the example for men. The ideal Christian character is like Christ, and so is like God. Thus we learn the moral qualities of God from what he has shown himself to be in Christ, and from what he has commanded his children to be, and promised that they shall become.[39]

The fact that Clarke discussed the character of God in terms of God's personality — goodness, holiness, love, and wisdom — is of course not signal. Most theologians did the same. But the fact that he sought to anchor in Christ each attribute of God set forth in the biblical revelation is worthy of especial note. We see in Christ what God is and what God does. For this reason, there is no tension in the character of God between his holiness and his love. "Love," Clarke said, "desires to impart the good, and holiness holds immovably to the right thought as to what the good is, and how it shall be imparted." [40]

Clarke also moved along orthodox lines in discussing the natural, or metaphysical, attributes of God, which he preferred to call God's "modes of activity." Such attributes as eternity, infinity, transcendence, immanence, omnipresence, omniscience, and omnipotence are duly and carefully examined. His remarks upon these cannot be noted in detail here.

The central point for emphasis is that Clarke discerned that the so-called natural attributes of God must be seen in relation to God's moral character. It is the Christlike God who is eternal and omnipotent, who "creates, sustains, and orders all." [41] "Christianity does not claim to have learned this from the universe, but from God himself, who has spoken in Christ and made his motive known. In Christ he has explained the universe by manifesting himself." [42]

Clarke was traditionally Protestant in his belief that God is the Creator of all things. He was not traditional in his belief about how God went about his work of creation. He accepted with equanimity the findings of scientific investigation which vastly enlarged the duration of the universe in terms of geologic ages. He thought that to regard the Genesis account of the Creation as literal history was obscurantist. He preferred to leave aside the question whether the physical universe ever had a beginning at all. The doctrine of Creation, he thought,

> . . . does assert that the existence of God is necessary to that of the universe, while the existence of the universe is not necessary to that of God. One of the two is self-existent and the other is not, and the one is the source of the other. Because of the will and work of God the universe exists. The Christian doctrine does not insist upon any account or description of God's creative activity, or any theory of the manner in which power went forth, or goes forth, from him to act upon that which is not himself. On these points it has no objection to agnosticism, for it has no means of knowing what to proclaim.[43]

Yet, while the question of origins lies beyond the reach of theological inquiry, Clarke was not as hesitant concerning the method by which God creates and rules the material order. In general, he said:

> God's method in the universe is evolutionary. A gradual, progressive method, operating from within, characterizes his work in creating, sustaining, and ordering all. It involves a continuous process of enfolding and unfolding, of formation and disintegration, of growth, ripening, and decay, followed by recurrence of the same long movement. As trees, animals, and men follow an order of growth and decay, so do worlds and systems; and so does the universe as a whole. God himself, in a manner beyond our present knowledge, ministers to his universe the indwelling force by which the incessant movement is carried on. . . . Whether the movement will ever end is known to him alone. Immeasurable ages are required for this method, and so is immeasurable, wise, and patient activity on the part of God. That this is God's method is certain, though concerning the process much is yet to be learned, and all will never be learned.[44]

Clarke was willing to concede that human beings might also have arisen from lower orders of life in the evolutionary process, or, on the other hand, by the direct creation of God. The resolution of the question, he thought, rests upon the evidence, and theology is indifferent to the answer. The point which theology insists upon is that the various orders of being and life came from the hand of God, by whatever process.

God is a purposeful God, working in the world processes to accomplish his great objectives, all of which are motivated by holy love. Because God loves his creatures and has bestowed upon man, in particular, his love beyond measure, the evolutionary process is divinely governed in such a way as to preserve the freedom of finite spirits, to hear and answer their prayers, and to direct his providences sometimes in such unusual ways as to allow for the possibility of "miracles." [45] Whether miraculous events ever happen or not, however, they are not in accord with the way in which God usually works. ". . . the truth is that God is present and is proved by the steady order and unfolding of creation, and would be commended to his creatures by his work if no miracle had ever been wrought." [46]

In his subscription to a belief in the divine immanence, Clarke was characteristically liberal. However, he was not a thoroughgoing immanentist, and he believed that the doctrine of God's immanence should be complemented by the doctrine of his transcendence. Although God works in the world and is not outside the universe, he is not to be identified with it, "is not shut up in it, not limited by it, not required in his totality to maintain and order it. . . . God is Source of all, and Lord of all." [47]

Clarke referred to God's triune mode of existence as the Triunity rather than the Trinity. Nowhere did he say that God is a trinity of persons in the sense that He embodies in his interior being three distinct centers of consciousness. Rather, the one God manifests himself in three modes of self-disclosure. The Trinity seems therefore in Clarke's understanding to be a trinity of manifestation rather than a trinity of essence. Even so, he conceived that each of these manifestations of God tells us something profoundly true about God, so that we are speaking correctly when we say that the one God is forever Father, Son, and Holy Spirit.

God going-forth is related to God original as word to mind, or as son to father; he is uttered, or begotten, or sent forth from the primal Being. The third element is the unifying Spirit, the common life of Father and Son, God completing his own being in eternal unity. These three modes of being, if indeed they rest upon essential elements in divine self-consciousness, are not shadowy or transient, but real, abiding, and eternal. They are not personalities, in the modern sense of the term, but are separate aspects of one personality.[48]

As the metaphysical attributes of God occupied a subordinate place in Clarke's thought, so did argument for God's existence. In the *Outline,* his discussion of "reasons for thinking that there is such a Being as this," occupies only twenty-six pages. In his great monograph on the doctrine of God, the question of "evidence" for God's existence occupies the fourth and last section of his treatment.[49] In his discussion of evidence for God's existence, Clarke made use of modified forms of the cosmological, rational, teleological, and moral arguments. He considered these arguments valuable, but not conclusive and not indispensable. "Religion," he said, "existed before argument; in fact, it is the preciousness of religion that leads to the seeking for all possible confirmations of the reality of God." [50]

While he did not believe that the existence of God can be conclusively proved by rational argument, he did believe that there are corroborative lines of evidence which render God's existence thoroughly plausible to an unprejudiced mind. He thought, for example, that the world's rational structure argues for a divine mind which gave it that structure.

> Life, consciousness, reason, far-reaching intellect—these form an ascending movement, rising toward resemblance to the original conceiving mind; and we never doubt that these qualities, slowly brought forth in the world, are qualities of the mind by which the entire process has been thought through. But to these is added goodness. Goodness, moral worthiness, grows up in men. . . . It is coming in as yet another form of resemblance to that great mind which is bringing forth its own likeness from the long process of the universe.[51]

But the ultimate test of God's existence, Clarke said, not surprisingly, is experience. One who would reach final certainty must take the good God who showed himself in Christ "for real." "Men have tested him by trusting him, and have found what they had been encouraged to expect." [52]

THE DOCTRINE OF MAN

That man has an animal nature, due to his biological inheritance, Clarke conceded with no reluctance. Man's ego, his personhood, is, however, in the realm of spirit. His spiritual nature separates him by a vast distance from the animal world.

Also man's spiritual endowment makes him akin to God. Although "his body is akin to the material universe . . . his spirit is akin to the eternal creative Spirit." God made man in his own image. He also made all men his children. Man cannot cease being God's child, even while in rebellion against God, except by the destruction of his spiritual personality.[53]

> Men are born his sons, and can become their true selves only by becoming his sons indeed, in moral and religious fellowship. . . . Since they are his sons by birth, he desires them to be his sons in fellowship and character,

and is satisfied with them only as they are giving themselves to the filial life.[54]

In endowing man with a spiritual nature, God made him also immortal — "the human personality is undying." [55] Clarke had no particular argument by which human immortality can be demonstrated. To deny it was simply unthinkable to him.

> If God is good and true, if the world is an honest world, if life has the meaning that we are compelled to find in it, if moral values hold and moral possibilities are precious, if existence itself does not deceive and defraud us, then it is incredible that personal life has been summoned out of the void, only to return so quickly to the void again.[56]

In view of Clarke's conviction that man is God's child, created in the divine image and destined in the divine purpose for everlasting fellowship with God, it was fitting that he should put strong emphasis upon man as a moral being. The God who revealed himself in Christ has shown himself to be a God of superlative moral qualities. He is a good God, which means that "moral goodness is the original of all things, the source of man, the starting-point of creation." [57] This aboriginal and creative goodness in God is the ground of obligation which constrains man to be like God. Man *ought* to have in himself those qualities of goodness which inhere in the divine Father.

The moral obligation which man has from God is not imposed upon him as a legal requirement which is alien to his spiritual constitution. Rather, this obligation is written into the constitution of man's spiritual life. He cannot be his true self without allowing God to cultivate in him those qualities of goodness which God has within himself.

However, the will of God does not override the will of man. Man possesses, to however limited a degree, the freedom to will the will of God for his life, or to deny God's will. He is a responsible being.

Clarke was keenly aware that man is not simply a lone individual in his capacities and responsibilities. Man is the recipient of hereditary and environing factors, and he finds himself in structured relationships, which both limit and implement his freedom. Yet these complex constellations of factors do not rob him of his responsibility either as a social being or as a child of God. "The race-connection," said Clarke, "is God's help to private and public virtue." It also projects man into "a world of infinite complication and involvement, where no one can extricate himself from the common lot or shake off its burdens." [58]

Concerning human origins, Clarke expressed his willingness to remand this inquiry to the investigations of modern science. It is plain, however, that to him mankind originated in the evolutionary process, through which he believed the divine purpose to be accomplished.

> From an origin in animal life, the human race has advanced, and is still advancing, by growth of the soul. Mental powers have been developed from lower to higher grade, and are still gaining in largeness and force. Personality has been attained, and is always receiving enrichment from experience. . . . Religion has become a constant element in life, and capacity for religion has grown as ages passed. Man is ever becoming more fully man. . . . The older view of humanity was that God created a being in his own likeness at a stroke; the newer view is that he brings a being to his own likeness by a process, through gradual development of his powers.[59]

THE DOCTRINE OF SIN

For those who believe the cliché that liberal theologians entertained a shallow conception of sin, Clarke's searching consideration of this problem might occasion some surprise. He realized the difficulty in reducing sin to one root, or in defining it in capsule form. His depiction of sin as "badness," that is, as unlikeness to the good, as the abnormal, as a departure from the standard of duty, as "the placing of self-will or selfishness above the claims of love and duty" [60] — this depiction is quite incisive. Moreover, sin is not only, in Clarke's view, personal and individual; it is also social and racial. "The race-connection itself," he said, "has been the means of perpetuating sin." [61]

There was certainly a deposit of the liberal view of sin in Clarke's belief that much of sin is to be accounted for by the survival of an animalism in man, which man is gradually outgrowing. However, "it is not so much the brute in man that is sin," he said, "as it is the preference of the man for the brute rather than for the spirit, or the yielding of the spirit to the brute." [62] Besides, "the spirit has subtle and dangerous sins of its own," which cannot be attributed to man's brute nature.[63]

A mysterious and fateful quality of sin is indicated by the fact that it arises both from man's brute nature *and* his spiritual nature. This is true not only of individual but also of racial sin.

> An infant is born with passions that are innocent while irresponsibility continues, but become wrong and pass insensibly into sin when the higher life of responsible age comes on and they are accepted as dominant in preference to what is better. So the race was born with passions of animalism and self-will that were not sinful until the higher life of the spirit had become developed. But when the estate of genuine humanity had been reached, animalism and self-will were not normal to it, but were false and degrading

elements, fatal to the higher life unless they were rejected; and through the consent of the human will to the now abnormal rule of lower powers, what had before been innocent passed into sin. Such is the course of the individual, and such seems to have been the course of the race, far back in the infancy of prehistoric life.[64]

Despite Clarke's sensitive understanding of the depth and destructive nature of sin, he viewed the plight of man with a sober optimism. The world is good at its core because it was made by a good God. Therefore, God's battle against evil will be triumphant. Clarke's evolutionary presuppositions enabled him to see this growing victory in the spiritual pilgrimage of mankind.

Humanity certainly is by nature a slowly rising race, with a native tendency to outgrow faults. Sin is of course a burden and a clog upon that upward tendency, and one that might become so heavy as to nullify all higher possibilities. But God has certainly endowed humanity with a tendency to rise; which is only another way of saying that nature is favorable to goodness.[65]

Clarke was hesitant to say that God punishes sin in the sense that this punishment is under His personal administration. He preferred to say that God "has so constituted the universe that sin brings penalty." [66] It is true to say that the penalty of sin is intended by God to serve a disciplinary purpose, but it is not true to say that penalty is wholly disciplinary. Penalty is also a fitting retribution for evil. Moral evil receives its fitting reward, unless its consequences are annulled through the forgiveness of God. If this annullment happens, it is because God has moved to effect man's salvation in Jesus Christ.

THE DOCTRINE OF CHRIST

The heart of Clarke's preoccupation with Christ may be seen in his view that Christ is the true and authoritative revelation of God. What has already been said in this chapter on Christ the revealer should therefore be presupposed here.

Clarke shared the concern of the liberals that the figure of Jesus should be allowed to shine forth from the Gospels in its pristine light, without *a priori* dogmatic assumptions. He believed that the first three Gospels present a substantially accurate picture of the figure of Jesus.

The picture there presented shows us the figure of a man. As a liberal, Clarke was intensely concerned that the humanity of Christ should be preserved in Christian theology.

He found in the New Testament, however, a clear witness that the believing community in some sense worshiped Christ as divine. "Their simple faith and straightforward love found him more than human, and it came to pass that they adored him with God, and God by means of him." [67] Since no explanation is given in the New Testament of how Christ could be both a human and divine being, Clarke recognized this question as being of pressing theological concern.

His formulation of the doctrine of the Person of Christ is that Christ is "true God — true man," and the doctrine would thus far be consistent with the Chalcedonian formula. It is significant, however, that, although he examined the New Testament witness carefully, he virtually ignored the early Christian creeds. His interpretation of the person of Christ was made, not in terms of divine and human substances, but in terms of the kinship of God and man.

Clarke stopped short of saying that this kinship is one of identity. In other words, there is no pantheistic identification of deity and humanity in his estimate of Christ's person. On the other hand, he held that the incarnation of God in human life is by no means unnatural or incredible.[68] Man is like God, he said, "in spiritual constitution." He is unlike God "in greatness, range, extent of being." [69] Man, he said, can never transcend his human limits to become God, but God may enter into these limits and become man.[70] According to the Logos-doctrine, he believed, there is in God a disposition to enter into humanity.

Clarke made use of the kenotic theory in his discussion of the Person of Christ. God "emptied himself" in order to accommodate himself to the requirements and limitations of human life.

To say that God became incarnate did not mean, however, that God became diminished or divided during the lifetime of Jesus of Nazareth. "The truth is rather this: that the God of infinitely varied activity added to his other self-expressions the act of becoming man — an additional form of activity in which he could engage without withdrawing himself from any other." [71]

Although Jesus Christ was both human and divine, he was one person. He had one will, not two wills. Jesus of Nazareth did not have the "eternal consciousness of God." He was neither omniscient, omnipotent, nor omnipresent. Yet he was aware of his unique relationship with the Father. He knew what it was necessary for him to know to accomplish his redemptive mission. The divine and human qualities in him were blended in perfect harmony, neither the divine nor the human element overpowering, or dominating, the other.[72]

The humanity of Christ was fully consistent with the fact that he was, unlike all other men, sinless, and, unlike all other men, in perfect fellowship with the Father. His divinity and his sinlessness by no means distorted or diminished his humanity. He was the ideal and typical man, "the truest man that ever lived" ". . . the second Adam, the head of a new and true humanity." [73] Indeed, he united God with essential humanity. Between the two he became "the living link." "To God, he is God's very self; to men, he is God-with-us, even while he is The Man." [74]

Because Christ was divine, he was able to incarnate not only the person of God, but also the holy love of God in its outreaching search for man; because he was man, he experienced the triumphs and tragedies of human life. He entered into the depths of the meaning of human sin, without himself becoming sinful.[75]

Clarke conceived that, even if man had never sinned, God would have incarnated himself in human flesh, as the crowning touch of glory to his creative work.[76] He nevertheless admitted that this thought was speculative, and he recognized that the sin of man has caused the incarnation to be seen rather in the light of God's redemptive effort.

The work of Christ is one of reconciliation. Clarke preferred this biblical term to the term "atonement," for Christ was the agent for the reconciliation of God and man. Reconciliation meant restoration of fellowship. It was a personal, not a legal, reconciliation. The obstacles to this reconciliation were to be found, not at all in God, but only in the stubborn heart of man. Therefore, there is no sense in which the work of Christ in his life or death was intended to render God willing to save, by satisfying the divine law or the justice of God on man's behalf.

It is true that God hates sin and has established a moral order in which sin brings punishment upon the offender. But the law of God is not an entity separate from God with which men must deal. It is rather an expression of the character of God which indicates the path of righteousness and the pitfalls of sin. The law, therefore, is in the service of grace. Its intention is not to set the terms of punishment, but to promote goodness. "Grace satisfies law by saving sinners." [77]

Although Clarke's intention was to set forth a positive conception of Christ's work, it is easy to see in his discussion a polemic against such legal theories of atonement as the theory of Anselm and its first cousin, the theory of penal substitution.

Neither with God who gives it nor with men who receive it, nor yet with Christ through whom it comes, is the Christian salvation a salvation by satisfaction of law. It is not procured, imparted, or received on the terms of law; that is to say, it is not procured by works or earned by merit, whether of men or of Christ. Men are not saved by payment of debt, or by legal satisfaction, or by transfer of merit from Christ to them. God does not deal with men through Christ in the character of lawgiver, or judge, or in any special character, but in his real character as God, his own very self, in personal relations with his creatures as their very selves; and the method of his saving work is that of grace, which does not wait for any one's merit or earning, but freely gives.[78]

If there is no antagonism between God's law and his grace, it must be said even more strongly that there is no disparity between God's action in salvation and the action of Christ. God was *in* Christ. What Christ felt, God felt. What Christ did, God did. The life and death of Christ were a true expression of what God eternally is.

. . . Christ's sin-bearing was not a separate thing, having its significance wholly within itself. It was not a service of his own offered to God who had no share in it. Here, as everywhere, God was the original and Christ the Word. Christ's sin-bearing was the expression of God's. As God's hatred of sin and God's saviour-heart found expression in Christ, so in Christ did the fact of his eternal sin-bearing find announcement and illustration. The sufferings of Christ were the true representative symbol and proclamation of what goes on perpetually in God. From them God wished the world to learn that sin is put away only through the redemptive suffering of holy love, which he himself is gladly bearing, and which Christ, his representative and expression, endured before the eyes of men.[79]

Clarke did not identify his own view of the work of Christ with the Moral Influence view, but it seems to be essentially that. This fact is indicated by the reason which he assigns for the "necessity" of the death of Christ.

His death was necessary, because nothing short of death could represent, in a human career and effort, the spirit of self-sacrifice with which God bears sin that he may save. By going to this extremity God sufficiently declared his condemnation of sin . . . and sufficiently manifested his redeeming love.[80]

In answer to the manifestation of the divine love which God makes in Christ, the response which is required on the part of man is "the sacrifice of self-offering to him, confession of the evil of sin, consent to his holy will, and self-sacrificing fellowship with his redeeming purpose." [81] ". . . nor can any man be completely saved except by becoming like him." [82]

THE DOCTRINE OF THE HOLY SPIRIT

Clarke believed that the Holy Spirit is the presence of God in the spirit of man. He is in no sense a derived, diminished, impersonal presence, but the very God himself in direct and vital communication with living persons. He is also the living Christ returned, for the purpose of carrying on the redemptive mission of Christ in the world.

Clarke did not believe that the Spirit is present only in the Christian community. It is inconceivable that the God who loved the world could find no way to make himself present in the larger life of the world. "All good," Clarke said, "that appears in men grows up under the fostering care of the Holy Spirit." [83]

God's work in humanity is sometimes most difficulty to identify as the express work of the Holy Spirit. His most characteristic work is making real the life of Christ within the human soul.

> He himself moves upon the souls that he has created, and abides in the very secret of their life. The profoundest and most inseparable indwelling with men best consummates the relation in which he and they exist. This perfect inhabitation of human souls by himself is what he is seeking to bring to pass: all that he has done through Christ is one long endeavor to this end.[84]

The work of the Holy Spirit is frequently discussed in theology in connection with the doctrine of the church. Clarke quite properly followed this order of development. His concern was principally about the intimate relationship between the Holy Spirit and the Christian life. It is in the church, he said, considered not as an institution but as the community of Christian people, that the Holy Spirit does his deepest work in the world.[85] In this community His work may be generally described as follows: "He reveals and glorifies Christ, he brings to remembrance what Christ has taught, he guides the Christian people into the full Christian truth, he calls out testimony from men to Christ, and by all means he quickens piety in fellowship with God." [86]

It is in individual human beings that the Holy Spirit creates and sustains the divine life in its intensest form. In discussing the Spirit's creation of the spiritual life within individuals, Clarke illuminated the traditional doctrines designated regeneration, repentance, faith, justification, sanctification, and the like.

His concepts of the spiritual realities called by these terms were not unusual and will not require elaboration here. Clarke was wise enough to see that they were all figurative terms which refer to a single and central reality in its various aspects — that is, to life in Christ. Clarke's treatment therefore is free of the damaging method of an older theology which sought to make each term represent a different stage or process in the work of salvation. His treatment also preserves a wholesome balance between the work of God and, at every step, the free response of the individual person.

Clarke's doctrine of salvation, while not minimizing the relevance of God's saving work to the next world, is strongly oriented toward the present life. "Likeness to Christ," he said, "is the goal of the Spirit's leading and increasing conformity to Christ's character and life is the way through which he leads." [87] Sanctification is, therefore, conceived in intensely ethical terms. It is to regeneration "what growth is to birth."

> The Holy Spirit nourishes and strengthens the holy love that he has awakened. He makes Christ ever more truly known, taking what is his and manifesting it to the soul. He constantly calls out new faith in Christ, new love toward God and men, new hope of further blessing and progress. He brings home to the heart the truths that are helpful to the growth of holiness.[88]

So central is the work of divine grace in the sanctification of the soul that death does not end it. Both the discipline and challenge of Christian growth will continue into the next world.

THINGS TO COME

Although Clarke's treatment of eschatology is marked by a luminous faith and by pointed convictions, few features of his thought show so plainly his departure from biblical literalism. His conclusions regarding the millennial question are a case in point. His examination of the grounds for both the premillennial and the postmillennial positions is careful and respectful. Nevertheless, he believes, the figurative and apocalyptic language upon which these positions are built suffers distortion if it is literally interpreted. So both positions are without valid foundation.

Similar conclusions may be reached concerning the Second Coming of Christ. Again apocalyptic vision and language have been misunderstood by biblical literalists. The emphasis upon the Second Coming has caused the church to think of Christ in terms of absence instead of in terms of presence. The church thinks of herself as Christ's widow instead of as his bride.[89] The Second Coming of Christ was not a far-off event of the future; it was the day of Pentecost. At the heart of Christian faith is the fact that Christ has returned, and is powerfully present, in the Holy Spirit.[90]

However, Clarke did not think that the coming of Christ is accomplished in any single event. It is rather a process which includes innumerable events. "No visible return of Christ to earth is to be expected, but rather the long and steady advance of his spiritual kingdom." [91] However, this advance is not some sort of escalator of automatic progress, but it is accomplished as the forces of Christ give themselves to mighty exertion to battle and overcome evil.[92]

The soul has no more "invincible surmise," and the Christian faith is radiant with no stronger promise, than that of life after death. The resurrection of the dead is a doctrine of precious truth, but it is not to be taken literally. The spiritual person will retain its integrity in the world to come, but the physical body which it left will not be revivified. Likewise, we need not expect a general resurrection of dead bodies at some looked-for descent of Christ on the clouds of heaven. Rather, we may believe that each man, "complete in all that personality requires, stands up alive beyond the great change that we call death, having in the same hour died and risen again." [93]

The judgment of God in the life to come need not refer to a great assize at which the assembled multitudes of human souls will stand before the judgment bar of God. It is rather likely that each individual person receives his judgment from God immediately following the experience of death.[94]

Although judgment is in the hands of God, Christ is also said to be the Judge. This means that Christ is the standard by which judgment is to be given. It also means that the God who judges will do so in the character of Christ. "So the judgment at the end of life is an estimating of men according to the life that they have lived, viewed in the light of the standard of Christian love." [95]

Clarke noted that there was a trend in the theology of his period which held out some hope in the world to come for those who have not been redeemed in this life. Upon this supposition Clarke refused to dogmatize. It is certain, he believed, that God's antagonism to sin is everlasting. The soul which persists in his defiance of God in the future life will continue, as long as his defiance lasts, to suffer the retribution which he has brought upon himself. However, God's dealing with his creatures after death may even then pursue the offices of discipline and reformation which seek the extension of mercy. If so, it must be firmly held that in time or in eternity there is no salvation except by "transformation into the likeness of the good God." The possibility that God may carry on his redemptive efforts in the world to come in no sense diminishes the responsibility of the church to seek the salvation of the world by "an intense, unconquerable, self-sacrificing love." [96]

CLARKE — THE MAN AND THE THEOLOGIAN

William Newton Clarke was a man of fervent Christian piety, of great catholicity of mind, and of lovable spirit. A contemporary, Markham W. Stackpole, said of him:

> Though a fearless progressive in his thinking, he had a sweetness of nature and a devoutness of spirit that forbade the bitterness of controversy. He kept himself above factions. He preserved personal friendships in spite of theological differences, and he was too large of mind and heart to confine his interest or friendships to a single party or denomination. He belonged to the "Christian Brotherhood." [97]

Although Clarke was opposed by some of the conservatives in the Christian fellowship, this opposition was surprisingly small. The comparative lack of antagonism which attended his pathway is to be explained by more than his sweetness of temper. His own background and early views had been conservative. He could have fellowship with many conservatives because he understood them, and because, when he differed from them, he nevertheless respected them as persons. Moreover, at many points he remained conservative himself. A close student of Clarke's life and thought, Claude L. Howe, Jr., makes the following observation:

> Sharing the conservative theological outlook of a majority of his denominational contemporaries for many years, he responded slowly to forces that brought about a theological transition in this country, at last becoming the first systematic theologian of theological liberalism in America. A strange mixture of conservatism and liberalism in his thought is accounted for by this gradual development. [98]

Clarke's talent for clear statement, his pungent thought, and his deep feeling combined to make him that rarity among theologians — a theologian with a readable and luminous literary style. Though not himself a great or profoundly original thinker, his gifts as a Christian theologian made him an admirable spokesman for a point of view and won him a hearing not only among his fellow-scholars, but also among a large circle of intelligent laymen.

As a teacher, he was much beloved and much respected by most of his students. This was particularly true of his students of more liberal outlook. Harry Emerson Fosdick, one of Clarke's aptest and most perceptive pupils, said of his teacher:

> There are doubtless many who can say, as I can, that but for Doctor Clarke they would not be to-day in the Christian ministry. When the old theology was clashing with the new, and bitterness was deeply felt upon both sides; when, watching the conflict, the young men of undergraduate years saw clearly that for them it was no longer a question of old or new theology, but of new or no theology, Doctor Clarke stood as the proof to us that it was possible to be a Christian and reasonable, a disciple and a modern man, at once devout and intelligent. . . . How many of us are chiefly thankful

for this, that he did not leave us to be driven from faith and the church by reactionaries, but made it possible for us to become in the new generation preachers of the Gospel of Christ.[99]

In his autobiography written many years later, Fosdick appeared to be as grateful to Clarke as ever: "Looking back on the conventional orthodoxy of those days, I can understand now why the diehards hated him, and why we youngsters turned to him for help." [100]

An estimate of Clarke's influence among the Baptists must take account of the fact that he spent his whole public career as a pastor of Baptist churches and as a teacher in Baptist institutions. The theological convictions which have been elaborated in the foregoing pages of this chapter were the convictions which Clarke taught to Baptist students and which he preached in Baptist pulpits, for a whole generation. These views were also widely disseminated among Baptists, as well as among others, through his books. He became a theological mentor to a host of Baptist ministers, as well as to many thoughtful laymen.

Considering his close and lifelong identification with the Baptists, it is surprising that he says so little about his own denomination. However, he wrote most of his books as a theological liberal, and that liberalism was self-consciously ecumenical in outlook, not to say non-denominational.

Mrs. Clarke remarked that, up to about 1871, Clarke had never questioned the commonly accepted beliefs of his denomination. He was a mild Calvinist, and he believed that immersion was the method of baptism used in the New Testament and therefore of perennial validity. He was even a close communionist.[101]

By the 1880's Clarke realized that his spiritual pilgrimage was taking him away from many traditional Baptist viewpoints. In 1881 he wrote: "I do not regard myself as a champion of denominational orthodoxy, but I do regard myself as a Baptist and as a humble champion of my Master's truth." [102] This seemed to have been the attitude which he retained toward the denomination for the rest of his life. He urged many young men, in this period and in later years, to remain in the denomination even when some of their convictions were not consistent with those of a majority of Baptists.[103] Occasionally, angry voices in the churches were raised in opposition to his retaining his professorship at Hamilton. During one such period, Clarke remarked to Harry Emerson Fosdick, "They will get me yet." "They never did, however," said Fosdick. "He went from strength to strength." [104]

Of course, as a liberal, Clarke did not stand alone in the Baptist denomination of his time. Kenneth Cauthen, in his study entitled *The Impact of American Religious Liberalism* (1961), examines the thought of the following outstanding liberals: William Adams Brown, Harry Emerson Fosdick, Walter Rauschenbusch, A. C. Knudson, Eugene W. Lyman, Shailer Mathews, Douglas Clyde Macintosh, and Henry Nelson Wieman. Of these, Fosdick, Rauschenbusch, Mathews, and Macintosh were Baptists. Other prominent Baptist liberals contemporary with Clarke were Crawford H. Toy, William Rainey Harper, Shirley Jackson Case, and George B. Foster. Of these scholars, the theological positions of Mathews, Macintosh, Toy, Case, and Foster were considerably to the left of the position of Clarke.

During Clarke's lifetime, theological liberalism among Baptists was largely to be found, not in the denomination as a whole, but in institutions of higher learning. A. H. Newman, a leading Baptist historian, estimated in 1906 that in the New England and Middle states not one Baptist in ten was "conscious of any important change in theology or departure from the old Baptist orthodoxy." In the western and southeastern states he thought the ratio would be hardly one in twenty; in the South, one in a hundred would be a liberal estimate.[105]

Newman observed that the Divinity School of the University of Chicago had a number of distinguished liberal Baptist scholars, although some of the members of the faculty of that school were thoroughgoing conservatives. In some of the Baptist universities in the East (notably Brown), the faculties were almost as liberal as the faculty of Chicago. Moreover, Baptist students in large numbers, Newman noted, had graduated in nondenominational universities and seminaries noted for their liberal thought, such as Harvard, Yale, Columbia, Cornell, Union, and the Universities of Michigan and Wisconsin, and had no doubt been affected by this exposure.

At Rochester, the president and professor of theology was Augustus Hopkins Strong, who was, like Clarke, one of the most noted systematic theologians in the Baptist denomination. Although Strong remained conservative in many of his theological views, he became hospitable toward "higher criticism," and toward theological views associated with evolutionism. At Rochester, also, were men like Benjamin O. True and Walter Rauschenbusch, who were generally in accord with Strong's views of the Scriptures. Rauschenbusch was one of the greatest of the liberals.

At Newton Theological Institution several members of the faculty were moderately inclined toward higher criticism, as was its president, Nathan E. Wood. After the departure of Crawford Toy from the Southern Baptist Theological Seminary because of his advanced views on the Bible, the faculty of the institution remained quite generally conservative for some years, although John A. Broadus, an outstanding New Testament scholar, encouraged his students to study German exegetical works and to pursue graduate studies in German universities.

In his study of "Baptists and Changing Views of the Bible," Norman H. Maring notes a growing receptivity of Baptist seminary faculties in the early part of the twentieth century toward the historical-critical approach to the Scriptures.

> Although there were still a few staunch opponents of the methods and conclusions of higher criticism on the faculties, they were a minority and belonged to a generation which was rapidly vanishing. By 1918 adoption of the critical approach to the Bible had been virtually completed in the older theological schools. The attitudes of professors varied from grudging concession of the right of Biblical criticism to do its work to enthusiastic advocacy of its conclusions, but only a few were still its declared foes.[106]

Clarke died some years before the outbreak of the Fundamentalist controversy, which tended to polarize the liberal and conservative elements in several of the leading American Protestant denominations, including the Northern Baptist Convention.[107] Clarke therefore had no direct part in the conflict which was to have tragic results for several great denominations, including his own denomination. When the controversy came, the strength of the liberals in the Northern Baptist Convention was entrenched principally in the older seminaries and in northern urban churches. On the other hand, the influence of liberals in the Southern Baptist Convention was negligible.

Clarke, if he had lived during this conflict, would have deplored it; he would have been conciliatory and brotherly toward those who certainly would have opposed him. On one point, however, he would have remained adamant. He would have held that the Christian message must be given intelligent expression in the cultural forms of every given era and that it must and can do so without losing its distinctiveness and integrity. He would have said with candor that the Christian message is destined to survive every theological system which attempts to give it expression, including that of William Newton Clarke.

8-WALTER RAUSCHENBUSCH-
Prophet of Social Christianity

The name of Walter Rauschenbusch is often associated with the social gospel. The social gospel movement in America began in the latter decades of the nineteenth century under the leadership of an influential group of Protestant leaders who were concerned about the serious social problems arising out of the industrial revolution. The social gospel was basically a reaction to the inequities of capitalism which were evident in the industrial society as it developed during this period. Therefore, issues which arose concerning capital and labor, property, corporations, and monopoly were of prime interest to the leaders of the social gospel movement. Other matters of social importance, such as the family, race, democracy, housing, and war, were discussed only as they related to the economic issues.[1]

An interest in social Christianity had quickened in Europe during about the same period in which the American movement developed, but Americans were more familiar with the work of men such as Chalmers, Maurice, Kingsley, and Henry Scott Holland in Britain.[2]

The American movement was, however, in a real sense distinctive. It was shaped by patterns of thought and action which had long characterized Protestantism in this country. Its temper was readily merged with American moral idealism and optimism.[3] It shared the optimistic mood created by the dramatic achievement of technological science, rather naïvely believing that human problems were also subject to progressive solution.

The term "social gospel" did not attain common usage until after 1900. The social gospel movement reached its peak in the first two decades of the twentieth century and declined after World War I, although it left a treasured heritage in the main body of American Christianity.

Not all Protestant liberals were adherents of the social gospel. Yet virtually all of the leaders in the movement were Protestant liberals. This fact can be seen by noting the main emphases and convictions which the advocates of social Christianity shared.

These include a conviction that the social principles of the historical Jesus could serve as reliable guides for both individual and social life in any age. Central to his teachings, so these liberal social Christians believed, was a stress on the immanence of God, the goodness and worth of man, and the coming kingdom of God on earth. Indeed, they affirmed, at the very heart of his gospel was the message of the kingdom, which they interpreted as a possibility within history. Though the church had long ago lost the true key to the kingdom, now that key had been recovered. The spokesmen for the social gospel expected that, through the efforts of men of good will, the kingdom of God would soon become a reality, bringing with it social harmony and the elimination of the worst of social injustices. . . . Spokesmen for the social gospel believed wholeheartedly in progress. Their faith was not, as a rule, in automatic or inevitable progress, for they normally saw progress as conditional upon man's response to divine leading. But along with liberal theologians generally, they were so confident of human goodness as to be sure that men could be educated to choose the good and to contribute directly to "the building of the kingdom." Sin they regarded primarily as selfishness. Through education, men could be led to prefer social good to private advantage. The spokesmen for the social gospel were aware that sin could be transmitted corporately through social institutions, yet they believed that these institutions too could come under the law of love. Through determined moral effort, men could hasten the day of the coming of the empire of law and love, the kingdom of God. The ethics of the social gospel stressed Christ's way of love, which could lead men toward the glorious reign of love. In this coming order, socialized and enlightened men would work for the good of all.[4]

A widespread interest in social religion resulted in the proliferation of organizations and activities dedicated to the advancement of social reformation. This interest manifested itself in a great variety of sermons, books, tracts, conferences, magazine articles, theological school curricula, and social evangelism. Societies of Christian socialists, most of them of passing tenure, sprang up. There were more specifically religious organizations which were longer lived — like the Brotherhood of the Kingdom, of which Walter Rauschenbusch was the leading spirit. The Christian Social Union and the Church Association for the Advancement of the Interests of Labor were enduring and effective organizations in their own spheres of interest. The Federal Council of Churches of Christ in America, organized in 1908, from the beginning embodied a vital social interest. Their social concern drew many capable persons from the churches to places of leadership in social work. It established an unofficial but definite liaison between socially focused Christianity, on the one hand, and both the Socialist party and the labor movement on the other.[5]

By 1900, men such as Washington Gladden, Josiah Strong, Richard T. Ely, Francis G. Peabody, and George Herron had brought the social gospel to a mature development. However, with the publication of *Christianity and the Social Crisis* in 1907, Walter Rauschenbusch became the most outstanding exponent in the United States of the social gospel. He continued to be its leading advocate during its period of greatest influence.[6]

WALTER RAUSCHENBUSCH — BIOGRAPHICAL SKETCH

Walter Rauschenbusch (1861–1918), a son of German immigrant parents, was born into a cultured home. His father was a member of the faculty of Rochester Theological Seminary, in which institution he had special responsibility for the training of pastors for German-American churches.

Like his father, Rauschenbusch became a Baptist minister. In 1886 he finished his theological education at Rochester Seminary and volunteered for service as a foreign missionary. This possible direction of his life was closed, however, when one of his professors at Rochester affirmed that Rauschenbusch's views on the Old Testament were unorthodox. When a strong midwestern church turned him down as pastor, apparently also because of his liberal views, he became the pastor of a small German Baptist church in New York City, on the edge of "Hell's Kitchen."

From 1886 to 1897 Rauschenbusch labored among his people in the squalid tenement section in which the church was located. He came to see that the social problems of urban, industrial America demanded a searching reappraisal of the conservative Christianity which he had embraced from his childhood. In 1886 the campaign of Henry George for the mayoralty of New York contributed to his social awakening. He found himself in quest of a concept of Christianity which would be comprehensive enough to embrace both personal and social problems. When he rediscovered the concept which was so central in the teachings of Jesus, the kingdom of God, he felt that he had recovered a vision of Christianity which was all-embracing. In 1892 he and two other close friends, Leighton Williams and Nathaniel Schmidt, organized a society which they called "The Brotherhood of the Kingdom." This fellowship, never large in membership, was destined to play a crucial part in the development of some of the principal leaders of American social Christianity.

In 1897 Rauschenbusch became a member of the faculty at

Rochester Seminary. He became a professor of church history in this institution in 1902, and he remained in this position until his death.

Prior to his coming to a rather sudden fame, Rauschenbusch had been fairly well known in his own denomination. But with the publication of *Christianity and the Social Crisis* in 1907, he quickly attained recognition among the Christian forces of the whole nation.

The volume just mentioned turned out to be the most widely known of all Rauschenbusch's books, and it put him at the forefront of the leadership of the social gospel movement. Rauschenbusch in this book first gave his attention to an analysis of the ethical and social message of the Old Testament prophets. He also gave serious attention to the social message of Jesus, and he pointed out the relevance of Jesus' message to the social conditions of twentieth-century America. He contrasted the irrelevance of much of contemporary Christianity with the social power of Christianity in the early church. He sought to define the role of the church in modern society and concluded with a chapter on "What to Do."

Rauschenbusch's second book on the theme of social Christianity was entitled *For God and People: Prayers of the Social Awakening,* published in 1910. These prayers, which manifested their author's deep feeling and concern for the acute problems and the human casualties of the social system, were a unique contribution to the social gospel cause. Ernest Trice Thompson said:

> Nothing like these prayers had ever been published before; no prayers combining so successfully social passion with profound religious insight and soul-stirring expression have been published since. All recent Protestant liturgies reflect their influence. For many ministers and laymen prayer breathes a new spirit; it has taken on a new dimension.[7]

The next of Rauschenbusch's works was published in 1912. It was entitled *Christianizing the Social Order.* This cogent book was his most carefully thought-out work on the application of Christian principles to the problems of society. "Our semi-Christian social order" was examined, and this examination was followed by a trenchant critique of capitalism on the basis of frankly socialistic presuppositions. Rauschenbusch urged social justice and economic democracy as minimal elements required for the establishment of Christian social order.

In 1916 Rauschenbusch published a brief study book for the International YMCA on *The Social Principles of Jesus.* While this volume was not as ambitious as his longer works, its wide circulation among college young people made it very influential. It proved to be, indeed, the most popular of all his books.

The last and possibly the greatest of Rauschenbusch's books was his Nathanial W. Taylor Lectures at the Yale Divinity School in 1917. These lectures were published under the title *A Theology for the Social Gospel*. Affirming that "we need a systematic theology large enough to match the social gospel and vital enough to back it," Rauschenbusch sought to inquire what light the social gospel could throw upon the Christian doctrines of sin, salvation, God, Christ, the Holy Spirit, revelation, inspiration, baptism, the Lord's Supper, eschatology, and the atonement.

A THEOLOGY FOR THE SOCIAL GOSPEL

The home from which Rauschenbusch came was one of deep piety. In his subsequent life, he never lost this profound element of Christian devotion. His experience in "Hell's Kitchen" caused him to doubt the adequacy of the conservative theology which had been a part of his theological background. In 1891 he took leave from his pastoral charge to study social movements in England and to study the New Testament in Germany. During and after this period of study his theology became more liberal. He adopted a more critical approach to the Scriptures and became especially open to the insights of thinkers like Schleiermacher, Ritschl, Wellhausen, Bushnell, and Harnack. He also became broadly acquainted with the writings of the critics of capitalism, and he came to have a deep affinity for socialism (not Marxism). He became a thinker of wide learning, rich experience, and singular courage. More than any other leader in the social gospel movement, he stood as a mediator between the older evangelicalism and the new learning and theology.[8]

It should be remembered that Rauschenbusch was never a professional theologian. He was a specialist in church history. His work is not marked by great constructive theological power; yet it is rich in historical detail, historical illustration, and critical analysis. It is marked by a vivid, and at times eloquent, literary style, and sometimes by a striking originality.

Rauschenbusch became convinced that the social gospel demanded a reassessment of Christian theology and a partial restructuring of the body of theology to accord with the new social insight which was rapidly developing in his own day. He shared the conviction of Schleiermacher that theology must be rethought and rewritten in each era of history, in order to reflect the problems and insights of new Christian experience. Theology, therefore, is not a static discipline. It must be alert to the world in which it lives, and it must be flexible to the demands of each new time. "When the progress of humanity creates new tasks," he said, "such as world-wide missions, or new problems, such as the social problem, theology must connect these with the old fundamentals of our faith and make them Christian tasks and problems." [9] Theology must therefore be "large enough to contain the social gospel, and alive and productive enough not to hamper it." [10]

Rauschenbusch thought that theology should take intelligent account of new learning, particularly that growing out of the historical interpretation of the Bible. Scholarly historical interpretation, he believed, had given the Bible back to men of "modernized intelligence." Theology should also respect the fresh growing minds of young college and seminary students. It is not fair to these young people to force them to choose "between an unsocial system of theology and an irreligious system of social salvation." [11] The social gospel emphasis should make theology more eager to come to grips with the problems of this world. Theology should therefore be profoundly ethical in orientation. It should force no dichotomy between the personal and the social, but it should take full account of both the personal and the social dimensions of life at the same time. While it should never "pare down its thought to the rudimentary ideas of untrained people," [12] it should deal with the problems with which the common man is familiar. It should deal with the sin, sickness, tragedy, injustice, ignorance, and destitution of real men and women, as these problems express themselves in private and public spheres.

THE DOCTRINE OF SIN

Having asserted the need for a theology which meets the challenge of the social gospel, Rauschenbusch was concerned to "pass in review" the doctrines of the Christian faith which would be most affected by the social challenge. The first doctrine was the doctrine of sin. The doctrines of sin and salvation, he believed, "are the starting-point and goal of Christian theology." [13]

The Christian understanding of sin, he believed, should be modified to take account of a deepening and sharpening Christian consciousness of sin. If sin is perceived in the light of the standards of the kingdom of God, the inadequacies of a merely individualistic conception of sin appear.

If the exponents of the old theology have taught humanity an adequate consciousness of sin, how is it that they themselves have been blind and dumb on the master iniquities of human history? During all the ages while they were the theological keepers of the conscience of Christendom, the peasants in the country and the working class in the cities were being sucked dry by the parasitic classes of society, and war was damning poor humanity. Yet what traces are there in traditional theology that the minds of old-line theologians were awake to these magnificent manifestations of the wickedness of the human heart? How is it that only in the modern era, since the moral insight of mankind has to some extent escaped from the tuition of the old theology, has a world-wide social movement arisen to put a stop to the exploitation of the poor, and that only in the last three years has war been realized as the supreme moral evil? [14]

The social gospel does not deny or condone the sins of individuals, but it is concerned to call attention to the larger questions of public morality, to the "wrongs done by whole classes or professions of men," which have been sidestepped by the old theology. [15]

The doctrine of the fall of man, Rauschenbusch thought, has been given altogether too much attention by traditional theology. He noted that the prophets and Jesus were far more interested in present evil than in a speculative interpretation of the story of the fall as recorded in the early chapters of Genesis. Jesus himself recognized the terrible reality and universality of sin. His interest, however, was practical instead of speculative, religious and ethical, instead of philosophical. He was concerned with the actual sources of sin which he saw operative in the world around him. [16]

The doctrine of the fall has been so accentuated in theology that the sinful contributions of later generations have received all too scant attention.

Consequently theology has had little to say about the contributions which our more recent forefathers have made to the sin and misery of mankind. The social gospel would rather reserve some blame for them, for their vices have afflicted us with syphilis, their graft and their wars have loaded us with public debts, and their piety has perpetuated despotic churches and unbelievable creeds. [17]

In searching for the nature of sin, Walter Rauschenbusch was not satisfied with those definitions which identified the sin of man with unsublimated animal passions, inertia, or ignorance. All of these doubtless are woven into the pattern of sin. However, the nature of sin cannot be grasped without viewing the human condition in the light of the positive ideals of social righteousness which are seen in the person and teachings of Jesus, and in the kingdom of God.

When it is seen in comparison with the righteousness and love of Christ, the essence of sin appears to be selfishness. Sin is preferring one's own will to the will of God and to the well-being of one's fellows. The sinful mind is the unsocial and antisocial mind.

> To find the climax of sin we must not linger over a man who swears, or sneers at religion, or denies the mystery of the trinity, but put our hands on social groups who have turned the patrimony of the nation into the private property of a small class, or have left the peasant labourers cowed, degraded, demoralized, and without rights in the land. When we find such in history, or in present-day life, we shall know we have struck real rebellion against God on the higher levels of sin.[18]

While he made little of the doctrine of the fall, Rauschenbusch acknowledged that he took very seriously the Christian doctrine of original sin. This doctrine was one point, he believed, at which an individualistic traditional theology had attempted seriously to come to grips with a solidaristic involvement of all mankind in sin. There is more than a hint that Rauschenbusch did not believe that sin entered the bloodstream of the human race as a fatal disease in the fall of two historical figures named Adam and Eve. Side by side with this orthodox view he set the theory arising from evolutionary science to the effect that the alimentary and reproductive impulses, which have formed a part of the biological heritage of all human beings, have not been altruized, socialized, and spiritualized. "In either case," he says, "a faulty equipment has come down to us through the reproductive life of the race."[19]

Theology, Rauschenbusch thought, has done much harm in concentrating upon "the biological transmission of evil," however true this insight may be in part. In so doing, theology has diverted our minds from the power of the social transmission of evil. The social channel of sin, he thought, is at least as important as the channel of biological inheritance. Indeed, it is "far more susceptible of religious influence and control. Original sin deals with dumb forces of nature; social tradition is ethical and may be affected by conscious social action."[20]

Many factors enter into the social transmission of sin. One is the human instinct of imitation, by which evil example is passed on to others. A sinful practice or custom is communicated by the authority of the social group, whose condonation or idealization of a wrong blinds its individual members to its reprehensible nature. The most potent motive for the perpetuation and transmission of sin is, however, its profitableness.

Ordinarily sin is an act of weakness and side-stepping, followed by shame the next day. But when it is the source of prolific income, it is no longer a shame-faced vagabond slinking through the dark, but an army with banners, entrenched and defiant. The bigger the dividends, the stiffer the resistance against anything that would cut them down. When fed with money, sin grows wings and claws.[21]

A grave shortcoming of individualistic theology has been its incapacity to recognize how collective groups transcend the individual person and become themselves deadly instruments of sin. Any group which wields a collective power may become the repository and agent of evil. The group may be a corporation, a trade union, a church, or a nation. The list might be endlessly extended.

It is important to realize that these "super-personal forces of evil" are seldom formed initially for evil purposes.

. . . a small corrupt group in a city council, in order to secure control, tempts the weak, conciliates and serves good men, and turns the council into a force of evil in the city; an inside ring in the police force grafts on the vice trade, and draws a part of the force into protecting crime and browbeating decent citizens; a trade union fights for the right to organize a shop, but resorts to violence and terrorizing; a trust, desiring to steady prices and to get away from antiquated competition, undersells the independents and evades or purchases legislation.[22]

Rauschenbusch believed that solidaristic conceptions of evil point to and converge upon a terrible reality, namely, the "Kingdom of Evil." It is not necessary, he believed, to hold in modern times to the conviction that the world is rife with evil spirits, or that the hosts of wickedness are led and presided over by a personal devil. Yet the traditional beliefs that there is a hereditary racial unity in sin and that there is a supernatural power of evil behind all sinful human conditions and actions point to a profound truth — that each man and all men are bound together in a solidaric and organic network of sin and guilt.[23]

This network of evil is to be interpreted in terms of both personal and social responsibility. It is to be seen, not in terms of what superhuman powers do to mankind, but in terms of the harm which men do to each other. The evil powers are social powers to which we give the names lovelessness, injustice, exploitation, and hatred. "The sin of all is in each of us, and every one of us has scattered seeds of evil, the final multiplied harvest of which no man knows." [24] By solidarity of action and spirit we enter into a solidarity of guilt. "If in the most restricted sphere of life we act on the same sinful principles of greed and tyranny on which the great exploiters and despots act, we share their guilt." [25]

SOCIAL SALVATION

Rauschenbusch, who was interested in the vast social evils of an industrial society, was concerned also to search for their remedies in terms of a social salvation. This search was made by interpreting the Christian message in terms of social redemption.

> The new thing in the social gospel is the clearness and insistence with which it sets forth the necessity and the possibility of redeeming the historical life of humanity from the social wrongs which now pervade it and which act as temptations and incitements to evil and as forces of resistance to the powers of redemption.[26]

While Rauschenbusch considered a salvation "confined to the soul and its personal interests" an imperfect and inadequate salvation, it would be unfair to him to minimize the great importance which he assigned to personal regeneration. By emphasizing the social aspects of salvation, he did not mean to denigrate the crucial value of the individual. Harry Emerson Fosdick has shown how Rauschenbusch's concern for the individual and the social environment were joined.

> As for his parish work, he expended himself with tireless dedication in the service of individuals. Despite his attack on the old "individualism," it was to persons one by one that his major interest and devotion were given. It was because he identified himself with persons that he cared so intensely about what an evil social order was doing to them. It was because personality was to him the supreme treasure that he wanted so passionately a juster, more co-operative society which would help fulfill personality's possibilities. So for him personal and social Christianity were blended; they were one gospel indivisible. When he attacked corrupt politics, teamed up with Jacob Riis to secure playgrounds, fresh-air centers, decent housing, helped organize the Brotherhood of the Kingdom to give voice to the Christian revolt against social wrongs, and in sermons, lectures, articles pleaded for a more socialized, co-operative economic order as against the cut-throat, laissez-faire competition which then prevailed, he counted himself as much a Christian evangelist as when he proclaimed to individuals, "Ye must be born again." [27]

Rauschenbusch always considered his work to be that of a Christian evangelist.[28] His concept of evangelism included the regeneration of individual persons *and* the salvation of society. The social gospel and the individual gospel were not two gospels. They were two phases of the one gospel. The gospel in its social dimension, Rauschenbusch thought, had been tragically neglected.[29] Personal salvation is not an experience of an atomistic individual, standing alone before God. Genuine salvation "turns a man from self to God and humanity." [30] "Salvation is the voluntary social-izing of the soul." [31]

Rauschenbusch was intrigued by the classical passage on regener-ation in John 3. Here personal regeneration is closely bound with the kingdom hope.[32] The converted man is the man who henceforth makes the kingdom of God his life and his goal. Like-wise, faith, as set forth by Paul, was not a subscription to a rigid doctrinal creed, or submission to the teaching of the church. It was rather "expectancy and confidence in the coming salvation of God." [33]

> It is faith to assume that this is a good world and that life is worth living. It is faith to assert the feasibility of a fairly righteous and fraternal social order. In the midst of a despotic and predatory industrial life it is faith to stake our business future on the proposition that fairness, kindness, and fraternity will work. When war inflames a nation, it is faith to believe that a peaceable disposition is a workable international policy. Amidst the dis-unity of Christendom it is faith to look for unity and to express unity in action. It is faith to see God at work in the world and to claim a share in his job. Faith is an energetic act of the will, affirming our fellowship with God and man, declaring our solidarity with the Kingdom of God, and repudiating selfish isolation.[34]

As regeneration and faith have social content and implications, so does sanctification, that process of transformation and educa-tion by which the human personality is made a more willing and effective agent of Christ. Personal sanctification, Rauschenbusch believed, "must serve the Kingdom of God." Therefore, any Chris-tian asceticism or mysticism which isolates the Christian from re-deeming labor among his fellowmen is "dangerous religion." [35]

Rauschenbusch believed that a strategy for bringing redemption to the social order would have to deal with the salvation of the "super-personal forces" which historically have been massive de-positories of evil. In *Christianizing the Social Order,* Rauschen-busch noted that certain of these "super-personal forces" in Amer-ican society have been "Christianized." When he discussed "the Christianized sections of our social order," however, he did not mean that the family, the church, the school, and the state had attained a state of Christian perfection. He meant that they had come under the suasion of Christian influences, to which they had been measurably and markedly responsive.[36] Doubtless he was too optimistic concerning the outlook for a continued progress of their "Christianization."

When he turned to the workings of the capitalistic system, how-ever, Rauschenbusch saw little evidence of the influence of Chris-tianity.

It is in commerce and industry that we encounter the great collective in-humanities that shame our Christian feeling, such as child labor and the bloody total of industrial accidents. Here we find the friction between great classes of men which makes whole communities hot with smoldering hate or sets them ablaze with lawlessness. To commerce and industry we are learning to trace the foul stream of sex prostitution, poverty, and political corruption.

Business life is the unregenerate section of our social order. If by some magic it could be plucked out of our total social life in all its raw selfish-ness, and isolated on an island unmitigated by any other factors of our life, that island would immediately become the object of a great foreign mission crusade for all Christendom.[37]

The massive indictment which Rauschenbusch leveled against the evils of the capitalistic system cannot be discussed in detail here. This indictment, amplified in *Christianizing the Social Order,* was renewed on a smaller scale in *A Theology for the Social Gospel.* The effectiveness of capitalism in the production of wealth, he said, is of course unquestioned. But so is its effective-ness in the production of "human wreckage."

Its one-sided control of economic power tempts to exploitation and oppres-sion; it directs the productive process of society primarily toward the crea-tion of private profit rather than the service of human needs; it demands autocratic management and strengthens the autocratic principle in all social affairs; it has impressed a materialistic spirit on our whole civilization.[38]

Rauschenbusch's critique of capitalism was made upon the basis of socialistic positions. Rauschenbusch was never a member of the socialist party, although he referred to himself upon occa-sion as a Christian socialist. He was not a Marxian socialist, how-ever. He rejected the revolutionary methods, the materialism, the atheism, and the dogmatism of the Marxists.

In keeping with his socialist beliefs, Rauschenbusch advocated government ownership of natural resources, the public ownership of railroads, communication systems, waterways, and gas and elec-tric power; he believed in breaking up the accumulations of mas-sive wealth by a steeply graded inheritance tax; he believed that the income derived from publicly owned wealth and services should be used to promote the welfare of the public in the exten-sion of education, libraries, museums, parks, playgrounds, and the like. Labor legislation, he thought, should carefully protect the working people by maintaining living wages, shortening working hours, improving the sanitary and safety conditions of laborers, preventing child labor, and restricting female labor. He believed in labor organization, in social insurance, in pensions for the aged, and in pure food and drug laws.[39]

Rauschenbusch's dissatisfaction with capitalism was responsibly considered; his support of socialist measures of correction was not doctrinaire. To him the test of any social institution or system was its conformity to the law of the kingdom of God.

> The fundamental step of repentance and conversion for professions and organizations is to give up monopoly power and the incomes derived from legalized extortion, and to come under the law of service, content with a fair income for honest work. The corresponding step in the case of governments and political oligarchies, both in monarchies and in capitalistic semi-democracies, is to submit to real democracy. Therewith they step out of the Kingdom of Evil into the Kingdom of God.[40]

The tendency of liberalism to slight the importance of the church in its interpretation of the Christian message is also to be seen in Rauschenbusch. He had a keen awareness of the weaknesses and shortcomings of the institutional church. His ideas of the church were free-church in character. He seems to have had little concern for church polity. Yet he called the church "the social factor of salvation."

He paid tribute to the church for its preservation, in certain historical periods, of the spiritual treasures of mankind, including those of education, history, art, music, and philosophy. The church nourished and passed on the great ideals of the spiritual life concerning God, the soul, sin, duty, and holiness — ideals which would have been lost if the church had not preserved them.[41] The church has come into contact with God through the living memory of its Lord and through the continuing fellowship which ever finds Jesus Christ as its center. Thus, "the new life of the individual is mediated by the social organism which is already in possession of that life." [42] The saving power of the church does not depend upon its institutional forms, upon its ministry, its doctrine, or its impeccable historical continuity, but upon the presence of the kingdom of God within it. "The saving qualities of the Church depend on the question whether it has translated the personal life of Jesus Christ into the social life of its group and thus brings it to bear on the individual." [43]

THE KINGDOM OF GOD

To Rauschenbusch, the kingdom of God is itself the social gospel. The doctrine of the kingdom is the central doctrine of Christian theology, the very "marrow of the gospel." [44] Salvation is to be understood in terms of the kingdom.

Rauschenbusch thought that the doctrine of the kingdom of God had become so attenuated and weakened through vast periods of Christian history that disastrous consequences had followed.

"Traditional theology and the mind of Jesus Christ became incommensurable quantities." [45] The ethical principles of Jesus disappeared from Christian ethics. As the kingdom diminished in Christian recognition, the church superseded it. The sacramental and the priestly took the place of the kingdom's fight for righteousness and justice. When the church was exalted to be the supreme good, the supremacy of the church over the state was asserted. The church lost the norm and conscience of its own life, with "no conditions and obligations to test and balance" its claims. The revolutionary power of the kingdom gave way to the reactionary influence of the church. The forces of democracy and social justice were denied a religious backing in the world and became secular. Secular life itself was lowered in status below the religious realm, and thereby became less important. Christian theology, in its loss of the doctrine of the kingdom, lost its fire and its "boundless horizons." [46]

The kingdom of God is "divine in its origin, progress, and consummation." It was founded by Christ and is sustained by the Holy Spirit. The doctrine of the kingdom therefore relates our moral actions to our faith, and it gives those actions a religious quality. The kingdom sets out the objectives, aims, and spirit of the Christian religion and furnishes flexible but definite norms for the Christian life. It is always present and future, the eternal in the midst of time, "the energy of God realizing itself in human life." It is always impinging upon the present, always coming, always "big with possibility," always demanding action.

The kingdom of God is "humanity organized according to the will of God." Its subjects in the world fight for the freest and highest development of human personality, whose divine worth has been revealed by Christ. It fights for a progressive reign of love in human life and society, and it fights against any system of social organization or exploitation which denies human brotherhood. It seeks the progressive unity of mankind in a fellowship which preserves individual freedom and "the opportunity of nations to work out their own national peculiarities and ideals." The kingdom, far from being superseded by the church, is the end and aim of the church's existence. It is the church's task and responsibility, therefore, to interpret salvation, whose agent it is in the world, in the light of the nature and goals of the kingdom. Lastly, the kingdom of God is not confined to the church. Rather, it embraces the whole life of man. "It is the Christian transfiguration of the social order." [47]

THE DOCTRINE OF CHRIST

Since the chief interest of social Christianity is the kingdom of God, advocates of the social gospel "want to see the Christ who initiated the Kingdom of God." [48] Rauschenbusch felt that the social viewpoint upon Christianity made many of the speculative problems of christological dogma seem remote or superfluous. The problem of the social gospel is not how the divine and human natures can be united in one person, but how "the divine life of Christ can get control of human society." [49] It is the problem of social salvation.

Christology is to be viewed in terms of the purpose which shaped Christ's life and ministry, and for which he died — the kingdom of God. The social gospel "would have more interest in basing the divine quality of his personality on free and ethical acts of his will than in dwelling on the passive inheritance of a divine essence." [50]

The great failing of traditional Christology is that Jesus does not appear in it to be a true personality. He appears merely as a part of a scheme of salvation, "the second premise in a great syllogism."[51] Consequently, the things which Jesus himself was passionately interested in have been left aside in conventional Christianity.

Jesus lived his life in loving communion with God. Thus he "set love into the centre of the spiritual universe, and all life is illuminated from that centre." [52] And thus the reign of God in his kingdom was a reign in which all human life was to be bound in a universal fellowship of love, righteousness, and justice.

What Jesus achieved in his own person permeated and penetrated the fellowship of his followers. "What was personal with him became social within the group of the disciples. His life became a collective and assimilating force and current of historic tradition." [53]

Jesus brought the kingdom of God into the world not as a concept or ideal merely, but as a living force. It is a power in history, present, moving, dynamic, fighting evil, redeeming men individually, and redeeming the social structures which shape human life.[54]

THE DOCTRINE OF GOD

Sin and redemption, considered in the framework of social change, are the acknowledged themes with which Rauschenbusch sought to deal in his search for a reconstruction of theology. He sought to suggest, however, how the social gospel would influence the doctrines of God, of the Holy Spirit, of inspiration, of the sacraments, of eschatology, and of the atonement. Several of these topics will now be dealt with briefly.

Rauschenbusch pointed out that the social relations in which men have lived have exercised a determinative influence upon their ideas of God. When men have lived under despotic regimes, for example, they have thought of God as a despot. If God is an autocrat, then tyrannical power and arbitrary decision in God are to be expected. "This spiritual influence of despotism made even the face of Christ seem hard and stern." [55]

In a famous passage, Rauschenbusch described what Jesus did to change the human conception of God.

> When he took God by the hand and called him "our Father," he democratized the conception of God. He disconnected the idea from the coercive and predatory State, and transferred it to the realm of family life, the chief social embodiment of solidarity and love. He not only saved humanity; he saved God. He gave God his first chance of being loved and of escaping from the worst misunderstandings conceivable. . . . We have classified theology as Greek and Latin, as Catholic and Protestant. It is time to classify it as despotic and democratic.[56]

In the course of Christian history, Jesus' understanding of God the Father has been repeatedly distorted and obscured. The aim of the social gospel is to bring back Jesus' understanding of God and to put it to work in human affairs. Modern men can believe in this kind of God as "their chief fellow-worker, the source of their energies, the ground of their hopes." [57] There are some, Rauschenbusch thought, who "would be willing to think of God as less than omnipotent and omniscient if only he were working hard with us for that Kingdom which is the only true Democracy." [58]

The kingdom toward which God and his children are working together is a kingdom of justice. Rauschenbusch left unresolved the theoretical question concerning how a good God could permit the suffering of the innocent. To explain suffering merely on the supposition that it is the reward of sin, or an instrument of divine chastisement, is not an explanation but a form of "dope" which is used to narcotize the restless questionings of innocent sufferers. God is a fighter for the relief of the sufferings of oppressed masses. He is opposed to the status quo in a social system which lines the pockets of the few while wrecking the lives of multitudes.[59]

The kingdom for which God and his children are working is also a kingdom of brotherhood. While religion is ordinarily used to sanction the bond of social groups which regard all other groups intolerantly, the Christian religion in its pure form insists that all races and social groups belong to a common humanity and are beloved creatures of one God. The God who is the breaker of barriers has committed to those who have had a Christian experience the task of expanding human fellowship by the breaking down of barriers between men.[60]

THE HOLY SPIRIT

The work of the Holy Spirit frequently has been interpreted as belonging to the most private and mystical traffic of the soul with God. Actually, the social nature of religious experience is shown decidedly in the work of the Holy Spirit. Prophets and apostles were not persons who stood in lonely isolation before God. Rather, they spoke for groups of men and women who have now receded into oblivion, but who shared the Spirit with the prophets and apostles. Pentecost was significant, not for the number who received the Spirit, but for the fact that the Holy Spirit became the common property of the group.

Rauschenbusch became manifestly impatient with the view which restricts the doctrine of inspiration to the Holy Spirit's inspiration of the pages of the Scriptures. The historical-critical study of the Bible has made a valuable contribution by endeavoring to uncover the social background and the conditioning environment of the inspired personalities of biblical history. The enterprise of historical-critical study does not derogate from the divine inspiration of the outstanding figures of the Bible but rather shows that the inspiring work of God extends beyond them to nameless men and women who comprised the prophetic circles in which the great prophets lived and moved.

Traditional Christianity has done a disservice in seeking to limit inspiration to the words of a book, and to stamp the imprimatur of infallibility upon the biblical text. Primarily, it was men whom God inspired, not books. And the Holy Spirit still inspires men. The view that inspiration communicates infallible truth to the minds of fallible men is itself a curious error. The Holy Spirit still speaks through the Sacred Book, but "to suppose that we can work out a living knowledge of the truth from a sacred book without the enlightening energy of the spirit of God is sub-christian and rationalistic." [61]

BAPTISM AND THE LORD'S SUPPER

Rauschenbusch clearly was not sympathetic with views which

confer saving properties upon the sacraments or which relate the sacraments' validity or efficacy to the administration of a special ministerial class. Baptism is an act of dedication to a religious and social movement — to the spirit and aims of the kingdom of God. Baptism

> . . . has always been an exit and an entrance; why not the exit from the Kingdom of Evil and the entrance into the Kingdom of God? That would, under right teaching and with the right people, give it solemn impressiveness. It would make it a truly Christian act. Baptism has always been dogged by superstitions, and thrust down into paganism. The individualistic interpretation of it as an escape from damnation tainted it with selfishness. Contact with the kingdom of God would restore baptism to its original ethical and spiritual purity.[62]

Likewise, the Lord's Supper should be a celebration not only of the Lord's death, but also of his life in the fellowship of men.

> In the Lord's Supper we re-affirm our supreme allegiance to our Lord who taught us to know God as our common father and to realize that all men are our brethren. In the midst of a world full of divisive selfishness we thereby accept brotherhood as the ruling principle of our life and undertake to put it into practice in our private and public activities. We abjure the selfish use of power and wealth for the exploitation of our fellows. We dedicate our lives to establishing the Kingdom of God and to winning mankind to its laws. In contemplation of the death of our Lord we accept the possibility of risk and loss as our share of service. We link ourselves to his death and accept the obligation of the cross.[63]

ESCHATOLOGY

Rauschenbusch took note of the fact that traditional eschatology is a mosaic containing fragments of non-Christian and pre-Christian systems, combined with genuine Christian ideas. What has authority for us, he believed, "is the ethical and religious light of men who had an immediate consciousness of the living God, and saw him now and hereafter acting for righteousness, for the vindication of the oppressed classes, and for the purging of the social life of the nation." [64]

Both caution and sanity are needed in the interpretation of the Christian eschatological hope. Even so, this hope is an indispensable part of the Christian faith. Eschatology should be interpreted in the framework of the kingdom of God and with the mind of Christ as the criterion of interpretation.

With the character of the kingdom in mind, it is apparent that eschatology has both a this-worldly and an other-worldly reference. That is to say, the Christian faith dreams of and works for a social order upon this earth which will bind men into a fellowship of brotherhood

. . . for a social order in which the worth and freedom of every least human being will be honoured and protected; in which the brotherhood of man will be expressed in the common possession of the economic resources of society; and in which the spiritual good of humanity will be set high above the private profit interests of all materialistic groups. We hope for such an order for humanity as we hope for heaven for ourselves.[65]

Eschatology also looks to a life to come. Rauschenbusch lightly dismissed the doctrine of purgatory. The doctrine of hell fared little better. The doctrine of hell was tolerable only when God was thought to be an autocratic sovereign ruling over his subjects. It became intolerable when men found God to be a Father dealing with his children.

All the most Christian souls in heaven would get down there and share the life of the wicked, in the high hope that after all some scintilla of heavenly fire was still smouldering and could be fanned into life. And they would be headed by Him who could not stand it to think of ninety-nine saved and one caught among the thorns.[66]

Heaven will be a place where incomplete personalities will grow in spiritual stature, where love and service and labor will mark the fellowship which was all too imperfect on earth.

THE DOCTRINE OF ATONEMENT

Rauschenbusch ended his *Theology for the Social Gospel* with a chapter on the atonement. His discussion is interesting and significant.

It is apparent that he was dissatisfied with the principal theories by which this doctrine has been elaborated. Many of the fundamental terms and ideas of these theories, he said, like "satisfaction," "substitution," "imputation," and "merit," represent post-biblical concepts and are alien to the spirit of Christianity.[67]

Rauschenbusch observed that the historic interpretations of the doctrine of the atonement were heavily influenced by the social and political realities and structures which existed at their time of origin. Since his own era, he thought, was dominated by ideas of personality and social solidarity, he believed that any reinterpretation of the atonement should take account of these ideas.

His first inquiry was to ask how Jesus bore the sins of mankind. His answer was that Jesus in his own experience felt the brutal and crushing weight of the six great public sins of organized society, "great permanent evils which have blighted the life of the race and of every individual in it." [68] These were religious bigotry, the combination of graft and political power, the corruption of justice, mob spirit and mob action, militarism, and class contempt. Though Jesus did not contribute to these sins, he really and personally bore their impact upon his body and soul. Since we have all repeated the sins which killed Jesus, we are linked with all other men in a solidarity of guilt.[69]

Rauschenbusch was careful not to isolate the death of Jesus from his life, and by so doing to assign prime significance to the former. His life and death had the same significance — the fulfillment of the will of God and the initiation of the kingdom of God. His death was the culminating point of his life, a "focus-point of blazing light," in which the character and purpose of his life stood revealed.

Rauschenbusch asked: How can the death of Christ be said to have affected God? We cannot conceive that the sacrifice of Christ changed the mind of God toward man from an attitude of antagonism to one of love. Yet because we have to think of God in a human way, it is legitimate for us to say that the manifestation of the love and purpose of God which Christ effected on the plane of history was a meaningful experience to God the Father — an experience purposed and cherished by the Father himself.[70]

Rauschenbusch's view of the atonement stands closer to the Moral Influence Theory than to any other prominent theory. The atonement affected men, he said, primarily in two ways: First, it was the conclusive demonstration of the power of sin in human life. Second, it was the supreme revelation of love.[71]

> Thus the death of Christ was the conclusive and effective expression of the love of Jesus Christ for God and man, and his complete devotion to the Kingdom of God. The more his personality was understood to be the full and complete expression of the character of God, the more did his death become the assurance and guarantee that God loves us, forgives us, and is willing to do all things to save us.[72]

Jesus starkly illuminated God's attitude toward sin, and he adopted that attitude as his own. He showed that God bears our sin while loving us and that he resists that sin with the sovereign opposition of a love which expresses itself in the cross.[73] By his own sacrifice, Christ drew others into the circle of the holy and loving will of God, "so that they too freely loved God and appropriated his will as their own."[74]

The important point is that the moral influence theme is in the thought of Rauschenbusch socialized. The redeemed live out in the world the self-giving, self-sacrificing life which Christ lived in the world. Thus they embody in the world's life-structures what Rauschenbusch liked to call "prophetic religion."

> The prophet is always the predestined advance agent of the Kingdom of God. His religion flings him as a fighter and protester against the Kingdom of Evil. His sense of justice, compassion, and solidarity sends him into tasks which would be too perilous for others. . . . The cross of Christ put God's approval on the sacrificial impulse in the hearts of the brave, and dignified it by connecting it with one of the central dogmas of our faith. The cross has become the motive and the method of noble personalities.[75]

WALTER RAUSCHENBUSCH AS A BAPTIST

Rauschenbusch was definitely a free churchman both by instinct and theological conviction. He was prejudiced against sacerdotalism, hierarchicalism, priesthood, and priestcraft. He had few words of approval for the Roman Catholic church and seemed to prefer the radical sects of the Reformation to the great reformers. Of the sects, for example, he said, with apparent approval:

> They all tended toward the same type, the type of primitive Christianity. Strong fraternal feeling, simplicity and democracy of organization, more or less communistic ideas about property, an attitude of passive obedience or conscientious objection toward the coercive and militaristic governments of the time, opposition to the selfish and oppressive Church, a genuine faith in the practicability of the ethics of Jesus and, as the secret power in it all, belief in an inner experience of regeneration and an inner light which interprets the outer word of God. . . . Their communities were prophetic. They have been the forerunners of the modern world.[76]

Rauschenbusch became a very influential member of the liberal wing of the Northern Baptist Convention. He made his influence felt not only through his writings, but also through the pulpit and the platform. The Baptist Congress, an unofficial denominational forum which held its first meeting in 1882, featured many young Baptist ministers who were articulate spokesmen for social Christianity. Rauschenbusch occupied its platform first in 1888. Other Baptists whose social interest was marked were also heard from, such as Leighton Williams, Samuel Zane Batten, Shailer Mathews, Charles R. Henderson, E. B. Andrews, Norman Fox, P. S. Moxom, Francis Wayland, and W. H. P. Faunce.[77]

The Brotherhood of the Kingdom, a small fellowship of friends who were interested in the social gospel, originated in the late 1880's with three young Baptist ministers — Rauschenbusch, Leighton Williams, and Nathaniel Schmidt, the last named of whom became a famous Old Testament scholar. In the course of time, the fellowship was enlarged and many men of other denominations came into it. Many of the leaders of social Christianity were brought into contact with this influential fellowship. Writing to the group in 1907 while he and Mrs. Rauschenbusch were in Europe, Rauschenbusch made the following illuminating comments about what the Brotherhood of the Kingdom had stood for:

> I am impressed with the amazing changes in public thought since the Brotherhood was founded. All those things for which we then stood, according to our light, have come to the front and fill more and more of the horizon, like a hill toward which an express train is running. We stood for Christian union, and today that sentiment has spread so that kindred groups of churches are coalescing by formal vote, and what is so conservative and tenacious of its corporate identity as a church body? We stood for an historical study of the Bible, and today that method is triumphant among all Biblical scholars, and reactionary movements against it show that at every point how completely they rest on the inertia of past convictions only. We stood for purer politics, for the abolition of privilege, for the rights of the people against the corporations, and today the United States are moving with almost revolutionary speed toward a new political era. We stood—though not unanimously—for Christian socialism, and today that is capturing the heart of the intellectual and moral aristocracy of our people. We stood for the pre-eminence of the Kingdom of God in Christian thought, and thereby—perhaps more than we realized—tended to substitute a power, more ethical, more synoptic, of a more Christian type of doctrine for the old "scheme" of salvation, and all theology is drifting that way.[78]

It is clear that Rauschenbusch was a very independent Baptist who made little effort indeed to follow a denominational party line. He was a devout Christian and a good churchman; yet it would appear that denominational affairs were not at the center of his personal interests. Occasionally, as a professor in a Baptist seminary, he came under fire from more conservative individuals in the denomination and even from members of the board of trustees of Rochester Seminary. In each case, he was defended staunchly by his president, Augustus Hopkins Strong, a noted theologian in his own right, who held for Rauschenbusch both a devoted personal friendship and a deep respect for him as a scholar, teacher, and thinker.[79]

The series of articles which Rauschenbusch wrote under the title "Why I Am a Baptist" uniquely illuminates his Baptist convictions and is, in the words of S. L. Stealey, *"one of the best statements ever written on our distinctive principles."* [80]

Rauschenbusch acknowledged that he was a Baptist because his father was a Baptist before him. However, he had come to be a Baptist by conviction, and "could not well be anything else." [81] Beyond this accident of cultural and family heritage which made him a Baptist were three determinative reasons.

The first was that "the Christian faith as Baptists hold it sets spiritual experience boldly to the front as the one great thing in religion." [82] Baptist churches are composed upon the basis of the Christian experience of their members. Baptism of believers is practiced, not to insist upon a mere external form, but to protest the emptiness of any external form which has no experience to back it up. A prerequisite to admission to the Baptist ministry is the Christian experience of conversion. Baptists also want to know of their ministers whether they have received a call of God to the ministry. This is another example of Baptist insistence that a personal experience with God is a necessary qualification for Christian service.[83]

To make personal experience the "only essential thing in religion," is not to minimize rituals, creeds, and forms as important parts of church life. It is only to insist that these should grow out of a vital religious experience and should be organs of its expression.[84] "I am a Baptist, then," said Rauschenbusch, "because in our church life we have a minimum of emphasis on ritual and creed, and a maximum of emphasis on spiritual experience, and the more I study the history of religion, the more I see how great and fruitful such a position is." [85]

The second reason he was a Baptist, Rauschenbusch affirmed, was because Baptists embody Christian social principles in their church organization. This is not to say that Baptist church organization is perfect, for in many ways it is faulty and "creaks and groans as it works along." [86] But among the noble guidelines of its life, the following may be mentioned:

1. Baptist organizational life attempts to create an organization of people who are genuinely Christian. Its membership is voluntary, the main term of membership being that one has met Christ and loves him.

2. Baptist churches are democracies. This means that the church membership itself is sovereign, under God. Although there is room for everyone to make his own contribution in the church, authority is held by the whole congregation.

3. Baptist churches have no priestly class. There is no essential difference between the minister and the layman. The sharp line of demarcation is not between the ministry and the laity, but between the church and the world.

4. There is no hierarchy in the Baptist ministry. This polity allows for a genuine fraternity in the ministry, while allowing room also for differing capacities for leadership, different levels of piety, insight, etc., which the fraternity may freely recognize and honor.

5. Although Baptist churches have home rule, the sovereignty

of each church in its own affairs does not hinder free association with other churches, whenever the membership deem these attachments to be needed and wise.

6. Baptist churches decline all formal alliances with the state. This means that they accept no dictation from the state in spiritual matters. The state should allow the churches to work with moral and spiritual problems which extend beyond the right and competence of the state. Also, the state should be free in its own sphere from the pressures of ecclesiastical politics.

Of these six principles, Rauschenbusch freely admitted that Baptist churches have not lived up to them. It is, however, "a great thing for a body of churches to have embodied such advanced Christian principles in their very constitution, even if individually or collectively they drop below them." [87]

The third reason for his being a Baptist Rauschenbusch connected with the Baptist view of worship. This view holds to a simplicity and directness of worship, which minimizes "holy places, holy times, holy formulas, holy experts" and maximizes direct fellowship with God and love for our fellows. "To become a disciple of Jesus means to learn to think of God and live with him as Jesus did, and to let all life be transformed by that new knowledge and faith." [88] By being a Baptist, Rauschenbusch thought, "I can help to bring humanity to that simple, ethical, spiritual worship which Jesus taught and which has been so sadly overlaid by the gilded and jeweled worship of a paganized church." [89]

To Rauschenbusch, creedalism was a denial of the freedom which should characterize faith and worship. Many denominations of Christendom have assumed the burden of subscription to ancient formulas, liturgies, and creeds. In this way they have stifled freedom and forestalled Christian growth. "It is fatal to make the religious thought of one age binding for a later age." [90]

Baptists have refused to adopt an authoritative creed. They have insisted that the Bible alone is their sufficient authority for faith and practice. "The strength of a creed is in its uniformity and its tight fit; the beauty of the Bible is in its marvelous variety and richness. A creed imposes a law and binds thought; the Bible imparts a spirit and awakens thought." [91] Although many Baptists have of course vitiated the Bible by making it a lawbook and a collection of proof texts, this use is not observed by those who have caught the true spirit of the Scriptures. "Baptists, in tying to the New Testament, have hitched their chariot to a star, and they will have to keep moving." [92]

One of the most challenging points in the way Rauschenbusch stated his Baptist convictions is the spacious horizon in which he placed them.

I do not want to make Baptists shut themselves up in their little clam-shells and be indifferent to the ocean outside of them. I am a Baptist, but I am more than a Baptist. All things are mine; whether Francis of Assisi, or Luther, or Knox, or Wesley; all are mine because I am Christ's. The old Adam is a strict denominationalist; the new Adam is just a Christian.[93]

CONCLUSION

World War I, during which Rauschenbusch died a troubled and saddened man, did a great deal to diminish the optimism, good will, and confidence in progress which had found expression in the social gospel. The social gospel was relentlessly opposed by conservatives of both the economic and theological camps. The tendency of the movement's left wing was to veer in the direction of humanism and certainly to lose the balance between evangelical Christianity and social concern which Rauschenbusch had always been careful to preserve. Neoorthodox theologians in later years criticized the social gospel for being overly optimistic about history, for tending toward humanism, for emphasizing God's immanence at the expense of his "otherness," for being theologically shallow, and for lacking a realistic comprehension of the human problem.[94]

Although Rauschenbusch's optimism about the future of the social gospel has proved to be unjustified, he retains at least the distinction of making what Kenneth Cauthen called "the classic statement of the social gospel." He was, says Reinhold Niebuhr, the "most brilliant and generally satisfying exponent" of social Christianity.[95]

During the first two decades of the twentieth century, Rauschenbusch, more than any other person, made American Christians aware of the abuses, injustices, and miseries arising out of the industrial revolution, and aware also of the relevance of the Christian message to them. More than any other leader, he guided a large segment of his own denomination into a lasting social concern. He was, as his biographer, Dores R. Sharpe, called him, "a great, good man." His prophetic stature has been little diminished by the passage of time. He remains a bright ornament in the history of the Baptists.

9 - MARTIN LUTHER KING, JR.-
Civil Rights Martyr

Martin Luther King, Jr., was one of the principal leaders in the struggle for civil rights as this struggle developed in the United States near the middle of the present century. This chapter will be devoted largely to an examination of his theological and ethical views in their bearing upon the massive problems in race relations to which King addressed himself. We shall attempt first to look at the social and historical context in which King's life and work were carried on.

THE CIVIL RIGHTS STRUGGLE

In 1944 Gunnar Myrdal wrote in his great study *The American Dilemma* that the race problem in the United States was on "the minds and consciences" of Americans. From the perspective of a quarter of a century later, Myrdal's observation would seem to have been unduly sanguine, for, in one third of the states in 1944, Negroes were not allowed to benefit from the advantages of the best schools, parks, and restaurants. They were made to sit in the rear of buses and in segregated railroad cars, and they could not vote in primary elections. Both in the North and in the South, they were employed largely in menial jobs. They served in segregated units of the armed forces. They were not permitted to sit down at a drugstore lunch counter or to view a movie in any of the downtown theaters in the nation's capital, Washington, D.C.

Ten years later, the situation had brightened somewhat. President Truman had ordered an end to segregation in the armed forces. A decision of the Supreme Court had made mandatory the integration of the public schools of the United States with all "deliberate speed." This ruling was especially portentous for seventeen southern states and the District of Columbia, in which the public schools had continued to operate on a segregated basis.

In 1954, despite considerable progress made during the previous decade, Negroes continued to suffer discrimination in voting, employment, housing, transportation, and in all the amenities which belong to a truly democratic society. Congress had not passed a civil rights bill in seventy-five years, and the lack of political action in the civil rights area reflected a profound apathy on the part of the American public.

Since 1954 the racial problem in the United States has received increasing attention. Several civil rights laws have been enacted by Congress, thus focusing the weight of federal authority upon questions of discrimination against the Negro. Segregation in buses and railroad cars has virtually ended. The issue of segregation in the public schools, though subject to evasive and delaying tactics, has been forced to the forefront of consideration all over the country. There has been a sharp increase in Negro political power, in both North and South. Rank discrimination is still practiced in all sections of the nation, but the Negro has found his voice and has subjected discriminatory practices to sharp, and many times effective, criticism and pressure.

In the meantime, the ferment, tension, and tumult which have arisen from the racial problem have been attended by great bitterness, as militant extremists both black and white have widened the rift between the races. The Negro struggle for better jobs, better education, and better housing — for indeed the full rights of American citizenship — goes on. At long last, perhaps the country is awakening to the fact that the great internal problem of the nation is the problem of race.

Daniel Thompson has pointed out in his book *The Negro Leadership Class* that the struggle for his rights has caused the Negro in the United States to develop three Negro leadership types: the "Uncle Tom," the "racial diplomat," and the "race man."[1] The "Uncle Tom" pattern characterized Negro leadership in the post-Reconstruction South. This kind of leader conformed to the leadership pattern expected by the whites. The "Uncle Tom" curried favor with the whites and was forced to come to terms with a second-class citizenship for the Negro race. He represented no real freedom of decision for the black race, no genuine power base distinct from that granted by the whites. His position was one of subserviency and accommodation.

The "racial diplomat" was, on the contrary, a Negro leader who was concerned with equal rights and equal dignity for his people. He was, however, also concerned to estimate the needs and rights of his own race in the context of the needs and rights of the whole American community. One of his main themes, therefore, was that of interracial cooperation for the good of the whole society.

The "race man" Negro leader also demands complete rights for Negro citizens in American society. In order to appeal to the pride of the Negro people, however, he is disposed to emphasize the worth and value of blackness. He regards himself as a champion of black rights, dedicated to improving the condition and to securing the rights of his own people by many kinds of legal and direct action. Without being a racist, he is much more active and militant for Negro rights than was the "racial diplomat."

The transition from the "Uncle Tom" to the "racial diplomat" type of leadership occurred in the early 1900's, when W. E. B. Du Bois began to attack the leadership of Booker T. Washington. The change from the "racial diplomat" to the "race man" pattern of leadership occurred about a half century later, when leaders like Roy Wilkins, Whitney Young, Martin Luther King, Jr., James Farmer, and Floyd McKissick emerged upon the American racial scene.[2]

Negro leaders of the recent past and of the present generally belong to the "race man" pattern, but this fact does not mean that the crisis in Negro leadership has become less acute. The debate which has transpired between the membership and the leaders of SNCC (Student Nonviolent Coordinating Committee), CORE (Congress on Racial Equality), SCLC (Southern Christian Leadership Conference), NAACP (National Association for the Advancement of Colored People), and the Urban League indicates a decided pluralism of interests in the Negro community itself.

To the above three types of Negro leadership should be added a fourth — the "black separatist." This type includes militant Negro leaders who have given up hope that the Negro can ever receive his rights in a white society. They believe that the United States is a white man's country and that the Negro's authentic allies are the other nations of the world which are struggling to rid themselves of the incubus of white oppression. These leaders appeal to strong anti-white sentiments in the Negro community. The late Malcolm X was an advocate of black separatism. Stokely Carmichael and Rap Brown have also been militant separatists.

The positions of militant leaders have aroused considerable anxiety among the leaders of the "race man" type. The latter have attacked the racism of the militants and have urged that American society must provide for whites and blacks to live amicably together in terms of complete equality. They renounce the disposition of the militants to repudiate the support of white moderates and white liberals in the achievement of this status for American blacks. They seek vigorously to pursue the goals of a just and equal society for all by the adoption of an intelligent legal strategy, and by the development of a moral power which will at the same time effectively challenge white prejudice and effectively arouse the black community to demand its rights.[3]

BIOGRAPHICAL SKETCH OF MARTIN LUTHER KING, JR.

Of all the civil rights leaders which have been projected upon the American scene so far in this century, Martin Luther King, Jr., is the figure of largest stature. To designate him as belonging to the "race man" pattern of Negro leadership is not to try to pigeonhole him neatly, but to identify his general position in the civil rights movement.

King was born in Atlanta, Georgia, on January 15, 1929. His father, Martin Luther King, Sr., was pastor of the Ebenezer Baptist Church in that city.

Martin, Jr., graduated from high school at the age of fifteen. In 1949 he received his B.A. degree from Morehouse College in Atlanta. He then entered Crozer Theological Seminary in Chester, Pennsylvania, and after his graduation from that institution won a fellowship to Boston University in Boston. He finished his Ph.D. degree at this school in 1955.

In 1953 King married Miss Coretta Scott, a graduate student at the New England Conservatory of Music. The Kings moved to Montgomery, Alabama, in 1954, where King became pastor of the Dexter Avenue Baptist Church.

When Mrs. Rosa Parks touched off the boycott of segregated buses in Montgomery in 1955, King assumed the leadership of the movement in the city by virtue of his election to head the Montgomery Improvement Association. By the time the boycott was called off 381 days later, King was a national figure — perhaps the best known Negro activist in the country.

In the early 1960's King maintained his leadership in civil rights activities by leading in voter registration drives and by carrying on desegregation campaigns in many localities. His showdown with the white establishment in Birmingham in 1963 was a massive confrontation of considerable importance. Later in the same year, he was a principal figure in a great integrated march on

Washington, D.C., in which perhaps 200,000 persons participated. This march was followed by the far-reaching Civil Rights Act of 1964. King's finest personal triumph also occurred in 1964, when he was called to Oslo to receive the Nobel Peace Prize.

At the very peak of his personal popularity, King's influence began to wane. When the Watts riot occurred in August, 1965, the main civil rights battlefield moved out of the South. Other inner-city riots occurred across the nation, many of them in northern cities. The influence of King, many have observed, was not transplanted easily in the northern ghettos.

The problems of the inner city, the Black Power movement, and the tragic U.S. buildup in Vietnam involved for the civil rights movement complex problems with which King was wrestling at the time of his untimely death.

In early April, 1968, King was in Memphis to aid the cause of garbage workers who were striking for higher wages. On the night of April 4 he was shot to death by an assassin's bullet at the Lorraine Motel. His tragic death made him the greatest martyr in the cause of the civil rights movement in the present century.

INTELLECTUAL PILGRIMAGE

Although King was brought up in the moderately comfortable home of his pastor father in Atlanta, early in life he became acquainted with the "varieties of injustice" in American society. He came "perilously close," he said, to resenting all white people.[4]

During his student days at Morehouse College, he was deeply impressed by Thoreau's *Essay on Civil Disobedience*. This essay was his first intellectual contact with the theory of nonviolent resistance. Early in his career at Crozer Seminary, he became acquainted with Walter Rauschenbusch's *Christianity and the Social Crisis*. Rauschenbusch made an indelible impression upon his mind in delineating a theological foundation for a Christian social concern. While he felt that Rauschenbusch had fallen victim to the nineteenth-century cult of inevitable progress, Rauschenbusch's profound insight concerning the relationship between the social and economic conditions of men, on the one hand, and their spiritual welfare on the other, made a permanent contribution to King's thinking.

During his seminary years, King also read widely in philosophy, searching through the social and ethical theories of great thinkers, such as Plato, Aristotle, Rousseau, Hobbes, Bentham, Mill, and Locke.

In 1949 he gave careful study to Karl Marx's *Das Kapital* and *The Communist Manifesto*. King rejected Marx's materialistic interpretation of history, his atheism, and his ethical relativism. He felt repelled by communism's political totalitarianism and its consequent denial of the right of individual freedom.

In certain respects, however, he found communism challenging. He was challenged by its protest against the hardship of the underprivileged. "Communism in theory," he said, "emphasized a classless society, and a concern for social justice, though the world knows from sad experience that in practice it created new classes and a new lexicon of injustice." [5] Marx sharpened King's consciousness of the gap between superfluous wealth and abject poverty, and of the consequent need for a more equitable distribution of wealth. Marx helped him to see the danger of the profit motive as the sole basis for economic life and enabled him to recognize that a capitalistic system can lead to a materialism which is just as pernicious as that of communism.

Nineteenth-century capitalism failed to see that life is social and Marxism failed and still fails to see that life is individual and personal. The Kingdom of God is neither the thesis of individual enterprise nor the antithesis of collective enterprise, but a synthesis which reconciles the truths of both.[6]

While he was a student at Crozer, King became interested in the life and thought of Gandhi. He was particularly fascinated by Gandhi's concept of Satyagrapa ("truth-force" or "love-force"). Prior to his reading of Gandhi, he had thought that the love ethic of Jesus applied only to relationships between individual persons. Gandhi convinced him that Jesus' ethic was a potent instrument for "social and collective transformation." Gandhi's principle of nonviolent resistance, King came to believe, "was the only morally and practically sound method open to oppressed people in their struggle for freedom." [7]

During his last year at Crozer, King discovered the thought of Reinhold Niebuhr. Niebuhr's critique of pacifism led King to evaluate more closely his own position in the light of his attraction to Gandhi. The weakness of Niebuhr's position, he saw, was Niebuhr's interpretation of pacifism as nonresistance to evil. Gandhi helped King to understand that true pacifism is not *nonresistance* to evil, but rather a positive, nonviolent *resistance* to evil.

Despite this disagreement, King found Niebuhr to be challenging and helpful by his extraordinary insight into human nature, by his refutation of the false optimism of liberalism and of what King considered to be the irrationalism and semi-fundamentalism of some of the neoorthodox theologians. Niebuhr also helped him to see the destructive power of sin at every level of human existence.[8]

In his graduate studies at Boston University, King came under the influence of an intellectual environment which had far-reaching effects upon his outlook. Walter Muelder and Allen Knight Chalmers were pacifists who had a passion for social justice and a deep faith in the noble potentialities of human beings. King came to believe that Niebuhr had overemphasized the corruption of human nature by making too much of sin and not enough of grace.

Studying philosophy and theology under Edgar Sheffield Brightman and L. Harold DeWolf, King found himself to be attracted permanently by the personalism of these teachers. Personal idealism, said King in 1958, "remains today my basic philosophical position."

> Personalism's insistence that only personality—finite and infinite—is ultimately real strengthened me in two convictions: it gave me metaphysical and philosophical grounding for the idea of a personal God, and it gave me a metaphysical basis for the dignity and worth of all human personality.[9]

Shortly before Dr. Brightman's death, King began with him the study of Hegel. Although he could not accept Hegel's absolute idealism, or, indeed, a number of Hegel's other ideas, Hegel's view that "truth is the whole" served to shape King's lifelong habit of looking for rational coherence in human situations. He was also permanently affected by Hegel's view that growth develops through struggle.[10]

King's ideas, of course, grew and sharpened after he left the relatively cloistered life of school to take his place in what proved to be a stormy career. Yet his career as a civil rights leader disclosed that he tenaciously adhered to many of the ideas which he had discovered in his academic life. These ideas formed the basic structure of his thought.

PRINCIPAL CONVICTIONS

Considering the fact that King was a preacher and a civil rights leader, it is not surprising that his theological views were not given systematic development in his addresses and writings. His ideas are informed by theological insight, but they reflect little concern for the technical points of theology. There is therefore little reason to try to dig out a systematic theology from his writings. Several of his theological convictions should, however, be briefly indicated, for they undergird much of his thought. The first was his belief in a personal God.

DOCTRINE OF GOD

In expressing a deeply felt personal credo, King said:

The agonizing moments through which I have passed during the last few years have . . . drawn me closer to God. More than ever before I am convinced of the reality of a personal God. True, I have always believed in the personality of God. But in the past the idea of a personal God was little more than a metaphysical category that I found theologically and philosophically satisfying. Now it is a living reality that has been validated in the experiences of everyday life. God has been profoundly real to me in recent years. In the midst of outer dangers I have felt an inner calm. In the midst of lonely days and dreary nights I have heard an inner voice saying, "Lo, I will be with you." When the chains of fear and the manacles of frustration have all but stymied my efforts, I have felt the power of God transforming the fatigue of despair into the buoyancy of hope. I am convinced that the universe is under the control of a loving purpose, and that in the struggle for righteousness man has cosmic companionship. Behind the harsh appearances of the world there is a benign power.[11]

DOCTRINE OF CHRIST

King's profoundly Christian conception of God was a central factor in his life and work. What might be called his christological interest is seldom given as explicit statement. King appears to have had the liberal's interest in Jesus as teacher and example. The revelational mission of Christ was prominent — any particular interest in a Chalcedonian Christ, who was of the "same substance" with the Father, was remote. Jesus was divine in the sense that "he was one with God in purpose. He so submitted his will to God's will that God revealed his divine plan to man through Jesus." [12] Again, King said:

Where do we find this God? In a test tube? No. Where else except in Jesus Christ, the Lord of our lives? By knowing him we know God. Christ is not only Godlike but God is Christlike. Christ is the word made flesh. He is the language of eternity translated in the words of time. If we are to know what God is like and understand his purposes for mankind, we must turn to Christ. By committing ourselves absolutely to Christ and his way, we will participate in that marvelous act of faith that will bring us to the true knowledge of God.[13]

DOCTRINE OF MAN

Man, King thought, was made in the image of God. The image of God, he said, may be interpreted in terms of fellowship, responsiveness, reason, and conscience. Man is also a sinner. He is a sinner not only individually but also collectively. Acknowledging his indebtedness to a Niebuhrian theme, King said:

Man collectivized in the group, the tribe, the race, and the nation often sinks to levels of barbarity unthinkable even among lower animals. We see the tragic expression of Immoral Society in the doctrine of white supremacy which plunges millions of black men into the abyss of exploitation and in the horrors of two world wars which have left battlefields drenched with blood, national debts higher than mountains of gold, men psychologically deranged and physically handicapped, and nations of widows and orphans. Man is a sinner in need of God's forgiving grace.[14]

King believed that human evil was attributable about as much to man's stupidity as to his deliberate badness. "If American democracy gradually disintegrates," he said, "it will be due as much to a lack of insight as to a lack of commitment to right." [15] The stupidity of man is derived not merely from a lack of information, however. It is due also to a tragic misuse of freedom. "The call for intelligence is a call for openmindedness, sound judgment, and love for truth. It is a call for men to rise above the stagnation of closed-mindedness and the paralysis of gullibility." [16]

King's high estimate of man's capacity for good marks him as a true liberal in his view of man. The high destiny of man is shown by man's ability to cooperate with God in the overthrow of evil and in the achievement of God's will for human life.

Moral victory will come as God fills man and man opens his life by faith to God, even as the gulf opens to the overflowing waters of the river. Racial justice, a genuine possibility in our nation and in the world, will come neither by our frail and often misguided efforts nor by God imposing his will on wayward men, but when enough people open their lives to God and allow him to pour his triumphant, divine energy into their souls.[17]

King's most distinctive interest may be termed ethical in nature, since it was directed toward the goal of a political and social community in which the basic human rights of all men, and particularly those of the black race, would be achieved. This kind of community must be realized, he thought, because its realization is the will of God. It must be achieved because the divinely intended destiny of man is frustrated without its fulfillment. It *can* be achieved because, despite the crippling effects of human evil, man still possesses the capacity for cooperating with God in the building of a just society.

LOVE

A basic ingredient of such a society is love. The love which King advocated as an instrument of social transformation was not a shallow preachment but a potent force. The story of the Montgomery bus boycott, King asserted, was the story of "50,000

Negroes who took to heart the principles of nonviolence, who learned to fight for their rights with the weapon of love, and who, in the process, acquired a new estimate of their own human worth."[18]

King attempted to define the kind of love he was advocating by referring to the three words for love found in the Greek New Testament. The first was *eros*, which "has come now to mean a sort of aesthetic or romantic love." The second was *philia*, an affection between personal friends. The third was *agape*, a word used to describe God's love, and to describe a quality of human relationships which are informed by the love of God. It is a spontaneous, creative, disinterested love. It is a love which loves others "for their sakes." It is a love which "discovers the neighbor in every man it meets."

This love springs from the need of the other person. As the love of God does not fail in time of need, so that of the neighbor-regarding person is constant and unfailing.

Agape is not a weak, passive love. It is love in action.
Agape is love seeking to preserve and create community. It is insistence on community even when one seeks to break it.
Agape is a willingness to sacrifice in the interest of mutuality.
Agape is a willingness to go to any length to restore community. It doesn't stop at the first mile, but it goes the second mile to restore community. It is a willingness to forgive, not seven times, but seventy times seven to restore community. The cross is the eternal expression of the length to which God will go in order to restore broken community. The resurrection is a symbol of God's triumph over all the forces that seek to block community. The Holy Spirit is the continuing community creating reality that moves through history.[19]

However difficult application of this ideal of human conduct might be, King had specifically in mind its reference to the bitter and explosive racial situation in America. Love, he said, is to be directed toward one's enemy. It involves forgiveness, for "he who is devoid of the power to forgive is devoid of the power to love." [20] It involves seeing one's enemy in a new light.

We recognize that his hate grows out of fear, pride, ignorance, prejudice, and misunderstanding, but in spite of this, we know God's image is ineffably etched in his being. Then we love our enemies by realizing that they are not totally bad and that they are not beyond the reach of God's redemptive love.[21]

One's enemy should be loved because this is the only possible way to win his friendship and understanding. ". . . we love every man because God loves him. At this level, we love the person who does an evil deed, although we hate the deed that he does." [22]

In the service of love for one's fellowman, suffering and sacrifice are to be expected. Suffering is to be accepted without retaliation. King liked to quote Gandhi's word to Gandhi's own people: "Rivers of blood may have to flow before we gain our freedom, but it must be our blood." Suffering is to be accepted because "unearned suffering is redemptive." It has indeed "tremendous educational and transforming possibilities." [23]

In the midst of various kinds of ideological conflict between races, nations, classes, and individuals, King saw love as the basis for the establishment of wholeness, community, and reconciliation. By its very nature, he said, "hate destroys and tears down; by its very nature, love creates and builds up. Love transforms with redemptive power." [24]

The insight of King in perceiving a healing, integrating power working at the heart of conflict quite likely owed much to the passion of Hegel to "see things whole." In any case, it made King to be what H. W. Richardson called "the most important proponent of a theology of reconciliation." In King's theology, says Richardson,

. . . faith affirms reconciliation in opposition to the relativism that denies its possibility. In intellectual discussion, faith hopes for agreement and not only dialogue. In war, faith expects and works for peace. In economic struggle, it calls for the common good. In the working together of churches, it anticipates ecumenical reunion. In all these acts, faith affirms something relativism cannot see, i.e., the power of divine unity working in all things to reconcile the ideological conflict generated by relativism itself. Quite concretely, too, faith as the affirmation of such a power of reconciliation also affirms that all those institutions and movements of our time which are working to overcome ideological conflicts are special instruments of redemptive power. One thinks immediately of King's support of the United Nations, and of his development of the Southern Christian Leadership Conference, and of his concern for peace and ecumenism.[25]

JUSTICE

While King's understanding of love was central to his thought and life, perhaps the spearhead of his life's work is to be seen in his eloquent and powerful demand for justice for his people. Racial injustice has seldom been more vividly portrayed for contemporary Americans than in King's famous "Letter from Birmingham Jail."

We have waited for more than 340 years for our constitutional and God-given rights. The nations of Asia and Africa are moving with jetlike speed toward gaining political independence, but we still creep at horse-and-buggy pace toward gaining a cup of coffee at a lunch counter. Perhaps it is easy for those who have never felt the stinging darts of segregation to say, "Wait." But when you have seen . . . hate-filled policemen curse, kick and even kill your black brothers and sisters; when you see the vast majority of your twenty million Negro brothers smothering in an airtight cage of poverty in the midst of an affluent society; when you suddenly find your tongue twisted and your speech stammering as you seek to explain to your six-year-old daughter why she can't go to the public amusement park that has just been advertised on television, and see tears welling up in her eyes when she is told that Funtown is closed to colored children, and see ominous clouds of inferiority beginning to form in her little mental sky . . .; when you are harried by day and haunted by night by the fact that you are a Negro, living constantly at tiptoe stance, never quite knowing what to expect next, and are plagued with inner fears and outer resentments; when you are forever fighting a degenerate sense of "nobodiness"—then you will understand why we find it difficult to wait. There comes a time when the cup of endurance runs over, and men are no longer willing to be plunged into the abyss of despair.[26]

King believed that the racial injustices of American society are rooted in an ideological racism which has cursed American history from its beginning. This racism was first a justificatory device for slavery, in which human beings were bought and sold for profit. The reaching out for some rationalization by means of which this system could be clothed in garments of righteousness gave birth to the theory of white supremacy.

King cited with approval Ruth Benedict's definition of racism as "the dogma that one ethnic group is condemned by nature to hereditary inferiority and another group is destined to hereditary superiority." [27]

The racist mentality, with its banner of white supremacy, enlisted the aid of white religion, logic, education, and even science to support itself.[28]

Thus through two centuries a continuous indoctrination of Americans has separated people according to mythically superior and inferior qualities while a democratic spirit of equality was evoked as the national ideal. These concepts of racism, and this schizophrenic duality of conduct, remain deeply rooted in American thought today. This tendency of the nation to take one step forward on the question of racial justice and then to take a step backward is still the pattern. Just as an ambivalent nation freed the slaves a century ago with no plan or program to make their freedom meaningful, the still ambivalent nation in 1954 declared school segregation unconstitutional with no plan or program to make integration real. Just as the Congress passed a civil rights bill in 1868 and refused to enforce it, the Congress passed a civil rights bill in 1964 and to this day has failed to enforce it in all its dimensions. Just as the Fifteenth Amendment in 1870 proclaimed Negro suffrage, only to permit its de facto withdrawal in half the nation, so in 1965 the Voting Rights Law was passed and then permitted to languish with only fractional and halfhearted implementation.[29]

Before the necessary steps can be taken to build a just society, the racism upon which injustice is built must be brought out of its hiding places and stripped of the rationalizations by which it has been justified. King believed that a cure could be effected, but not before the disease had been accurately diagnosed in all its hideous details. The nation which began its national life with a vision of a society of brotherhood can be redeemed, but not before there is a humble acknowledgment of guilt and an honest look at the national self.[30]

In seeking for a foundation upon which to build a just social order, King went back to the "pillars . . . soundly grounded in the insights of our Judeo-Christian heritage":

> All men are made in the image of God; all men are brothers; all men are created equal; every man is heir to a legacy of dignity and worth; every man has rights that are neither conferred by nor derived from the state, they are God-given.[31]

King insisted that justice for the black American must be not merely a high-sounding, abstract noun. It must find its content in concrete terms embracing all of America's public life. Justice demands not only the elimination of "brutality and unregenerate evil," but also the achievement of full equality for Negroes in American society.[32] Justice requires equal opportunity for blacks in a social order in which they have been exploited.

A just social order, King urged, would mean an end to job discrimination. It would mean an end to segregation in schools, housing, restaurants, and facilities of transportation, for segregation is a technique of racism for perpetuating the stigma of racial inferiority. A just social order requires a termination of "tokenism," gradualism, and "Tomism," for these are effective means by which a white racism postpones the day of a fully integrated American society and nourishes within the psyche of the Negro the vicious myth of his own incompetence and helplessness in a white man's world.

In an article written in 1962, James E. Sellers acknowledged his disappointment that King had, as Sellers believed, made justice the pinnacle of his "system," rather than love. "In King's reflections on the non-violent movement," Sellers said, "justice seems to stand as the highest goal of a Christian society, with love, accordingly, subordinated as the method or device by which the goal is to be attained." [33]

The tactical demands of King's leadership in the civil rights movement quite prevailingly caused him to speak more of justice than of love, and to emphasize definite goals which would embody and enforce at least a minimal degree of justice. However, he did not lose his vision of love as the supreme "unifying principle" of life. A worldwide fellowship, he said, which is capable of lifting human concern above the limits of tribe, race, class, and nation, is not possible except as it rises from a love for all men. King quoted Arnold Toynbee with obvious agreement. "Love," said Toynbee, "is the ultimate force that makes for the saving choice of life and good against the damning choice of death and evil. Therefore the first hope in our inventory must be the hope that love is going to have the last word." [34]

NONVIOLENT DIRECT ACTION

In the bus boycott in Montgomery, Alabama, in 1956, King had an opportunity for the first time to employ the method of non-violent direct action in the achievement of the immediate goals of the Montgomery Negroes. When he was called to the leadership of the black side of this struggle, King says that his mind was driven to the Sermon on the Mount and to "the Gandhian method of nonviolent resistance. . . . Christ," he said, "furnished the spirit and motivation and Gandhi furnished the method." [35]

The importance of nonviolence in King's mind cannot be seen, however, if it is viewed merely as the best pragmatic method by which a minority group may wrest some concessions from an unwilling majority. "Nonviolence," King said, "became more than a method to which I gave intellectual assent; it became a commitment to a way of life." [36]

King heartily embraced the principle of nonviolence because he believed it to be an effective instrument of both justice and love. Nonviolence, he said,

> . . . is the method which seeks to implement the just law by appealing to the conscience of the great decent majority who through blindness, fear, pride, or irrationality have allowed their consciences to sleep.[37]

When an angry crowd of Negroes gathered after the bombing of King's home in Montgomery, King sought to quiet them by an appeal to nonviolence. " 'We cannot solve this problem,' he said, 'through retaliatory violence. We must meet violence with nonviolence. . . . We must love our white brothers, no matter what they do to us. We must make them know that we love them.' " [38]

The large group of blacks who manned the resistance crusade in Birmingham several years later was called by King and other leaders an "army."

> But it was a special army, with no supplies but its sincerity, no uniform but its determination, no arsenal except its faith, no currency but its conscience. It was an army that would move but not maul. It was an army

that would sing but not slay. It was an army that would flank but not falter. It was an army to storm bastions of hatred, to lay siege to the fortresses of segregation, to surround symbols of discrimination. It was an army whose allegiance was to God and whose strategy and intelligence were the eloquently simple dictates of conscience.[39]

King saw six principles in the philosophy of nonviolence. First, nonviolent resistance is not a method for cowards. "It is not passive resistance to evil; it is active nonviolent resistance to evil." The nonviolent resister is not aggressive physically, but he is strongly active spiritually and intellectually. He is constantly attempting to convince his opponent.

Second, nonviolent resistance "does not seek to defeat or humiliate the opponent, but to win his friendship and understanding." Its aim is fellowship and reconciliation. "The aftermath of nonviolence is the creation of the beloved community, while the aftermath of violence is tragic bitterness."

Third, the nonviolent resister seeks to defeat the forces of evil, not the persons who happen to be doing the evil. King told his followers in Montgomery, "We are out to defeat injustice and not white persons who may be unjust."

Fourth, the nonviolent resister accepts suffering without retaliation, in the hope that his suffering will be redemptive.

Fifth, the nonviolent resister not only rejects outward violence, but also an internal violence of the spirit. He "not only refuses to shoot his opponent but he also refuses to hate him." "Along the way of life," King said, "someone must have sense enough and morality enough to cut off the chain of hate. This can only be done by projecting the ethic of love to the center of our lives."

Sixth, the nonviolent resistance springs from a faith that justice has cosmic backing. The universe upholds it and supports it.[40]

It must be acknowledged that in King's subscription to nonviolence there was an element of shrewd calculation. He was convinced that in a violent showdown, the Negro simply could not win. Even so, the prospect of violence he regarded with horror and revulsion. He well knew, of course, that not all Negroes who followed a course of nonviolence held to this course as a matter of principle. Nevertheless, he believed that nonviolent resistance was an immeasurably stronger moral position than was a position of violence.

. . . the nonviolent approach does something to the hearts and souls of those committed to it. It gives them new self-respect. It calls up resources of strength and courage that they did not know they had. Finally, it so stirs the conscience of the opponent that reconciliation becomes a reality.[41]

ADVERSARIES AND POTENTIAL ALLIES

Martin Luther King's passion for wholeness made him a bridge builder. He sought to span the chasms of misunderstanding, inequality, and hatred which for hundreds of years in America have divided the races. This passion led him to play the themes of love, justice, reconciliation, brotherhood, community, tolerance, and mutual understanding. For the sake of a society founded upon brotherhood and justice, he attacked a widely ramified host of evils which had set themselves tenaciously to destroy even the hope of genuine community, elements such as racism (white and black), exploitation, poverty, unequal job opportunity, discriminatory housing, disease, and segregation.

King was himself, in his role and person, something of a bridge between the black and white worlds in this country. However, during the last three years of his life, King's leadership was challenged in the black community by black militants, who considered him altogether too pacific and too moderate. His popularity among the Negro rank and file was still unrivaled, but strong militant leadership thought of him as an "Uncle Tom." On the other hand, the outbreak of riots in many northern cities confused many of the white moderates, seriously eroding the moderate center.[42]

With the rise of a black separatist movement, on the one side, and the development of a massive white backlash, on the other, King was acutely concerned to preserve the anchor points of his leadership in both the black and white communities.

It would seem to be appropriate here to notice King's measured appraisal of several of these groups which, he considered, threatened to obstruct the fragile movements of progress and community which he was trying to build, but which also held great resources for potential good.

THE BLACK POWER MOVEMENT

King was present in Greenwood, Mississippi, when Stokely Carmichael first raised in a public meeting the cry of "Black Power." From the first, King had serious misgivings about the slogan and about what a man like Carmichael might mean by it. He finally embodied his critique in 1967 in his book *Where Do We Go From Here: Chaos or Community?*

A part of King's evaluation was affirmative. It must be seen, he said, that Black Power is first of all a cry of disappointment. It is a cry born in the wounds of despair. It springs from the

Negro's conviction that a white society will never permit the
Negro to have equal opportunity and equal rights. The slogan also
arises from a deep disappointment with the federal government
because of the latter's timidity in making just laws and in im-
plementing those which are already on its books. The disappointment is heightened by the widening of the economic gap between
blacks and whites in northern cities, by the worsening of city
slums, and by the tenacity of segregated housing.

In the second place, Black Power is a "call to black people
to amass the political and economic strength to achieve their
legitimate goals." [43] Again King was convinced that the use of
political and economic power was to be commended for the attainment of legitimate objectives.

> There is nothing essentially wrong with power. The problem is that in
> America power is unequally distributed. This has led Negro Americans in
> the past to seek their goals through love and moral suasion devoid of
> power and white Americans to seek their goals through power devoid of
> love and conscience. It is leading a few extremists today to advocate for
> Negroes the same destructive and conscienceless power that they have justly
> abhorred in whites. It is precisely this collision of immoral power with
> powerless morality which constitutes the major crisis of our times. [44]

King was emphatically in favor of using the power of black people
to place blacks in key political posts, to alleviate poverty, and
to win full freedom and human dignity.

In the third place, King saw in the Black Power movement a
psychological call to manhood. Black Power was a call to the black
man to achieve his own identity and to rejoice in his blackness.
It was a call to stand erect in a system which still oppresses him,
while holding to a sense of his own value.

On the other hand, King believed that "Black Power is a
nihilistic philosophy born out of the conviction that the Negro
can't win." [45] It is a view that American society is so hopelessly
corrupt that there is no possibility of salvation inside of it.
The Black Power movement, so revolutionary in its pretensions,
still rejects the one element which all successful revolutionary
movements must have — "the ever-present flame of hope." King
called for a firm rejection of the bitterness, cynicism, self-pity,
defeatism, and disruption which Black Power had come to stand
for in militant circles.

> Our most fruitful course is to stand firm, move forward nonviolently, accept
> disappointments and cling to hope. Our determined refusal not [sic] to be
> stopped will eventually open the door to fulfillment. By recognizing the
> necessity of suffering in a righteous cause, we may achieve our humanity's

full stature. To guard ourselves from bitterness, we need the vision to see in this generation's ordeals the opportunity to transfigure both ourselves and American society.[46]

In the second place, Black Power is based upon an implicit and sometimes explicit belief in black separatism. King thought that few ideas in the racial struggle were more unrealistic. Just as the Negro cannot achieve political power in isolation, neither can he achieve economic power in separation from whites. What is needed, rather, is honest cooperation between blacks and whites in the attaining of mutually beneficial goals.

In the final analysis the weakness of Black Power is its failure to see that the black man needs the white man and the white man needs the black man. However much we may try to romanticize the slogan, there is no separate black path to power and fulfillment that does not intersect white paths, and there is no separate white path to power and fulfillment, short of social disaster, that does not share that power with black aspirations for freedom and human dignity. . . . The language, the cultural patterns, the music, the material prosperity and even the food of America are an amalgam of black and white.[47]

The Negro, said King, is neither wholly African nor wholly Western. He is Afro-American, a synthesis of two cultures. He cannot and must not separate himself from responsible participation in the life of America. "America must be a nation in which its multiracial people are partners in power." [48]

Finally, King thought that the most ominous feature of Black Power is its implicit or explicit sanction of retaliatory violence. But in a violent confrontation, King believed, neither side would win. "Violence," he said "only adds to the chaos. It deepens the brutality of the oppressor and increases the bitterness of the oppressed. . . . It destroys community and makes brotherhood impossible." [49] The power which is needed is not a retaliatory, destructive power. What is needed is a power "infused with love and justice, that will change dark yesterdays into bright tomorrows, and lift us from the fatigue of despair to the buoyancy of hope." [50]

THE WHITE MODERATE

In his "Letter from Birmingham Jail," King confessed that he had become gravely disappointed with the white moderate.

I have almost reached the regrettable conclusion that the Negro's great stumbling block in his stride toward freedom is not the White Citizen's Counciler or the Ku Klux Klanner, but the white moderate, who is more devoted to "order" than to justice; who prefers a negative peace which is the absence of tension to a positive peace which is the presence of justice; who constantly says: "I agree with you in the goal you seek, but I cannot agree with your methods of direct action"; who paternalistically believes he can set the timetable for another man's freedom; who lives by a mythical concept of time and who constantly advises the Negro to wait for a "more convenient season." Shallow understanding from people of good will is more frustrating than absolute misunderstanding from people of ill will. Lukewarm acceptance is much more bewildering than outright rejection.[51]

A serious trouble with the white moderate is his willingness to settle for a token solution, to settle for a snail's pace gradualism at a time when delay may be fatal, to settle for a half loaf instead of the whole. Moderates supported the Negro's push toward decency, but they wanted him to stop short of full equality. They wanted him to move out of his old ghetto, while the moderates were ready to build a new ghetto for him "with a small exit door for a few. . . . These moderates had come some distance in step with the thundering drums, but at the point of mass application they wanted the bugle to sound a retreat." [52]

The moderates, however, King did not consider to be "enemies." They were, he said, "our temporary obstacles and potential allies." [53]

THE WHITE CHURCH

King expressed also profound disappointment with the white church and its leadership. He spoke as one who had been nurtured in the bosom of the church and who continued to love it despite its failings.

When the historic bus boycott began in Montgomery, King thought that the cause of the Negroes would be supported by the white church. Instead, many churchmen opposed the movement. Ministers chose to remain silent behind their stained-glass windows. Others were the soul of caution and circumspection rather than of courage.

> In the midst of blatant injustices inflicted upon the Negro, I have watched white churchmen stand on the sideline and mouth pious irrelevancies and sanctimonious trivialities. In the midst of a mighty struggle to rid our nation of racial and economic injustice, I have heard many ministers say: "Those are social issues, with which the gospel has no real concern." And I have watched many churches commit themselves to a completely otherworldly religion which makes a strange, unbiblical distinction between body and soul, between the sacred and the secular.[54]

Far from being a prophetic voice in American society today, the church quite often is the arch-defender of the status quo. The power structure of the community, far from being threatened by the presence of the church, is frequently aided and abetted by the church in the rule of oppression. The church must recapture the sacrificial spirit of the early church. If it does not, it will become an irrelevant social club from which serious-minded people will turn away in disgust.[55]

STRATEGY

The strategy used by Martin Luther King to deal with the race problem in America resulted in the employment of a variety of techniques and methods — boycotts, mass demonstrations, sit-ins, and legal pressure. These techniques were very often directed toward concrete objectives, such as desegregation of transportation facilities, restaurants, and schools; voting rights; job opportunity on a nondiscriminatory basis; open housing; and relief of poverty.

All of the above techniques have become familiar and standard procedures in the advance of the civil rights movement in our time. King appears to have given most of his working effort to the problem of using them effectively. The point to be noticed was the overarching objective toward which King sought to direct them. This objective was a just society in which all individuals and groups would have full and equal rights, opportunities and privileges — a community in which all men were neighbors and brothers.

Several concepts shaped the concrete tactical techniques and actions which King employed in striving toward this goal. Some attention will be called to these concepts now.

A REVOLUTION OF VALUES

King called for a genuine "revolution" of values which would accompany the scientific and freedom revolutions now engulfing the earth. This revolution would involve a shift from a "thing"-oriented society to a "person"-oriented society. It would measure both communism and capitalism in terms of the contributions which each makes toward the development of personhood and brotherhood, rather than in terms of the stockpiling of wealth. It would not despise wealth, however, but would be concerned to use wealth for the enhancement of the good life rather than for a promotion of misery by means of exploitation and war. It would think of the nations of the world in terms of a worldwide fellowship instead of in terms of a destructive tribalism or nationalism.[56]

THE CREATIVE USE OF DISCONTENT

Oppressed people, said King, will not remain oppressed forever. Eventually the yearning for freedom will break into the open, and this is what has happened in the case of the Negro

American. Something in the *Zeitgeist* has reminded him that freedom belongs to him as a birthright and that this birthright is within his grasp. The American Negro is joining with the black men of Africa and with the brown and yellow men of Asia, South America, and the Caribbean in a quest for racial justice.

> If one recognizes this vital urge that has engulfed the Negro community, one should readily understand why public demonstrations are taking place. The Negro has many pent-up resentments and latent frustrations, and he must release them. So let him march; let him make prayer pilgrimages to the city hall; let him go on freedom rides—and try to understand why he must do so. If his repressed emotions are not released in nonviolent ways, they will seek expression through violence; this is not a threat but a fact of history. So I have not said to my people: "Get rid of your discontent." Rather, I have tried to say that this normal and healthy discontent can be channeled into the creative outlet of nonviolent direct action.[57]

THE ROLE OF CONFLICT

In the pursuit of goals which do not have the sanction of the status quo, conflict is a datum which is to be taken for granted. The problem is not to avoid conflict, but to make it purposive and constructive — and to determine that it will be nonviolent in nature.

> . . . I must say to you that we have not made a single gain in civil rights without determined legal and nonviolent pressure. Lamentably, it is an historical fact that privileged groups seldom give up their privileges voluntarily. Individuals may see the moral light and voluntarily give up their unjust posture; but, as Reinhold Niebuhr has reminded us, groups tend to be more immoral than individuals.[58]

King acknowledged that the creation of tension is sometimes necessary in order to so dramatize an issue that a community will be forced to confront it. "Nonviolent direct action," said King "seeks to create such a crisis and foster such a tension that a community which has constantly refused to negotiate is forced to confront the issue."[59] Nonviolent, constructive tension is necessary for growth and — in the civil rights struggle — for the attainment of justice.

In his appeal to the white moderate, King called attention to the constructive use of conflict. He had hoped, he said, that the white moderate would understand that law and order existed to promote justice and that, when they fail to do this, they can themselves become instruments of oppression. He had hoped that the white moderate would understand that social tension is a necessary phase in the transition from a negative peace, in which the Negro accepted his unjust plight with docility, to a positive peace, in which the Negro wins full dignity and respect in the

society of which he is a part. The white moderate should see that
the Negro who agitates for his rights is not the creator of tension.
Rather, he brings into the open air the hidden tensions which
are already rankling in oppressed lives, and he helps to effect an
honest settlement of them.[60]

BLACK IDENTITY AND BLACK UNITY

There can be no genuine community, no just society, as long
as one ethnic group within the society occupies an inferior status.

The Negro has been taught for centuries in white America that
he is a nobody, that he is innately inferior to the white man, and
that his proper position is one of subservience. For the sake of
himself, and for the sake of the larger society of which he is a
part, the Negro must learn to take pride in his historical background and in his racial heritage. "The Negro must be grasped by
a new realization of his dignity and worth. He must stand up
amid a system that still oppresses him and develop an unassail-
able and majestic sense of his own value. He must no longer be
ashamed of being black." [61]

Likewise, the attainment of the Negro's rights makes necessary
a strong sense of unity in the black community. This unity will
mean that Negroes will come to respect fully the blackness of
other blacks as well as their own. In other words, it will mean an
attack upon the Negro's demeaning self-image, as this image is
applied both to himself and to other Negroes.

> This plea for unity is not a call for uniformity. There must always be
> healthy debate. There will be inevitable differences of opinion. The dilemma
> that the Negro confronts is so complex and monumental that its solution
> will of necessity involve a diversified approach. But Negroes can differ and
> still unite around common goals.[62]

The unity for which King pleaded in the black community was
not only one in which the objective would be the attainment of
civil rights. It would be a unity around goals in the Negro community itself — goals like the raising of personal standards, the
elimination of crime, the best use of the freedom which the Negro
already has, the achievement of the highest excellence in the
various lines of endeavor which Negroes choose for themselves,
and respect for the dignity of labor and the laborer, no matter
how humble.[63]

BLACK STRENGTH

King did not like the term "Black Power" because it connoted black domination instead of black equality with whites. Yet he was intelligently aware that the black people must use power in the achievement of their rightful place in American society. Oppressed people, he said, realize deliverance when they accumulate enough power to force change. The compelling task is so to organize black strength that the American government and the whole American people cannot ignore or elude the Negro's just demands.

King believed in the development of black economic and political power, so that these might be concentrated upon the achievement of the Negro's fair share of the rights of citizenship, of education, and of economic opportunity.[64]

The Forming of Alliances

King's quarrel with black separatism was based upon his conviction that the blacks in American society could never go it alone. Separatism was economically and politically unfeasible, but, more than that, it was a denial of community. The Negro's best hope was not only to develop the self-reliance and competence which would demand respect and equal rights, but also to make alliances with other segments of society in the pursuit of common goals.

The Federal Government

The first alliance is the alliance of the civil rights struggle with the federal government. To be sure, governmental power cannot furnish a panacea for racial injustices, but its role is indispensable.

> Government action is not the whole answer to the present crisis, but it is an important partial answer. Morals cannot be legislated, but behavior can be regulated. The law cannot make an employer love me, but it can keep him from refusing to hire me because of the color of my skin. We must depend on religion and education to alter the errors of the heart and mind; but meanwhile it is an immoral act to compel a man to accept injustice until another man's heart is set straight. As the experience of several Northern states has shown, antidiscrimination laws can provide powerful sanctions against this kind of immorality.[65]

The White Liberal

In the civil rights cause, Negroes should also make alliances with the white northern liberals. This is "a substantial group who cherish democratic principles above privilege and who have demonstrated a will to fight side by side with the Negro against injustice." [66] This group must be liberal enough to push for the full rights of Negroes *now,* instead of stalling and temporizing as they have so often done.[67]

The Poor Whites

Another group with which Negroes can make alliance is the group of disadvantaged whites who have common needs with the Negro and who would benefit equally with him in social progress. Particularly is it possible for blacks to make common cause with these whites in the fight against poverty and the struggle for the improvement of wages and working conditions.

Organized Labor

The civil rights movement and the labor movement can be and must be mutually supportive. Few things would be so tragic as a schism between them.

> Strong ties must be made between those whites and Negroes who have problems in common. White and Negro workers have mutual aspirations for a fairer share of the products of industries and farms. Both seek job security, old-age security, health and welfare protection. The organized labor movement, which has contributed so much to the economic security and well-being of millions, must concentrate its powerful forces on bringing economic emancipation to white and Negro by organizing them together in social equality.[68]

The White Church

Unfortunately, the church "has been an accomplice in structuring racism into the architecture of American society." No one would deny, however, that individual church leaders from Catholic, Protestant, and Jewish bodies have been in the vanguard of the civil rights movement, especially in recent years. The church must confess its racism and acknowledge its truancy to its true heritage. It must lift up its voice to proclaim the rights of the black man. It must move out of the paralysis of its hesitations into a place of leadership in the cause of social reform.[69]

KING AS A BAPTIST

Martin Luther King, Jr., was born into a Baptist home, the son of a prominent Baptist minister. He graduated from a Baptist theological seminary, was ordained a Baptist minister, became pastor of one Baptist church, then became associate pastor of another, and remained a Baptist minister all his life.

The above summarizes the story of King as a Baptist. King's Baptist heritage showed up very little in the doctrinal beliefs which he came to hold at full maturity.

Baptist influences must be sought in King, not along doctrinal or ecclesiastical lines, but in the more informal origins and structures of the movement which he led. The sparks of the civil rights movement in its early phases under his leadership were frequently ignited and fanned to flame in rallies and services in local Baptist churches of Negro membership, as, for example, in Montgomery and Birmingham. Quite often, the ministers who sprang to places of leadership in the movement, including King and Ralph Abernathy, were ministers of Negro Baptist churches. When the Southern Christian Leadership Conference was formed, Negro Baptist ministers were prominent in the leadership positions within the group.

The creative role which King and other Negro religious leaders played in the Negro church community may be seen in their ability to turn the profound religious interest of multitudes of Negroes from an other-worldly to a this-worldly direction. The New Jerusalem which he sought, King affirmed, was not in the world to come (although he believed in this, too). It would be a New Montgomery, a New Birmingham, a New Atlanta. This ability to focus religious conviction upon the problem of human rights, and to do so with intensity, tenacity, and skill, was quite remarkable.

The result has been a rechanneling of the religious focus of a major segment of the Negro religious community. The Baptists have been distinctive in this change of emphasis only in the fact that their denomination has furnished not only a large part of the soldiers in the southern ranks of the movement but also has supplied a disproportionate percentage of its front-rank leadership.

The Negro Baptist churches have been churches of the people, and that relationship has been important to the civil rights movement by enabling it to strike fire among the Negro people at the common level. King and other Negro leaders took the spontaneity and informality of the Negro Baptist people and transferred them to the quest for civil rights, adding a discipline and an organizational skill and cohesion for which the Negro church had not theretofore been conspicuous.

A strong element in King's own thought was that of community, fellowship, and friendship. A great deal of his emphasis upon love carried the meaning of Christian friendship. The emphasis on love as friendship did not come, says H. W. Richardson, from the magisterial reformation, but "from the 'third wing,' the spiritualists, the Baptists." One can understand from this emphasis, says Richardson, how Harvey Cox could say that the life and work of King made him proud to be a Baptist.[70]

Despite his sophistication and wide appeal, there could be heard in the eloquent addresses of King the rhythmic oratorical cadences of the Negro preachers of the old South. He spoke from the deeps of the Negro religious experience, and his charisma for his own people owed much to this nonrational, emotional, subterranean attachment to the yearnings and aspirations of his people. There was in him the fire and thunder of the best Negro Baptist preachers, however much these were transmuted by the suavity and polish of a modern man.

For Baptists, the life and thought of King were pivotal in an area in which Walter Rauschenbusch had contributed brilliant illumination. It is an area in which the Christian gospel is given application and implementation to the torments of the modern world. King advanced beyond Rauschenbusch in selecting one of these torments, that of race relations, as the turbulent arena for his own witness.

"I'VE BEEN TO THE MOUNTAINTOP"

The night before he was brutally murdered, Martin Luther King said in a public address: "I've been to the mountain top. . . . And I've looked over, and I've seen the promised land. I may not get there with you, but I want you to know tonight that we as a people will get to the promised land." [71]

Perhaps the vision of this Moses will raise up enough Calebs and Joshuas to bring it to fulfillment. Perhaps the Amalekites, the Amorites, and the Philistines will be strong enough to keep the children of Israel out of the promised land. Or perhaps the children of Israel will elect to settle in the Edom of black separatism. Only time will tell.

It is too early fully to assess the stature and the contribution of Martin Luther King, Jr. Perhaps he was not as great a giant as some of his admirers have thought him to be. Certainly he was much larger than many of his detractors have imagined him to be.

Of all civil rights leaders in this century, King's interpretation of the problem of race relations has been the most Christian, and the most Christian projection of its resolution. The giving of his life must be seen as a part of the interpretation.

There was a wholeness about King's vision, an integrity about it, and a basic consistency, which witness to the fact that he was a thinker who thought his basic positions through. He delivered his message with prophetic fire when judgment was needed, and with gentleness when the "balm of Gilead" was called for. Richardson's judgment is worth considering. "King," he says, "was regarded as a civil rights leader and as a man of extraordinary personal valor, but he has not been understood as a brilliant and mature theologian. . . . He is the theologian for our time." [72]

The land which King saw from the mountaintop was a land in which his own people would be free, a land in which there would be justice for all men, and in which the society which comprised blacks and whites would be founded upon mutual respect, fellowship, goodwill, and love.

It may be that such a land is beyond the hope of complete realization; yet King's basic demands for social justice in a free society, in which men of all races and conditions have redress of grievances, nondiscriminatory opportunities, and first-class citizenship, make hardheaded good sense, however gilded with a touch of bright idealism.

It is encouraging to hear one of King's lieutenants say about himself and his colleagues in the SCLC:

> . . . you can be sure the nation hasn't seen the last of us. We are tougher and more deeply committed to his philosophies than we were when Dr. King was here to lead us. Now we are in a slump like the one after the 1961 Albany, Ga., campaign. Then, they said Dr. King was finished too. But after that came Birmingham. We are getting ready to work, and the nation better get ready for us. America still has to deal with Martin Luther King, Jr.[73]

King's figure casts a prophetic shadow of large proportions across the future history of this nation. It is to be hoped that King's own denomination will be in the vanguard of those of his countrymen who march out to meet the challenge for which that long shadow stands.

NOTES

CHAPTER 1—John Smyth

1. Alan Simpson, *Puritanism in Old and New England* (Chicago: The University of Chicago Press, 1955), p. 14.
2. Cited in Edmund S. Morgan, *Visible Saints* (New York: New York University Press, 1963), p. 14.
3. Perry Miller, *Orthodoxy in Massachusetts, 1630-1650* (Cambridge: Harvard University Press, 1933), p. 25.
4. *Ibid.*, p. 32.
5. Morgan, *op. cit.*, p. 6.
6. Miller, *op. cit.*, p. 36.
7. Morgan, *op. cit.*, pp. 17-18.
8. Cited in *ibid.*, p. 23.
9. Cited in Miller, *op. cit.*, p. 60.
10. Cited in Williston Walker, *The Creeds and Platforms of Congregationalism* (New York: Charles Scribner's Sons, 1893), pp. 71-72.
11. Walter H. Burgess, *John Smith the Se-Baptist, Thomas Helwys and the First Baptist Church in England, with Fresh Light Upon the Pilgrim Fathers' Church* (London: James Clarke & Co., 1911), pp. 45-46.
12. W. T. Whitley, *The Works of John Smyth* (Cambridge: At the University Press, 1915), vol. 1, p. 17.
13. *Ibid.*, p. 18.
14. *Ibid.*, p. 21.
15. *Ibid.*, p. 22.
16. *Ibid.*, cf. pp. 26-29.
17. *Ibid.*, p. 57.
18. *Ibid.*, p. 58.
19. Burgess, *op. cit.*, p. 52.
20. Whitley, *op. cit.*, p. 68.
21. *Ibid.*, p. 71.

22. *Ibid.*, p. 103.
23. *Ibid.*, p. 71.
24. *Ibid.*, p. 81.
25. *Ibid.*, p. 96.
26. *Ibid.*, p. 83.
27. *Ibid.*, p. 82.
28. *Ibid.*, p. 83.
29. *Ibid.*, p. 112.
30. *Ibid.*, p. 172. Cf. p. 113.
31. *Ibid.*, p. 166.
32. *Ibid.*
33. *Ibid.*, p. xliii.
34. Burgess, *op. cit.*, pp. 99, 105.
35. Whitley, *op. cit.*, p. 252.
36. *Ibid.*, p. 253.
37. *Ibid.*, p. 254.
38. *Ibid.*, p. 254.
39. *Ibid.*, pp. 254-255.
40. *Ibid.*, p. 255.
41. *Ibid.*, p. 256.
42. *Ibid.*, p. 258.
43. *Ibid.*, p. 259.
44. *Ibid.*, pp. 260-263.
45. *Ibid.*, p. 266.
46. *Ibid.*, p. 259.
47. *Ibid.*, p. 267.
48. *Ibid.*; cf. vol. 2, p. 329.
49. *Ibid.*, p. 343.
50. *Ibid.*, p. 357.
51. *Ibid.*, p. 343.
52. *Ibid.*, p. 354.
53. *Ibid.*, p. 383.
54. *Ibid.*, p. 373.
55. *Ibid.*, p. 466.
56. *Ibid.*, p. 468.
57. *Ibid.*, p. 490.
58. *Ibid.*, pp. 494-495.
59. *Ibid.*, pp. 515-516.
60. *Ibid.*, p. 437.
61. *Ibid.*

62. *Ibid.*, p. 403.
63. *Ibid.*, vol. 1, p. 277.
64. *Ibid.*
65. *Ibid.*
66. *Ibid.*, p. 282.
67. *Ibid.*, p. 303.
68. *Ibid.*, p. 280.
69. *Ibid.*, p. 291.
70. Burgess, *op. cit.*, p. 125.
71. Whitley, *op. cit.*, vol. 2, p. 565.
72. *Ibid.*
73. *Ibid.*, pp. 635-636.
74. *Ibid.*, p. 579.
75. *Ibid.*, p. 582.
76. *Ibid.*, pp. 611-612.
77. *Ibid.*, p. 648.
78. *Ibid.*, p. 587.
79. *Ibid.*, p. 655.
80. *Ibid.*, p. 657.
81. *Ibid.*, p. 659.
82. *Ibid.*, p. 660.
83. *Ibid.*, p. 666.
84. *Ibid.*, pp. 734-737.
85. *Ibid.*, p. 744.
86. *Ibid.*, p. 745.
87. *Ibid.*, p. 746.
88. *Ibid.*
89. *Ibid.*, p. 748.
90. *Ibid.*
91. *Ibid.*, p. 753.
92. *Ibid.*, p. 754.
93. *Ibid.*, p. 758.
94. *Ibid.*, p. 757.
95. *Ibid.*, pp. 759-760.
96. *Ibid.*, vol. 1, p. cxiii.
97. Cited in A. C. Underwood, *A History of the English Baptists* (London: Originally published by Kingsgate Press, 1947; now published by the Baptist Union of Great Britain and Ireland), p. 45.
98. *Ibid.*, pp. 45-46.

CHAPTER 2—Roger Williams

1. Cf. Ola Elizabeth Winslow, *Master Roger Williams* (New York: The Macmillan Company, 1957), pp. 3-34.
2. Cited in Irwin H. Polishook, *Roger Williams, John Cotton and Religious Freedom* (Englewood Cliffs, N.J.: Prentice-Hall, Inc., 1967), p. 46. Reprinted by permission.
3. Cf. Perry Miller, *Roger Williams* (Indianapolis: The Bobbs-Merrill Co., Inc., 1953), pp. 19-21.
4. Vernon L. Parrington, *Main Currents in American Thought* (New York: Harcourt Brace Jovanovich, Inc., 1927), vol. 1, p. 66.
5. H. Richard Niebuhr, *The Kingdom of God in America* (New York: Harper & Row, Publishers, 1959), pp. 68-69.
6. LeRoy Moore, "Roger Williams and the Historians," *Church History*, vol. 32, no. 4 (December, 1963), p. 442.
7. Miller, *op. cit.*, p. 23.
8. Cf. *ibid.*, p. 76.
9. John Cotton, *The Bloudy Tenent, Washed, and made White in the bloud of the Lambe: being discussed and discharged of bloud-guiltiness by just Defence. . . .* (London, 1647). Cited in Polishook, *op. cit.*, p. 71.
10. John Cotton, *A Practical Commentary, or an Exposition with Observations, Reasons, and Uses upon the First Epistle General of John.* Cited in Polishook, *op. cit.*, p. 77.
11. Cotton, *The Bloudy Tenent, Washed.* Cited in Polishook, *op. cit.*, p. 72.
12. Cotton, *ibid.* Cited in Polishook, *op. cit.*, p. 99.
13. Roger Williams, *The Bloudy Tenent of Persecution for Cause of Conscience Discussed and Mr. Cotton's Letter Examined and Answered.* Edited for the Hanserd Knollys Society by Edward Bean Underhill (London: J. Haddon, Castle Street, Finsbury, 1848), p. 286.
14. Williams, *The Bloody Tenent Yet More Bloody. The Complete Writings of Roger Williams* [1866] (New York: Russell & Russell, Publishers, 1963), vol. 4, p. 80.
15. *Ibid.*, p. 180.
16. Williams, *The Bloudy Tenent of Persecution.* Cited in Polishook, *op. cit.*, p. 61.
17. Alan Simpson, *Puritanism in Old and New England* (Chicago: University of Chicago Press, 1955), pp. 57-58.
18. Williams, *The Bloody Tenent Yet More Bloody*, p. 189.
19. *Ibid.*, p. 188.
20. Williams, *The Bloudy Tenent*, pp. 211-212.

21. *Ibid.*, p. 167.
22. William Warren Sweet, *Religion in Colonial America* (New York: Charles Scribner's Sons, 1942), p. 126.
23. Williams, *The Bloudy Tenent*, pp. 46-47.
24. Williams, *The Bloody Tenent Yet More Bloody*, p. 383.
25. Williams, *The Bloudy Tenent*, p. 397.
26. *Ibid.*, p. 399.
27. *Ibid.*, pp. 415-416.
28. *Ibid.*, p. 302.
29. *Ibid.*, p. 421.
30. *Ibid.*, p. 162.
31. Williams, *The Bloody Tenent Yet More Bloody*, p. 292.
32. Williams, *The Bloudy Tenent*, p. 23.
33. Williams, *The Bloody Tenent Yet More Bloody*, p. 143.
34. Cited in Miller, *op. cit.*, pp. 225-226.
35. Cf. *ibid.*, p. 32.
36. Williams, *The Bloudy Tenent*, p. 310.
37. *Ibid.*, p. 311.
38. *Ibid.*, p. 281.
39. *Ibid.*, p. 194.
40. *Ibid.*, p. 118.
41. *Ibid.*, pp. 119-120.
42. *Ibid.*, p. 266.
43. *Ibid.*, p. 196.
44. Williams, *The Bloody Tenent Yet More Bloody*, p. 261.
45. *Ibid.*, pp. 267-268.
46. *Ibid.*, p. 147.
47. Williams, *The Bloudy Tenent*, p. 58.
48. Williams, *The Bloody Tenent Yet More Bloody*, p. 230.
49. Williams, *The Bloudy Tenent*, p. 55.
50. Williams, *The Bloody Tenent Yet More Bloody*, p. 425.
51. Williams, *The Bloudy Tenent*, pp. 96-97.
52. *Ibid.*, p. 64.
53. *Ibid.*, p. 178.
54. *Ibid.*, p. 320.
55. Winslow, *op. cit.*, p. 175.
56. W. T. Whitley, *The Works of John Smyth* (Cambridge: At the University Press, 1915), vol. 2, p. 748.
57. Cited in A. C. Underwood, *A History of the English Baptists* (Lon-

don: Kingsgate Press, 1947), p. 47.
58. See Sidney E. Mead, *The Lively Experiment* (New York: Harper & Row, Publishers, 1963), pp. 16-38. Also, Thomas Cuming Hall, *The Religious Background of American Culture* (New York: Frederick Ungar Publishing Company, 1939, 1959), pp. 127-147.
59. Miller, *op. cit.*, p. 254.
60. John M. Mecklin, *The Story of American Dissent* (New York: Harcourt Brace Jovanovich, Inc., 1934), p. 115.
61. *Publications of the Narragansett Club.* First Series, vol. 4 (Providence: Providence Press Co., Printers, 1866-1874), p. viii.
62. Henry C. Vedder, *A Short History of the Baptists* (Valley Forge: Judson Press, 1907), p. 305.
63. Robert G. Torbet, *A History of the Baptists* (Valley Forge: Judson Press, 1963), p. 202.
64. A. H. Newman, *A History of the Baptist Churches in the United States.* The American Church History Series (Philadelphia: American Baptist Publication Society, 1915), vol. 2, p. 83.

CHAPTER 3—Isaac Backus

1. Isaac Backus, *A History of New England with Particular Reference to the Denomination of Christians Called Baptists*, 2nd ed., with notes by David Weston (Newton, Mass.: Published by Backus Historical Society, 1871), vol. 2, pp. 27-28.
2. Winthrop S. Hudson, "The Ecumenical Spirit of Early Baptists," *Review and Expositor*, vol. 55, no. 2 (April, 1958), pp. 182-195.
3. Cotton Mather, *Magnalia Christi Americana* (London, 1702), vol. 2, p. 531. Cited in John Mecklin, *The Story of American Dissent* (New York: Harcourt Brace Jovanovich, Inc., 1934), p. 150.
4. Backus, *op. cit.*, vol. 1, p. 439.
5. Edwin Scott Gaustad, *The Great Awakening* (New York: Harper & Row, Publishers, 1957), p. 42.
6. *Ibid.*, pp. 120-121. Gaustad says

that before the Great Awakening, there were five Baptist churches in Massachusetts. During the next half century, the number rose to one hundred and thirty-six. Between 1740 and 1796, Gaustad says, the number in Connecticut rose from two to sixty; in Rhode Island, from eleven to forty. Prior to the Revival, there were no Baptist churches in Vermont and New Hampshire. By 1800 over forty Baptist churches existed in each of these states.

7. C. C. Goen, *Revivalism and Separatism in New England, 1740–1800* (New Haven: Yale University Press, 1962), p. 4.

8. Joseph Tracy, *The Great Awakening* (Boston: Tappan & Dennet, 1842), pp. vii-ix.

9. Alvah Hovey, *A Memoir of the Life and Times of the Rev. Isaac Backus* (Boston: Gould and Lincoln; New York: Sheldon, Blakeman and Co., 1859), p. 57.

10. Cited in Tracy, *op. cit.*, p. 95.

11. Gaustad, *op. cit.*, p. 128.

12. Cited in Goen, *op. cit.*, p. 33.

13. Cited in Tracy, *op. cit.*, p. 316.

14. Hovey, *op. cit.*, p. 47.

15. Cited in Tracy, *op. cit.*, p. 318. From the Confession of Faith of the Separate church at Mansfield.

16. Backus, *op. cit.*, vol. 2, p. 107.

17. Hovey, *op. cit.*, p. 43.

18. Backus, *op. cit.*, vol. 2, p. 107.

19. Goen, *op. cit.*, pp. 217-218.

20. Backus, *op. cit.*, vol. 2, p. 89.

21. *Ibid.*, vol. 2, pp. 89-90.

22. *Ibid.*, p. 90.

23. Goen, *op. cit.*, pp. 208-209.

24. Backus, *op. cit.*, vol. 2, p. 110.

25. Cited in Hovey, *op. cit.*, p. 108.

26. Backus, *op. cit.*, vol. 2, pp. 114-115.

27. Tracy, *op. cit.*, pp. 320-325; 407-413.

28. Goen, *op. cit.*, p. 224.

29. Backus, *op. cit.*, vol. 2, p. 116.

30. Hovey, *op. cit.*, p. 130.

31. Cited in Goen, *op. cit.*, pp. 222-223.

32. T. B. Maston, *Ethical and Social Attitudes of Isaac Backus* (New Haven: Yale University, 1939). Cited in Goen, *op. cit.*, p. 223.

33. Backus, *op. cit.*, vol. 2, pp. 231-233.

34. Cited in Backus, *op. cit.* vol. 1, p. 9.

35. Cited in Goen, *op. cit.*, pp. 279-280.

36. Cited in *ibid.*, p. 280.

37. William G. McLoughlin, *Isaac Backus and the American Pietistic Tradition*. Edited by Oscar Handlin (Boston: Little, Brown and Company, 1967), p. 127.

38. Isaac Backus, *An Appeal to the Public for Religious Liberty, Against the Oppressions of the Present Day* (Boston: Printed by John Boyle in Marlborough Street, 1773), p. 4.

39. *Ibid.*, p. 13.

40. *Ibid.*, p. 16.

41. *Ibid.*, p. 42.

42. *Ibid.*, p. 54.

43. McLoughlin, *op. cit.*, pp. 167-193.

44. Wesley Marsh Gewehr, *The Great Awakening in Virginia* (Durham, N.C.: Duke University Press, 1930), pp. 134-135.

45. William L. Lumpkin, *Baptist Foundations in the South* (Nashville, Tenn.: Broadman Press, 1961), pp. 140-141.

46. Mecklin, *The Story of American Dissent*, chap. 9.

47. *Ibid.*, p. 225.

48. Samuel S. Hill, Jr., *Southern Churches in Crisis* (New York: Holt, Rinehart & Winston, Inc., 1967), p. 58.

49. Goen, *op. cit.*, p. 294.

50. Lumpkin, *op. cit.*, pp. 160-161.

51. *Ibid.*, p. 161.

CHAPTER 4—Andrew Fuller

1. Ernest F. Clipsham, "Andrew Fuller and Fullerism: A Study in Evangelical Calvinism," Part I, *The Baptist Quarterly*, vol. 20, no. 3 (July, 1963), p. 100.

2. A. C. Underwood, *A History of the English Baptists* (London: Kingsgate Press, 1947), p. 153.

3. *Ibid.*

4. *Ibid.*, p. 160.

5. *Ibid.*, pp. 134-135.

6. Cited in Sydnor L. Stealey, comp. and ed., *A Baptist Treasury* (New York: Thomas Y. Crowell Company, 1958), p. 86.

7. *Ibid.*, pp. 90-91.

8. S. Pearce Carey, *William Carey, D.D.* (London: Hodder and Stoughton, 1923), pp. 10-11.

9. Cited in Underwood, *op. cit.*, p. 160.

10. Cited in *ibid.*, p. 160.

11. Pearce Carey, *op. cit.*, p. 34.

12. Cited in Underwood, *op. cit.*, p. 161.

13. Edward Steane, at the B.M.S. Jubilee, Kettering. Cited in Pearce Carey, *op. cit.*, p. 311.

14. Underwood, *op. cit.*, p. 161.

15. *Ibid.*, p. 165.

16. For the following discussion of Fuller's theology, I am particularly indebted to the doctoral dissertation of my colleague, Professor John W. Eddins. Cf. John W. Eddins, "Andrew Fuller's Theology of Grace" (unpublished Th.D. dissertation, Southern Baptist Theological Seminary, 1957).

17. Arthur H. Kirby, "Andrew Fuller—Evangelical Calvinist," *The Baptist Quarterly*, vol. 15, no. 5 (January, 1954), p. 197.

18. Joseph Belcher, ed., *The Complete Works of the Rev. Andrew Fuller: with a Memoir of His Life* by Andrew Gunton Fuller. 3 vols. Reprinted from the third London edition; revised with additions (Philadelphia: American Baptist Publication Society, 1845), vol. 2, p. 334.

19. *Ibid.*, p. 338.

20. *Ibid.*, p. 339.

21. *Ibid.*, p. 343.

22. *Ibid.*, p. 344.

23. *Ibid.*, p. 347.

24. *Ibid.*, p. 348.

25. *Ibid.*, p. 349.

26. *Ibid.*, p. 351.

27. *Ibid.*, p. 352.

28. *Ibid.*, p. 353.

29. *Ibid.*, p. 354.

30. *Ibid.*, p. 355.

31. *Ibid.*, p. 358.

32. *Ibid.*, p. 359.

33. *Ibid.*, p. 360.

34. *Ibid.*, p. 371.

35. *Ibid.*, p. 367.

36. *Ibid.*, p. 373.

37. *Ibid.*, p. 367.

38. *Ibid.*, p. 373.

39. *Ibid.*, p. 374.

40. *Ibid.*

41. *Ibid.*

42. *Ibid.*, p. 376.

43. *Ibid.*

44. *Ibid.*, p. 377.

45. *Ibid.*

46. *Ibid.*, p. 378.

47. *Ibid.*, p. 380.

48. *Ibid.*, p. 384.

49. *Ibid.*, p. 385.

50. *Ibid.*, p. 387.

51. *Ibid.*, p. 390.

52. *Ibid.*, p. 393.

53. Fuller, *Antinomianism Contrasted with the Religion Taught and Exemplified in the Holy Scriptures. Complete Works of the Rev. Andrew Fuller*, vol. 1, p. 760.

54. *Ibid.*

55. *Ibid.*, p. 761.

56. Cited in John W. Eddins, *op. cit.*, p. 100.

57. Winthrop S. Hudson, ed., *Baptist Concepts of the Church* (Valley Forge: Judson Press, 1959), pp. 76-77.

58. Cited in *ibid.*, pp. 77-78.

59. Fuller, *Letters on Systematic Divinity. Complete Works of the Rev. Andrew Fuller*, vol. 1, p. 706.

60. Cf. Eddins, *op. cit.*, pp. 157-161.

61. Fuller, *The Calvinistic and Socinian Systems Examined and Compared as to Their Moral Tendency. Complete Works of the Rev. Andrew Fuller*, vol. 2, p. 154.

62. *Ibid.*

63. *Ibid.*, pp. 154-155.

64. *Ibid.*, p. 156.

65. Fuller, *Six Letters to Dr. Ryland. Complete Works of the Rev. Andrew Fuller*, vol. 2, p. 705.

66. *Ibid.*, p. 706.

67. Cited in Eddins, *op. cit.*, p. 176.

68. Fuller, *The Reality and Efficacy of Divine Grace, with the Certain Success of Christ's Kingdom. Complete Works of the Rev. Andrew Fuller*, vol. 2, p. 551.

69. Fuller, *The Gospel Its Own Witness. Complete Works of the Rev. Andrew Fuller*, vol. 2, p. 90.

70. W. T. Whitley, *A History of*

British Baptists (London: Charles Griffin & Company, Limited, 1923), p. 245.

71. Underwood, *op. cit.*, p. 166.

72. David Benedict, *Fifty Years Among the Baptists* (New York: Sheldon & Co.; Boston: Gould and Lincoln, 1860), pp. 135-145.

CHAPTER 5—Alexander Campbell

1. H. Richard Niebuhr, *The Social Sources of Denominationalism* (New York: Meridian Books, Inc., 1960. Reprinted by arrangement with The Shoe String Press. Copyright 1929 by Henry Holt and Company, Inc.), p. 146.

2. *Ibid.*, pp. 151-154.

3. *Ibid.*, pp. 155-161.

4. *Ibid.*, pp. 171-176.

5. Peter G. Mode, *The Frontier Spirit in American Christianity* (New York: The Macmillan Company, 1923), p. 120.

6. Winfred Ernest Garrison and Alfred T. DeGroot, *The Disciples of Christ* (St. Louis: Christian Board of Publication, 1958), pp. 205-206.

7. Cf. S. Morris Eames, *The Philosophy of Alexander Campbell* (Bethany, W. Va.: Bethany College, 1966), pp. 19-27.

8. Cited in Royal Humbert, ed., *A Compend of Alexander Campbell's Theology* (St. Louis, Mo.: The Bethany Press, 1961), p. 63.

9. Alexander Campbell, *The Christian System* (Bethany, Va.: A. Campbell, 1839), pp. 126-127.

10. Cf. Alexander Campbell, *The Millennial Harbinger*, vol. 17 (1846), pp. 634-636.

11. Alexander Campbell, ed., *The Christian Baptist*, revised by D. S. Burnet (Cincinnati: D. S. Burnet, 1852), vol. 1 (1823), p. 58.

12. Cited in Winfred Ernest Garrison, *Alexander Campbell's Theology* (St. Louis: Christian Publishing Company, 1900), p. 222.

13. Campbell, *The Millennial Harbinger*, vol. 2 (1831), p. 396.

14. Cited in Errett Gates, *The Early Relation and Separation of Baptists*

and Disciples (Chicago: The Christian Century Company, 1904), p. 119.

15. Campbell, *The Millennial Harbinger*, vol. 5 (1834), pp. 568-569. Cited in Humbert, *op. cit.*, p. 124.

16. Alexander Campbell, *A Debate on Christian Baptism, Between the Rev. W. L. Maccalla and Alexander Campbell, in Which are Interspersed and to Which are Added Animadversions on Different Treatises of the Same Subject Written by Dr. J. Mason, Dr. S. Ralston, Rev. A. Pond, Rev. J. P. Campbell, Rector Armstrong, and the Rev. J. Walker* (Buffalo: Published by Campbell and Sala, 1824), p. 135.

17. Campbell, *The Christian Baptist*, vol. 5 (1827), p. 416.

18. Garrison, *Alexander Campbell's Theology*, p. 246.

19. *Ibid.*, p. 247.

20. Winfred Ernest Garrison, *An American Religious Movement* (St. Louis: Christian Board of Publication, 1945), p. 104.

21. Campbell, *The Christian Baptist*, vol. 5 (1827), p. 455.

22. *Ibid.*, p. 454.

23. Cited in H. Shelton Smith, Robert T. Handy, and Lefferts A. Loetscher, eds., *American Christianity* (New York: Charles Scribner's Sons, 1960), vol. 1, p. 586.

24. Garrison, *Alexander Campbell's Theology*, p. 70.

25. Campbell, *The Christian Baptist*, vol. 4 (1826), p. 85.

26. Gates, *op. cit.*, p. 19.

27. Cited in B. H. Carroll, Jr., *The Genesis of American Anti-Missionism* (Louisville, Ky.: The Baptist Book Concern, 1902), p. 125.

28. Cited in *ibid.*, p. 131.

29. Cf. William Warren Sweet, *Religion on the American Frontier: The Baptists, 1783–1830* (Chicago: University of Chicago Press, 1931), p. 72.

30. Cf. Garrison and DeGroot, *op. cit.*, pp. 176-177.

31. Cf. Ray D. Lindley, "The Structure and Function of the Church in the Thought of Alexander Campbell" (unpublished Ph.D. dissertation, Yale University, 1945), p. 75.

32. Cf. Gates, *op. cit.*, p. 53.

33. Campbell, *The Christian Baptist*, vol. 2 (1824), p. 159.

34. *Ibid.*, p. 159.

35. *Ibid.*, p. 160.

36. Cited in *The Christian Baptist*, vol. 3 (1825), pp. 227-228.

37. Cited in Garrison and DeGroot, *op. cit.*, p. 194.

38. Cited in Gates, *op. cit.*, p. 53.

39. *Ibid.*, pp. 78-79.

40. Cited in J. H. Spencer, *A History of Kentucky Baptists* (Printed for the Author, 1886), vol. 1, pp. 638-639.

41. Jeremiah B. Jeter, *The Sermons and Other Writings of the Rev. Andrew Broaddus, with a Memoir of His Life* (New York: Lewis Colby, 1852), p. 292.

42. Cited in Spencer, *op cit.*, pp. 640-641.

43. W. E. Hatcher, *Life of J. B. Jeter* (Baltimore: H. M. Wharton and Company, 1887), p. 365.

44. John L. Waller, "Letters to a Reformer, Alias Campbellite," *The Christian Repository*, vol. 45 (September, 1855), p. 538.

45. Spencer, *op. cit.*, pp. 597-598.

46. Manly J. Breaker, "Causes of the Success of Campbellism," *Ford's Christian Repository and Home Circle*, vol. 4, no. 5 (May, 1893), pp. 335-336.

47. Jeter, *The Sermons and Other Writings of the Rev. Andrew Broaddus*, p. 374.

48. Cited in Spencer, *op. cit.*, p. 638.

49. J. B. Jeter, *Campbellism Examined* (New York: Sheldon, Lamport & Blakeman; Boston: Gould & Lincoln, 1855), p. 248.

50. *Ibid.*, p. 255.

51. Cited in Spencer, *op. cit.*, p. 638.

52. *Ibid.*, pp. 623-635.

53. A. M. Poindexter, "Campbellism Examined," *The Christian Repository and Literary Review*, vol. 39, no. 2 (March, 1855), p. 167.

54. *Ibid.*, p. 171.

55. A. P. Williams, *Campbellism Exposed* (Nashville, Tenn.: Southwestern Publishing House; New York: Sheldon & Company, 1860), p. 50.

56. J. B. Jeter, *Recollections of a Long Life* (Richmond, Va.: The Religious Herald Co., 1891), p. 138.

CHAPTER 6—J. R. Graves

1. James J. Burnett, *Sketches of Tennessee's Pioneer Baptist Preachers*. First Series, vol. 1 (Nashville, Tenn.: Press of Marshall and Bruce Company, 1919), p. 191.

2. James Robinson Graves, *Old Landmarkism: What Is It?* (Memphis, Tenn.: Baptist Book House, Graves, Mahaffy & Company, 1880), pp. xi-xii.

3. William Cathcart, ed., *The Baptist Encyclopedia*, rev. ed. (Philadelphia, Pa.: Louis H. Everts, 1883), p. 467.

4. William Wright Barnes, *The Southern Baptist Convention: 1845–1953* (Nashville, Tenn.: Broadman Press, 1954), p. 105.

5. O. L. Hailey, *J. R. Graves: Life, Times and Teachings* (Nashville, Tenn.: By the Author, 1929), pp. 65-66.

6. Burnett, *op. cit.*, p. 188.

7. J. R. Graves, *The Little Iron Wheel* (Nashville, Tenn.: Southwestern Publishing House, 1857), pp. 204-206.

8. Hailey, *op. cit.*, p. 69.

9. Cf. Graves, *The Little Iron Wheel*, p. 23.

10. Graves, *Old Landmarkism: What Is It?*, p. 39.

11. Amos Cooper Dayton, *Theodosia Ernest; Or, Ten Days' Travel in Search of the Church* (Philadelphia: American Baptist Publication Society, n. d.), vol. 2, p. 93.

12. Graves, *Old Landmarkism: What Is It?*, p. 38.

13. *Ibid.*, p. 32.

14. Cited in T. A. Patterson, "The Theology of J. R. Graves" (unpublished Th.D. thesis, Southwestern Baptist Theological Seminary, May, 1944), p. 34.

15. Dayton, *op. cit.*, p. 92.

16. Graves, *Old Landmarkism: What Is It?*, p. 33.

17. *Ibid.*

18. James Robinson Graves, *Intercommunion of Churches, Inconsistent, Unscriptural, and Productive of Evil*

(Memphis, Tenn.: Baptist Book House, 1881), p. 153.

19. James Robinson Graves, *The Great Iron Wheel; or, Republicanism Backwards and Christianity Reversed*, 17th ed. (Nashville, Tenn.: Graves, Marks, and Rutland; New York: Sheldon, Blakeman & Company, 1856), pp. 24-25.

20. *Ibid.*, p. 21.

21. Dayton, *op. cit.*, p. 176.

22. Graves, *The Great Iron Wheel*, p. 25.

23. Graves, *Old Landmarkism: What Is It?*, p. 31.

24. Graves, *The Great Iron Wheel*, p. 21.

25. Graves, *Old Landmarkism: What Is It?*, chap. 3.

26. Cf. James Madison Pendleton, *An Old Landmark Re-set*, 2nd ed. (Nashville, Tenn.: Southwestern Publishing House, 1857).

27. James Robinson Graves, *The Watchman's Reply* (Nashville, Tenn.: Published for the Tennessee Publication Society by Graves and Shankland, 1853).

28. Graves, *Old Landmarkism: What Is It?*, p. 31.

29. Graves, *The Great Iron Wheel*, p. 28.

30. *Ibid.*, p. 27.

31. Amos Cooper Dayton, *Pedobaptist and Campbellite Immersions* (Nashville, Tenn.: Southwestern Publishing House, Graves Marks & Company; New York: Sheldon, Blakeman & Company, 1858), pp. 126-127.

32. Graves, *Old Landmarkism: What Is It?*, p. 64.

33. James Robinson Graves, *The Act of Christian Baptism* (Copyright by J. R. Graves, 1881. Copyright by Baptist Sunday School Committee, Texarkana, Ark.-Tex., 1928), p. 52.

34. Pendleton, *An Old Landmark Re-set*, pp. 25-26.

35. Graves, *Old Landmarkism: What Is It?*, p. 65.

36. *Ibid.*, pp. 151-152.

37. *Ibid.*, p. 141.

38. Dayton, *Pedobaptist and Campbellite Immersions*, pp. 81-83.

39. Graves, *Old Landmarkism: What Is It?*, p. 152.

40. *Ibid.*, p. xiv.

41. *The Religious Herald*, Sept. 13, 1877, p. 1.

42. Cf. *Baptist Confessions of 1644, 1677, 1678, 1689*, etc.

43. John Leadley Dagg, *Manual of Theology, Second Part . . . Church Order* (Charleston, S.C.: Southern Baptist Publication Society, 1859), p. 113.

44. *The Western Recorder*, Oct. 14, 1880, p. 4.

45. Cf. the discussion of these sects by A. H. Newman, a Baptist historian, in *A Manual of Church History*, vol. 1 (Philadelphia: American Baptist Publication Society, 1914).

46. W. W. Everts, "The Old Landmark Discovered," *The Christian Repository and Home Circle*, vol. 37 (January, 1855), p. 34.

47. Cf. *The Western Recorder*, Sept. 20, 1854, p. 2.

48. Dagg, *Manual . . . Church Order*, p. 292.

49. *The Western Recorder*, April 25, 1855, p. 2.

50. Cf. James E. Tull, "A Study of Southern Baptist Landmarkism in the Light of Historical Baptist Ecclesiology" (unpublished Ph.D. dissertation, Columbia University, 1960), pp. 342-375.

51. Patrick Hues Mell, *Baptism in its Mode and Subjects* (Charleston, S.C.: Southern Baptist Publication Society, 1854), p. 194.

52. Cf. *The Baptist*, Jan. 29, 1876, p. 148.

CHAPTER 7—William Newton Clarke

1. Sydney E. Ahlstrom, ed., *Theology in America; The Major Protestant Voices from Puritanism to Neo-Orthodoxy* (New York: The Bobbs-Merrill Co., Inc., 1967), p. 64.

2. Clifton E. Olmstead, *History of Religion in the United States* (Englewood Cliffs, N.J.: Prentice-Hall, Inc., 1960), pp. 466-467.

3. *Ibid.*, p. 467.

4. James Ward Smith and A. Leland Jamison, eds., *The Shaping of American Religion*. Vol. 1, *Religion in*

American Life (Princeton, N.J.: Princeton University Press, 1961), pp. 290-291.

5. Kenneth Cauthen, *The Impact of American Religious Liberalism* (New York: Harper & Row, Publishers, 1962), p. 32.

6. *Ibid.*, p. 29; cf. Henry P. Van Dusen, *The Vindication of Liberal Theology* (New York: Charles Scribner's Sons, 1963), pp. 21-25. Lloyd J. Averill says that modernism was largely a post-World War I development. "No major figure of the liberal movement before 1917 qualifies for designation as a modernist." Lloyd J. Averill, *American Theology in the Liberal Tradition* (Philadelphia: The Westminster Press, 1967), p. 100.

7. H. Shelton Smith, Robert T. Handy, and Lefferts A. Loetscher, eds., *American Christianity* (New York: Charles Scribner's Sons, 1963), vol. 2, p. 256.

8. Lloyd J. Averill, *op. cit.*, p. 95.

9. Smith, Handy, and Loetscher, eds., *op. cit.*, p. 258.

10. Smith and Jamison, *op. cit.*, p. 291.

11. Cited in Emily Clarke, *William Newton Clarke* (New York: Charles Scribner's Sons, 1916), p. 70.

12. *Ibid.*, pp. 185-186.

13. William Newton Clarke, *An Outline of Christian Theology* (New York: Charles Scribner's Sons, 1909), p. 1.

14. *Ibid.*, p. 2.

15. *Ibid.*, p. 8.

16. *Ibid.*, p. 5.

17. *Ibid.*, pp. 8-9.

18. *Ibid.*, p. 11.

19. *Ibid.*, p. 15.

20. *Ibid.*, p. 18.

21. *Ibid.*, p. 19.

22. *Ibid.*, p. 21.

23. William Newton Clarke, *Sixty Years with the Bible* (New York: Charles Scribner's Sons, 1909), p. 80.

24. *Ibid.*, p. 108.

25. *Ibid.*, p. 184.

26. Clarke, *Outline*, p. 40.

27. Clarke, *Sixty Years with the Bible*, p. 200.

28. Clarke, *Outline*, p. 45.

29. William Newton Clarke, *The Use of the Scriptures in Theology* (New York: Charles Scribner's Sons, 1906), pp. 64-65.

30. Emily Clarke, *op. cit.*, p. 233.

31. Clarke, *Sixty Years with the Bible*, pp. 210-211.

32. Clarke, *Outline*, p. 47.

33. Emily Clarke, *op. cit.*, pp. 239-240.

34. Clarke, *Outline*, p. 47.

35. *Ibid.*, p. 48.

36. William Newton Clarke, *The Christian Doctrine of God* (New York: Charles Scribner's Sons, 1909), pp. 265-266.

37. *Ibid.*, p. 4.

38. Clarke, *Outline*, p. 66.

39. *Ibid.*, p. 78.

40. *Ibid.*, p. 72.

41. *Ibid.*, p. 75.

42. *Ibid.*, p. 72.

43. Clarke, *The Christian Doctrine of God*, pp. 284-285.

44. Clarke, *Outline*, pp. 131-132.

45. *Ibid.*, pp. 132-134.

46. *Ibid.*, p. 134.

47. *Ibid.*, p. 130.

48. *Ibid.*, p. 175.

49. Clarke, *The Christian Doctrine of God*, pp. 357-431.

50. Clarke, *Outline*, p. 104.

51. William Newton Clarke, *Can I Believe in God the Father?* (New York: Charles Scribner's Sons, 1899), pp. 52-53.

52. Clarke, *Outline*, p. 125.

53. *Ibid.*, pp. 191-192.

54. Clarke, *Can I Believe in God the Father?*, p. 145.

55. Clarke, *Outline*, p. 192.

56. *Ibid.*, p. 196.

57. *Ibid.*, p. 204.

58. *Ibid.*, p. 221.

59. Clarke, *The Christian Doctrine of God*, p. 177.

60. Clarke, *Outline*, p. 238.

61. *Ibid.*, p. 242.

62. *Ibid.*, p. 232.

63. *Ibid.*

64. *Ibid.*, p. 240.

65. *Ibid.*, p. 245.

66. *Ibid.*, p. 249.

67. *Ibid.*, p. 285.

68. *Ibid.*, p. 290.

69. *Ibid.*, p. 292.

70. *Ibid.*

71. *Ibid.*, p. 295.
72. *Ibid.*, pp. 298-300.
73. *Ibid.*, p. 307.
74. *Ibid.*, pp. 306, 308.
75. Cf. *ibid.*, pp. 308-315.
76. *Ibid.*, pp. 302-303.
77. *Ibid.*, p. 329.
78. *Ibid.*, p. 337.
79. *Ibid.*, p. 346.
80. *Ibid.*, p. 353.
81. *Ibid.*, p. 354.
82. *Ibid.*, p. 355.
83. *Ibid.*, p. 380.
84. Clarke, *The Christian Doctrine of God*, pp. 245-246.
85. Clarke, *Outline*, p. 382.
86. *Ibid.*, p. 383.
87. *Ibid.*, p. 410.
88. *Ibid.*, p. 409.
89. *Ibid.*, p. 445.
90. *Ibid.*, p. 441.
91. *Ibid.*, p. 444.
92. *Ibid.*, p. 447.
93. *Ibid.*, p. 458.
94. *Ibid.*, p. 463.
95. *Ibid.*, p. 462.
96. *Ibid.*, p. 480.
97. Cited in Emily Clarke, *op. cit.*, p. 115.
98. Claude L. Howe, Jr., "William Newton Clarke: Systematic Theologian of Theological Liberalism," *Foundations*, vol. 6, no. 2 (April, 1963), p. 124.
99. Cited in Emily Clarke, *op. cit.*, p. 118.
100. Harry Emerson Fosdick, *The Living of These Days* (New York: Harper & Row, Publishers, 1956), p. 56.
101. Emily Clarke, *op. cit.*, p. 41.
102. *Ibid.*, p. 143.
103. Howe, *op. cit.*, p. 129.
104. Fosdick, *op. cit.*, p. 65.
105. Albert H. Newman, "Recent Changes in the Theology of Baptists," *American Journal of Theology*, vol. 10, no. 4 (Oct., 1906), p. 608.
106. Norman H. Maring, "Baptists and Changing Views of the Bible, 1865–1918 (Part II)," *Foundations*, vol. 1, no. 4 (Oct., 1958), p. 45.
107. For an account of this controversy as it affected the Northern Baptist Convention, see Norman F. Furniss, *The Fundamentalist Controversy, 1918–1931* (New Haven: Yale University Press, 1954), pp. 103-119; Cf. Torbet, *A History of the Baptists*, rev. ed. (Valley Forge: Judson Press, 1965), pp. 425-430.

CHAPTER 8—Walter Rauschenbusch

1. Charles Howard Hopkins, *The Rise of the Social Gospel in American Protestantism, 1865–1915* (New Haven: Yale University Press, 1940), p. 319.
2. Robert T. Handy, ed., *The Social Gospel in America* (New York: Oxford University Press, 1966), p. 4.
3. Cf. *ibid.*, pp. 4-5.
4. *Ibid.*, pp. 10-11.
5. Hopkins, *op. cit.*, pp. 319-320.
6. Kenneth Cauthen, *The Impact of American Religious Liberalism* (New York: Harper & Row, Publishers, 1962), p. 87.
7. Ernest Trice Thompson, *Changing Emphases in American Preaching* (Philadelphia: The Westminster Press, 1943), p. 201.
8. Cf. Cauthen, *op. cit.*, p. 87.
9. Walter Rauschenbusch, *A Theology for the Social Gospel* (New York: The Macmillan Company, 1917), p. 7.
10. *Ibid.*, p. 9.
11. *Ibid.*, p. 7.
12. *Ibid.*, p. 17.
13. *Ibid.*, p. 167.
14. *Ibid.*, p. 34-35.
15. *Ibid.*, p. 36.
16. *Ibid.*, p. 40.
17. *Ibid.*, pp. 42-43.
18. *Ibid.*, p. 50.
19. *Ibid.*, p. 59.
20. *Ibid.*, p. 60.
21. *Ibid.*, p. 66.
22. *Ibid.*, p. 72.
23. *Ibid.*, p. 90.
24. *Ibid.*, p. 91.
25. *Ibid.*, p. 92.
26. *Ibid.*, p. 95.
27. Benson Y. Landis, ed., *A Rauschenbusch Reader: The Kingdom of God and the Social Gospel*. With an Interpretation of the Life and Work of Walter Rauschenbusch by Harry Emerson Fosdick (New York: Harper & Row, Publishers, 1957), p. xvii.

28. Dores R. Sharpe, *Walter Rauschenbusch* (New York: The Macmillan Company, 1942), p. 393-394.

29. Cf. *ibid.*, p. 192.

30. Rauschenbusch, *A Theology for the Social Gospel*, p. 97.

31. *Ibid.*, p. 99.

32. *Ibid.*, p. 100.

33. *Ibid.*, pp. 101-102.

34. *Ibid.*, p. 102.

35. *Ibid.*, p. 105.

36. Walter Rauschenbusch, *Christianizing the Social Order* (New York: The Macmillan Company, 1914), chap. 2, part 3.

37. *Ibid.*, p. 156.

38. Rauschenbusch, *A Theology for the Social Gospel*, p. 111.

39. Cf. Landis, *op. cit.*, pp. xx-xxii; Vernon Parker Bodein, *The Social Gospel of Walter Rauschenbusch and Its Relation to Religious Education* (New Haven: Yale University Press, 1944), p. 65.

40. Rauschenbusch, *A Theology for the Social Gospel*, p. 117.

41. *Ibid.*, p. 121.

42. *Ibid.*, p. 125.

43. *Ibid.*, p. 128.

44. *Ibid.*, p. 131.

45. *Ibid.*, p. 133.

46. *Ibid.*, pp. 133-137.

47. *Ibid.*, pp. 133-145.

48. *Ibid.*, p. 147.

49. *Ibid.*, p. 148.

50. *Ibid.*, p. 151.

51. *Ibid.*, p. 149.

52. *Ibid.*, p. 154.

53. *Ibid.*, p. 164.

54. *Ibid.*, pp. 146-147.

55. *Ibid.*, p. 174.

56. *Ibid.*, pp. 174-175.

57. *Ibid.*, p. 179.

58. *Ibid.*, p. 180.

59. *Ibid.*, pp. 180-184.

60. *Ibid.*, pp. 184-187.

61. *Ibid.*, p. 193.

62. *Ibid.*, p. 201.

63. *Ibid.*, pp. 206-207.

64. *Ibid.*, p. 216.

65. *Ibid.*, p. 224.

66. *Ibid.*, p. 234.

67. *Ibid.*, p. 243.

68. *Ibid.*, p. 247.

69. *Ibid.*, pp. 248-259.

70. Cf. *ibid.*, p. 264.

71. *Ibid.*, pp. 267 and 270.

72. *Ibid.*, p. 273.

73. *Ibid.*, pp. 262-263.

74. *Ibid.*, p. 265.

75. *Ibid.*, pp. 277-278.

76. *Ibid.*, p. 195.

77. Hopkins, *op. cit.*, p. 112.

78. Letter published in *The Kingdom*, vol. 1, no. 2 (Sept., 1907). Cited in Bodein, *op. cit.*, p. 26.

79. Sharpe, *op. cit.*, p. 156.

80. Sydnor L. Stealey, comp. and ed., *A Baptist Treasury* (New York: Thomas Y. Crowell Company, 1958), p. 163.

81. *Ibid.*, p. 164.

82. *Ibid.*, p. 166.

83. *Ibid.*, pp. 166-167.

84. *Ibid.*, pp. 168-169.

85. *Ibid.*, p. 169.

86. *Ibid.*, p. 171.

87. *Ibid.*, pp. 170-174.

88. *Ibid.*, pp. 175-176.

89. *Ibid.*, p. 178.

90. *Ibid.*, p. 180.

91. *Ibid.*, p. 182.

92. *Ibid.*, p. 183.

93. *Ibid.*, pp. 183-184.

94. Thompson, *op. cit.*, pp. 220-221.

95. Reinhold Niebuhr, *An Interpretation of Christian Ethics* (New York: Harper & Row, Publishers, 1935), preface.

CHAPTER 9—Martin Luther King, Jr.

1. Daniel C. Thompson, *The Negro Leadership Class* (Englewood Cliffs, N.J.: Prentice-Hall, Inc., 1963), pp. 58-79.

2. Joseph C. Hough, Jr., *Black Power and White Protestants* (New York: Oxford University Press, 1968), pp. 86-89.

3. Cf. *ibid.*, pp. 90-91.

4. Excerpts from *Stride Toward Freedom* by Martin Luther King, Jr. (New York: Harper & Row, Publishers, Perennial Library, 1958), p. 72. Copyright © 1963 by Martin Luther King, Jr. Reprinted by permission of Harper & Row, Publishers, Inc.

5. *Ibid.*, p. 75.
6. *Ibid.*, p. 77.
7. *Ibid.*, p. 79.
8. *Ibid.*, pp. 79-81.
9. *Ibid.*, p. 82.
10. *Ibid.*, p. 82.
11. Excerpts from *Strength to Love* by Martin Luther King, Jr. (New York: Harper & Row, Publishers, 1963), p. 141. Copyright © 1963 by Martin Luther King, Jr. Reprinted by permission of Harper & Row, Publishers, Inc.
12. Cited in J. Rohler, "Life and Death of Martin Luther King," *Christianity Today*, vol. 12 (April 26, 1968), p. 39.
13. King, *Strength to Love*, p. 76.
14. *Ibid.*, p. 91.
15. *Ibid.*, p. 32.
16. *Ibid.*, pp. 32-33.
17. *Ibid.*, p. 125.
18. King, *Stride Toward Freedom*, p. ix.
19. *Ibid.*, pp. 86-87.
20. King, *Strength to Love*, p. 35.
21. *Ibid.*, p. 36.
22. *Ibid.*, p. 37.
23. King, *Stride Toward Freedom*, p. 85.
24. King, *Strength to Love*, p. 38.
25. H. W. Richardson, "Martin Luther King—Unsung Theologian," *Commonweal*, vol. 88 (May 3, 1968), pp. 201-202; also Martin E. Marty and Dean G. Peerman, eds., *New Theology No. 6* (Collier-Macmillan, Ltd., London: The Macmillan Co., Ltd., 1969), pp. 178-185.
26. Excerpts from *Why We Can't Wait* by Martin Luther King, Jr. (New York: Harper & Row, Publishers, 1964), pp. 83-84. Copyright © 1963 by Martin Luther King, Jr. Reprinted by permission of Harper & Row, Publishers, Inc.
27. Excerpts from *Where Do We Go From Here: Chaos or Community?* by Martin Luther King, Jr. (New York: Harper & Row, Publishers, 1967), p. 69. Copyright © 1967 by Martin Luther King, Jr. Reprinted by permission of Harper & Row, Publishers, Inc.
28. *Ibid.*, pp. 72-75.
29. *Ibid.*, pp. 80-81.

30. *Ibid.*, p. 83.
31. *Ibid.*, p. 84.
32. *Ibid.*, p. 4.
33. James E. Sellers, "Love, Justice, and the Non-Violent Movement," *Theology Today*, vol. 18 (January, 1962), pp. 422-434.
34. King, *Where Do We Go From Here?*, p. 191.
35. King, *Strength to Love*, p. 139.
36. *Ibid.*
37. King, *Stride Toward Freedom*, p. 192.
38. *Ibid.*, p. 117.
39. King, *Why We Can't Wait*, p. 59.
40. King, *Stride Toward Freedom*, pp. 83-85.
41. King, *Strength to Love*, p. 139.
42. Rohler, *op. cit.*, p. 37.
43. King, *Where Do We Go From Here?*, p. 36.
44. *Ibid.*, p. 37.
45. *Ibid.*, p. 44; cf. pp. 38-44.
46. *Ibid.*, pp. 46-47.
47. *Ibid.*, pp. 52-53.
48. *Ibid.*, p. 54.
49. *Ibid.*, p. 61.
50. *Ibid.*, p. 66.
51. King, *Why We Can't Wait*, pp. 87-88.
52. *Ibid.*, p. 130.
53. *Ibid.*
54. *Ibid.*, pp. 94-95.
55. *Ibid.*, pp. 96-97.
56. King, *Where Do We Go From Here?*, pp. 186-191.
57. King, *Why We Can't Wait*, pp. 91-92.
58. *Ibid.*, p. 82.
59. *Ibid.*, p. 81.
60. *Ibid.*, p. 88.
61. King, *Where Do We Go From Here?*, p. 41.
62. *Ibid.*, p. 124.
63. *Ibid.*, pp. 125-128.
64. Cf. *ibid.*, chap. 5, pp. 135-167.
65. King, *Stride Toward Freedom*, p. 175.
66. King, *Where Do We Go From Here?*, p. 51.
67. King, *Stride Toward Freedom*, pp. 176-177.
68. *Ibid.*, p. 181.
69. King, *Where Do We Go From Here?*, pp. 96-101.

70. Richardson, *op. cit.*, p. 203.
71. *Newsweek*, April 15, 1968, p. 35.
72. *Ibid.*
73. George Goodman, "He Lives, Man!" *Look* (April 15, 1969), p. 31. Copyright 1969 by Cowles Communications, Inc.

INDEX OF PERSONS

250

SUBJECT INDEX

DATE DUE

PRINTED IN U.S.A

GAYLORD